14.50

The Dynasty

The
Dynasty

The
Rise and Fall
of Social Credit
in Alberta

John J. Barr

McClelland and Stewart Limited

ISBN 0-7710-1015-X

McClelland and Stewart Limited
The Canadian Publishers
25 Hollinger Road, Toronto

Dedication

To Grant Davy, – above all, a great teacher.

Table of Contents

Preface   9

PART ONE: THE CRUCIBLE
Chapter One – The Tradition of Revolt   13
Chapter Two – The Depression   18
Chapter Three – The Collapse of the Old Order   25
Chapter Four – Aberhart and the Young Manning   37
Chapter Five – Prairie Fire   50

PART TWO: THE YEARS OF POWER
Chapter Six – The Alberta Experiment   83
Chapter Seven – The New Leader   120
Chapter Eight – How Manning Used Power   132
Chapter Nine – How Manning Kept Power   149

PART THREE: FALL
Chapter Ten – Succession   167
Chapter Eleven – Reluctant Messiah   185
Chapter Twelve – The Rise of Lougheed   215
Chapter Thirteen – Last Hurrah   224

Index   250

Preface

Most of the really interesting things that have happened in Canadian history have happened in the West, the motherlode of our best folklore. And few western events have prompted as much folklore as Social Credit in Alberta.

This book is a personal search for the real Social Credit as opposed to the folklore of Social Credit we have all read about so many times. Social Credit is badly in need of demythologization – and indeed, it need not fear the consequence of it: the real Social Credit was every bit as interesting as (and in some ways more appealing than) its folklore counterpart.

This book began in 1965 and was originally conceived as a biography of Ernest Manning. As a journalist at the time, I was intrigued by this clever but distant and elusive man; but the more I got into the subject, the more I realized that Manning could not be properly understood except in the context of the movement that spawned him. And, at that time, the movement was at the peak of its power – or so it seemed. So I waited for further political events to indicate where the movement was going, and deepened my research.

Then, in late 1968, I was offered a position as advisor to the young new Social Credit Education Minister, Robert Clark. I accepted, and was privileged to spend the next three years – the last three years of Social Credit, as it turned out – actively involved in the struggle to reform the party and the government. This struggle ended on the night of August 31, 1971, and so if I was not yet present at Social Credit's creation, I can at least claim to have been present at its Armaggedon.

Those three years added depth and understanding to my analysis of Social Credit – so, at least, I believe.

Although many Social Crediters and ex-Social Crediters are my friends, and although I was a member of their team for a time, and although I gave the movement what I had, I never wish to be (and indeed was never accepted by older party people as) a "true Social Crediter." But while I am not a Social Crediter, I think I understand Social Crediters.

Parts One and Two of this book were written, substantially, before my internship with Social Credit; they were written as a journalist and amateur historian, and are based upon interviews, newspaper searches and the like. During these researches many people were helpful and deserve my thanks: the people of Rosetown, Saskatchewan, including Roy Manning and his wife; members of the original staff of the Prophetic Bible Institute; Aberhart's daughter, Mrs. Ola McNutt; Dr. Elmer Roper, onetime leader of the C.C.F., and Senator J. Harper Prowse, onetime leader of the Liberal Party; a host of senior civil servants over the years including Bob Andison, Clerk of the Legislature, and Dr. Ken Pugh, onetime Deputy Minister of Labour, and finally Ernest Manning himself, who, when he was still premier, made time in a busy schedule to give me several long interviews.

For insights gained during the post-1968 period of Social Credit I was indebted to a wide range of colleagues and friends – including, most especially, Bob Clark and Preston Manning. I alone, of course, am responsible for the conclusions in this book.

John J. Barr, Edmonton, March 1974.

Part One

The Crucible

CHAPTER ONE

The Tradition of Revolt

The problem was simple enough. It had been decided long ago that it was vital to Canada's future as a nation that the West be settled. But no one gave much thought to the possibility that the settlers might want to create the West in their own way.

The nation went shopping all over the world for settlers. Finally, by the turn of the century, they started to come in a flood. They brought with them a desire to begin again, to make a better life their own way. They were experimenters by nature. They had no particular loyalties to the fine old traditions (and fine old political parties) of Ontario. So when they found themselves in an economic and political system that undermined their rosy frontier hopes and their pioneer belief in simple democracy, they took the future into their own hands and set about creating their *own* solutions to their difficulties.

They were a cussed people, full of ideas about social co-operation and direct majority rule, but they found themselves living in an economic colony dominated by faceless people thousands of miles away. There was a conflict between their aspirations and their environment; it lasted two full generations: it resulted in a unique Western politics, and led eventually to Social Credit.

Between 1899 and 1910 the last great continental land rush took place in the Canadian West. The settlers came from the Ukraine; from Germany and Scandinavia; there were Mormons from Utah, Hutterites from the Dakotas, Finns from Minnesota and Belgians from Grosse Pointe, Michigan. In a last gasp of British emigration, thousands came from the United Kingdom.

By 1910 most of the West's aching emptiness had been filled. By 1920 one Canadian in every four lived in the West.

In the cold, clear air of this lonely last frontier, this society of immigrants began to define its own identity.

A major part of that identity was the experience the American settlers brought with them from the fast-disappearing U.S. frontier. By 1920 Alberta was thirty per cent foreign-born, and over half the settlers were Americans. With them they brought ideas about temperance, women's rights, radical social democracy.* Many of them had worked in The Grange, fought the U.S. railways and grain companies, supported the Non-Partisan League. A number had worked in William Jennings Bryan's great populist Presidential campaign in 1896, which came heartbreakingly close to victory.

South of the border the frontier was closing, and an ugly industrialism was starting to appear. On the Canadian frontier, they hoped, they would find or create the old life with its solid agrarian values.

The first clashes between this radical frontier society and the oppressive economic and political system in which it found itself, were not long developing. By the early 1920s the West had begun to spawn its own distinctive political leadership; not surprisingly, the first province in which this new leadership broke through to power was Alberta. In 1921 the United Farmers of Alberta, a populist movement founded on the work of a group of agrarian innovators who initiated the Alberta Wheat Pool and the United Grain Growers, swept the Liberals from office in Edmonton.

The alienation of the prairie frontier took three important forms. There was political alienation, which led to the creation of new political parties and movements. There was economic alienation, which led to the creation of new economic structures of self-help to protect farmers' interests. And finally, running through the whole period, there was *intellectual* alienation – an alienation that led to the development of a distinctively Western Canadian ideology of protest.

From the turn of the century until the rise of Social Credit itself, a long line of editors, political leaders, agrarian philosophers defined and elaborated on the causes of Western discontent. They did not all agree on causes or solutions. But by the coming of the Depression, there was in the Western provinces, and especially in Alberta, the mother-lode of Western protest, a broadly-based folklore of protest about the economic and political structure of Confederation.

* The three movements frequently coincided: Alberta was a hotbed of women's liberation and produced a score of early feminist leaders, including the Empire's first female magistrate. Some of the most important Social Credit figures in the early years were female reformers and temperance supporters.

The central features of this folklore were these:

First: That most of the vital economic decisions having a bearing on Western interests were made in Eastern Canada, whether the decisions affected interest rates for credit, freight rates or the price of farm implements.

Second: That most of these decisions were unjust because they took no account of peculiar needs and problems in the West.

Third: That the "old-line parties" in Canada – the Liberals and Conservatives – were captives of the Eastern commercial and industrial establishment, could not be counted upon for assistance in remedying Western grievances, and that the only political solution for the West was in its own popularly-controlled political parties committed to putting pressure on the federal government for solutions.

For the first third of the twentieth century these three forms of alienation coalesced into a variety of organizations and movements to protect Western interests. The dependency of the prairie economy on outside decisions and changes was a sore point with every Western farmer, retailer, cattle-grower. The power of the banks, the grain companies, the railways, the elevator and implement companies, had to be challenged, and was.

All of this agitation had some effect. In 1897 Ottawa had agreed to the Crowsnest Pass rates for freight. This agreement provided government help to the C.P.R. in exchange for reduced rates on the westward shipment of farm implements and the eastward movement of grain. In the 1920s the agreement was modified further to pacify the Progressives in the House of Commons. The government in Ottawa agreed to inspect the grain elevators more rigorously. The private monopoly on the grain trade was pushed back somewhat.

But on other issues there was little if any progress. The protective tariff, created to protect Eastern industry, had the effect of driving up the price of badly-needed farm implements and closing off foreign markets for wheat; little progress was made in ending it. In 1911 the Laurier Liberals made free trade with the United States the central issue in a national election. The Liberals took Alberta and Saskatchewan solidly, but lost the country.

One of the problems on which the prairie reformers put their finger early was the structure and philosophy of the banking system. In contrast to American frontier banks, which tended to be locally-owned, small, adapted to local needs and financially weak, the West's banks were simply an extension of the enormously large, secure, inflexible and oligopolistic Canadian chartered banking system.

In the minds of Westerners, the banking system had profound

inadequacies. In time of recession, it called in Western loans regardless of the needs or committments of farmers; in good times, it skimmed off funds from the West and put them into the national credit pipeline. Initially it refused to accept land as security for large loans, with the result that the mortgage and trust companies moved into the lending field with higher interest rates. (By 1914 $200,-000,000 worth of mortgages on Western farms were held by mortgage, insurance and trust companies.) Often the interest rates were so high that the borrower had little chance to repay the loan in full even in uninterrupted good times; when bad times intervened, foreclosure stalked the countryside.

It was argued that the nation needed a solid, secure banking system – that U.S. banks were notoriously unstable, and failures frequent. There was some limited truth to this. The other side of the argument was that Canadian banks were not only secure, they were also stodgy and unimaginative and autocratic. And, most important, Eastern – always Eastern. The important decisions in the banking industry were always being made elsewhere, and there was little way to influence those decisions.

And so the banks became a prime target of the developing agrarian protest movements. The federal government was very tardy in responding to these attacks: the Canadian Farm Loans Board was not established until 1929 and public control of money and credit was not enforced, even nominally, until the creation of the Bank of Canada in 1934. The Western governments were more responsive. Beginning in 1913, they launched investigations into credit practices and policies. Saskatchewan led the way with a Commission on Agricultural Credit. During the First World War, the governments of Manitoba, Saskatchewan and British Columbia slapped moratoria on farm takeovers by lenders.

The Western governments were not able to significantly effect the operation of the banking and credit system, partly because they were unable to get at the headquarters of the banks' operations, partly because the Western provinces *needed* credit and had nowhere else to turn for it. Several of the governments tried making farm loans themselves during the War, but soon found they had neither the funds nor the expertise. And so, going into the Depression years, the only points that the dissatisfied Western provinces had been able to score on the banking system were academic ones. As William Aberhart was to find out, any attack on the banking system *purely in the West* was going to be doomed to failure; the system would be changed by national action or not at all.

Against the backdrop of this agitation and debate, the Western economy was going through its birth pangs. While booms and busts came and went, millions of acres were being broken and brought into production. Between 1896 and 1920 the general trend was toward increased world wheat prices and decreased transportation costs. The result was a steady growth in population and income.

After 1914 land pressure drove farmers to expand into the old Palliser Triangle in southern Saskatchewan and eastern Alberta, areas in which less than eight inches of rain per year had fallen in at least thirty-five per cent of previous years. The first years were wet, and crops were good. Later there was to be drought, and disaster.

By 1920 the rudiments of Alberta's economy had been built – land cleared, houses, schools, hospitals and businesses erected, roads cut. People were beginning to realize some return on their sweat.

But the Alberta economy was still perched precariously on a single fragile pillar, the price system. Wheat was still the backbone of the economy, and farmers were dependent utterly on the whims of the world wheat market. A drop of several cents per bushel in world wheat prices meant a loss of millions to the total economy.

The agrarian radicals first saw the grain speculator as the chief villain; the answer, they said, was for farmers to pool their crops and sell them at the best time to take advantage of fluctuating prices. This "pool" principle worked, but only to a limited extent: on a competitive international market, the buyer is still in the dominant position. So the farmer's income fluctuated while his expenses (bank interest, mortgage payments, freight charges, implements) remained steady or increased. The farmer was at the mercy of nature and of man.

The wheat market went up and down like a roller-coaster. Between 1913 and 1928 the price of wheat went as high as $2.73½ a bushel and as low as $1.07 a bushel.

And year after year, the Western provincial governments went deeper and deeper into debt, along with their people. By 1935 the government and private debt of Albertans was three-quarters of a billion dollars, and there was no income to make payments on it.

In the last years before the Depression, then, this was Alberta: a euphoric land of raw novelty, backbreaking work, boom and bust, high hopes and high debts, a precarious economic base, and above all a popular tradition of questioning "tradition" and experimenting with new ways to improve the lot of man. Alberta was a society already dissatisfied with the structure of "the system"; Albertans were a people who had tried to change that structure, largely failed, and who were willing to try again.

Alberta was a society ripe for a crisis – and for an original response to crisis.

CHAPTER TWO

The Depression

In 1932, in the coal town of Blairmore in the Crowsnest Pass, communist-led miners persuaded the municipal government to dig up the centre of Main Street, plant it with trees and flowers, and rename it "Tim Buck Boulevard".

Alberta had seen depressions before, but never anything like this. By 1932 and 1933, the province of hope seemed to have been cursed.

In December 1932, over a thousand unemployed reliefers and destitute farmers met in Market Square in Edmonton for a hunger march on the Legislature. They sent a delegation to see Premier John Brownlee, who sternly told them that while he would always be available to talk to representatives of any legitimate group, the government was not prepared to submit to mob rule; no mass march would be allowed. The delegation returned to Market Square and relayed the news; the crowd became angry. One of the leaders shouted, "This afternoon we saw Brownlee and he told us we couldn't parade and that he had issued an order forbidding it. We demand the right to use the King's highways, our *own* highways!" With this, an angry mob of more than 2,000 men began pouring out of the Square and moved toward Jasper Avenue.

At 101A Avenue, the police – some on foot, some on horseback – were waiting for them. Under the eyes of more than 10,000 people who had gathered to watch, the mixed force of city police and mounted R.C.M.P. charged into the mob swinging billies and blackjacks.

The first charge broke the marchers' formation; when they retreated to the Square to re-form, a second charge broke them again, and they drifted away.

In April 1933, 1,500 men on relief in Calgary marched in parade formation to Mission Hill, where seventy men were doing road work for the city relief administration. The strikers shouted that the men working were "scabs"; a violent melee occurred, and police moved in to break it up. Here is the newspaper account:

> Women ran about screaming while the men slashed at each other with picks and shovels. Some of the workers fled but others lined up shoulder to shoulder and fought the strikers until baton-wielding police swept into the mob striking left and right until quiet was restored.

In May 1934, eight relief strikers (one of many groups who protested, through the period, that relief payments were too small to keep families alive) were arrested, trying to pass out handbills on a street corner near the offices of the Relief Department in Edmonton. The crudely-printed pamphlet said, "Fight the bankers' dictatorship and its lackey, [Mayor] Dan Knott. Let's demand the 50 per cent increase in relief allowances. We need it! We demand it! No begging for handouts! Our demands are just! Bring your wives and children!"

The men were charged with contravening an obscure 1917 Edmonton bylaw prohibiting the distribution of "signs, posters, dodgers, handbills or other advertising matter" on any public street, warned by a magistrate and then released.

It is not recorded whether anyone actually starved to death in Alberta during the Depression; certainly many were hungry. By the mid-thirties, the thing they were hungriest for was *hope*. "The Great Depression", as they referred to it in later years, was a much harder blow to their lives than Albertans had ever experienced. For instance: in the previous busts of 1910-15 and 1924, the lowest wheat had gone was down to $1.07 a bushel, Number One Northern; by 1932, the same grade of wheat was fetching between twenty-five and thirty-five cents a bushel.

The collapse was bad in Alberta – worse than anywhere in Canada, save Saskatchewan – because so many bad events took place simultaneously.

First, there was the sickening skid of world grain prices.

The price of meat was next: there are authenticated cases where stockmen shipped cattle to market only to learn later that the total price fetched at the packing plant wasn't enough to pay the freight charges.

Then, there were the natural disasters. History finally caught up with the Palliser Triangle. It entered a cycle of dry years that affected much of the western half of the continent, and by the early 1930s the

Triangle was turning into a howling desert: at its peak, 300,000 acres of land were "blowing out of control", topsoil gone, subsoil eroded into gaunt gullies, millions of acres nearby under attack, farmsteads abandoned, miles of country road literally drifted in with fine, blowing topsoil, the sun obscured for hundreds of miles by the haze.

Then there were massive outbreaks of wheat rust, and grasshoppers. It was like a Biblical plague. By 1939, 60,000 square miles of Alberta were grasshopper infested, and the farmers were fighting off sawflies as well.

On August 1, 1931, the Canadian Red Cross launched a national appeal for food and clothing for 125,000 farm families in the Palliser Triangle (many of them in the Alberta part of it) who had suffered three consecutive crop failures. By the early 1930s, hundreds of farm families were moving out of the Palliser Triangle and into the cities, to British Columbia, to northern Alberta and Saskatchewan.*

Here is how the Depression affected the lives of the people:

The backbone of the Alberta economy was agriculture. The vast majority of Albertans either worked the land or served those who did. When grain production and prices dropped it drained the whole economy of income; there was less and less money in circulation. In 1927, net income per farm in Alberta was $1,975. In 1933, it was fifty-four dollars. At a time when the average income of Canadians fell forty per cent, the average income of farmers fell *ninety-four per cent.*

In entire rural districts, virtually every farm family that could qualify for relief was on it. The province and many municipalities gave out free seed grain and potato seed. There was little point in trying to market crops some years, and in those years farm families kept their wheat and burned it for stove fuel. In some areas, families experimented with various ways of cooking and eating gophers. (The practice, it is said, was not as bad as it sounded; gophers are distantly related to squirrels and, although inclined to be scrawny, were fair eating.)

Many families found a new use for the lowly flour sack, using it for curtains, slip-covers, washcloths and – sometimes – girl's blouses.

Between 1929 and 1933, 14,000 cars and trucks simply disappeared from Alberta roads, many of them simply abandoned. Cars towed by teams of horses became a fairly common sight.

In the cities, small businessmen went into bankruptcy or clung to solvency by their fingernails. Lists of bad debts grew longer and

* See James H. Gray, *Men Against the Desert* (Saskatoon: The Western Producer, 1967)

longer. A merciless war of cost-cutting developed among the large department and chain stores; wages paid by suppliers and manufacturers were forced down, and down.

All across Western Canada, hundreds of miles of rural telephone lines went out of service and remained that way. Half of Alberta's registered telephones went permanently out of service between 1930 and 1937.

The tremendous increase in urban unemployment and the migration of displaced farmers caught the country's creaky and primitive unemployment and welfare system completely unprepared. Between 1932 and 1936, the relief budget of the province almost doubled – at a time when the government itself was on the verge of bankruptcy. In 1934, there were 20,000 applications for relief. Major government programs had to be created overnight, from inadequate resources of money and civil service manpower.

Ottawa began to move into the breach with emergency loans to the provinces and grants of forty cents a day for feeding and sheltering each unemployed single man. Many men were put to work on makeshift public works projects to earn their relief. In 1932, the Alberta government employed twenty doctors full time to travel and provide medical care for reliefers and their families in central and southern Alberta.

By 1935, eighteen public works camps had been built in the foothills and flatlands by the Unemployment Relief Commission, chiefly for unemployed single men, who were put to work clearing brush and building roads. Hundreds of despondent men drifted from camp to camp, sometimes being blacklisted for "agitating". "Many will remain a permanent charge on the province," said the Commission Chairman in his 1935 report.

In Edmonton and Calgary and other cities, city streets began to be punctuated by decaying abandoned houses, vacated by their owners after foreclosure.

In many rural areas, doctors were paid in produce. Many families went without medical care for fear of unpayable bills.

School boards tightened up mercilessly on education budgets; in rural areas, annual supplies in many schools totalled one box of chalk and one package of foolscap. Teacher tenure was endangered. City teachers did not suffer as badly, but in many rural areas teacher salaries were uncollectable. A 1937 letter to the magazine of the Alberta Teachers Alliance stated a typical problem:

> I should like your advice regarding the difficulty I have in drawing my salary . . . this school district cannot raise taxes to pay any salary, except three or four dollars in a month. It is absolutely

impossible for the majority of the people to pay any taxes at all at this time of the year . . . the board has not, or does not, know how to go about getting a loan to pay the teacher's salary . . . In my present boarding place the people have been refused further credit at the store [just] on the strength of my [teacher] grant . . . What should I do?

In many parts of Alberta, people reverted to a barter economy, trading produce for goods and services. One rural reader paid his subscription bill to the *Edmonton Bulletin* with a piece of home-painted currency promising to pay to the bearer "10 pounds of Grade A Turkey on demand."

By 1934 a colony of unemployed men had moved into Edmonton to live in cardboard boxes, and shacks made from licence-plates and packing crates, on the edge of the municipal dump and near the Legislative power house on the bank of the North Saskatchewan. They built their shanties from materials they scavenged in the shadows, cadged meals at back doors, tried to find odd jobs. Some panned gold on the riverbank. Some went from door to door sharpening knives and scissors.

A man from the "hobo colony" at Red Deer painted prairie and mountain landscapes on pieces of cardboard cut from the inside of old cornflake boxes, and sold them like hotcakes. An Edmonton man earned seventy-five cents a day collecting old paint cans, scouring out the insides, and selling them back to the paint companies for a few cents apiece. At Christmas, farm wives went door to door in the cities selling cleaned turkeys for a dollar each.

The situation in Saskatchewan was even worse, of course, because the Saskatchewan economy was even more totally dependent on agriculture. In Alberta, there were tiny pockets in the economy where a little income continued to come in – the coal mines in the Crowsnest Pass, the Coalbranch and Drumheller continued to produce, the railroads continued to run.* Lumber brought in a trickle. But on the whole, things were desperate. The fact that Alberta had prospered in the late 1920s made it all the harder to bear.

From 1929 until 1933, farm income dropped ninety-four per cent. In the same period, how did others in Canada fare? The income of small businessmen and professionals dropped thirty-six per cent, the salaries and wages in industry (mostly in the East) dropped thirty-seven per cent, and stock dividends dropped forty per cent.

---

* In 1949, the Canadian Federation of Agriculture presented a brief to the Royal Commission on Transportation claiming that in 1939, the average farmer had earned $586 – the average railwayman $1,549.

One group of Canadians experienced a rise in income during this period. Income from bond interest, life insurance and farm mortgages increased by thirteen per cent.

Men of all descriptions, men who had always looked to their own strength, their own skills, their own initiative, for advancement, began to find that the old certitudes no longer worked; skill, ambition, imagination were no longer a guarantee of anything. Thousands of tough, hard men were, for the first time in their lives, afraid. In a thousand businesses, a thousand minor employees discovered they could live with unreasonable bosses, shrinking pay, longer hours – because if they couldn't, there was a lineup of men waiting at the gate each morning who could.

Bitterness grew. Land wrenched from the prairie by backbreaking effort was turned over to mortgage companies for arrears. Farms were abandoned to drifting soil and howling winds. Careers and plans were postponed, forgotten.

By 1932 it was obvious that the Depression wasn't going to simply fade away into another epoch of quick prosperity. It was here for the long haul, and governments were openly admitting their inability to understand or solve it. The foundations of the political order were beginning to crumble.

When the police beat down the Edmonton hunger march in December 1932, the stragglers drifted back to Market Square to sing *The Red Flag* and give three cheers for the Communist Party of Canada. Special detachments of police were assigned to move around the province breaking up demonstrations. Two alleged communists, Andrew Irvine and Charles Stewart, were arrested and tried for unlawful assembly. Irvine got two months in prison, Stewart got a year. Stewart told the court, "As long as I am regarded as a leader of the workers, I will expect to be arrested, convicted and sentenced. All that I ask is that those who remain shall carry on the work." Said Mr. Justice Ives: "I intend to give you the opportunity to do some work. You are sentenced to serve one year at Fort Saskatchewan at hard labour."

In the face of this crisis some stubbornly tried to make the old values work – like the thousands of young men who rode the rails looking for work in every city.

Others turned to political solutions. And while there was little large-scale violence, considering social conditions, political radicals made deep inroads into the consciousness of many men and women. When eight hundred hunger marchers trudged through the snow down Jasper Avenue during a 1932 demonstration, they sang the *Internationale.*

As Eric Hoffer has pointed out*, it isn't historically correct that revolutions are set in motion to realize radical changes; "actually, it is drastic change which sets the stage for revolution." By 1933 and 1934, the old economic and political order in Alberta was discredited. The U.F.A. government – in conjunction with its sister provincial governments and the federal government – had run out of answers. Conditions were growing worse, and disorder was on the rise. In several cities, fights were breaking out between militant unemployed men and reliefers at work on city projects. The warning sign went up in April 1935: more than two thousand unemployed reliefers walked off their city public works jobs in Edmonton and refused to come back until relief allowances were raised. The strike lasted five weeks. The city administration, its resources already stretched to breaking, equivocated. A riot took place at the city potato-patch between strikers and reliefers who remained on the job. On May 17, police had to wade into a demonstration of strikers who were trying to prevent reliefers from leaving the C.N.R. station to board trains to go to work camps in the mountains. The strikers threw rocks, the policemen swung clubs. The policemen won.

Men are held back from radical change by fear of the unknown, belief in old values, ignorance, comfort. Only when the old values are discredited, comfort gone, and ignorance and fear of the unknown is replaced by a sense of desperation and a new, hopeful idea, is the time ready for rebellion.

That time had come.

---

* *The Ordeal of Change* (New York: Harper & Row, 1964), pp. 4-5.

CHAPTER THREE

The Collapse of the Old Order

1. *The Prophet.*

A key figure in every revolt or rebellion is the prophet – the man whose ideas speak to the needs of the time.

Such a man was Major Clifford Hugh Douglas, Scottish engineer, cost accountant, and the unlikely prophet of Social Credit. Douglas was the man who shaped and fashioned the ideas that William Aberhart was to hurl, like thunderbolts, at the political and economic establishment.

It is worthwhile to re-examine Douglas's ideas today because he is a neglected figure in the literature of economic and political theory, and it is impossible to understand Social Credit's appeal without understanding what it offered to the people.

Douglas was a non-socialist critic of capitalism. He admired many things about capitalism, chiefly its stress on competition, its striving after innovation, its rewarding of initiative and success, its great development of productive power. The great success of capitalism, he argued, was that it had raised production to unprecedented levels and provided a galaxy of goods and services to meet every conceivable human need. Its great failure was that it had not provided a means for people to *consume* this production.

Douglas's *bête noire* was an obscure economic theory called Say's Law. The French economist Jean-Baptiste Say had argued that in a competitive market economy production always would equal consumption because production created sufficient purchasing power to buy itself back. (Many people feel this today, Douglas, J.M. Keynes and others having made little impact on their theoretical consciousness.)

Douglas was in his late thirties and working as assistant director of the Royal Aircraft Works in England when he came across the facts on which he built a theory to challenge Say's Law. A thorough study of industrial cost-accounting at the Royal Aircraft Works and in a number of other industries led Douglas to believe that the monetary and credit system would continually drain off vital purchasing power; production would *not* generate sufficient income to buy itself back; there would be a chronic deficiency of purchasing power, and never enough fully to go around.

The Achilles heel of capitalism, Douglas argued in a score of books, speeches and pamphlets, was its monetary system – a system so flawed in its concept and very nature that it would be the sole cause of chronic crises of "poverty in the midst of plenty."

The "proof" of Douglas's theory was said to reside in his famous "A plus B Theorem." It worked like this: every manufacturing establishment has two kinds of costs – "A" costs (payments made to individuals for salaries, wages and dividends) and "B" costs (payments made to institutions for raw materials, purchases, machinery and bank charges). To recover its costs, the factory must put both into its price. The price is therefore "A plus B." But inasmuch as individual purchasing power is only "A", "A" obviously cannot buy back "A" plus "B". Therefore, there is always a shortage of purchasing power in the economy and a chronic condition of under-consumption.

But don't "B" payments (payments to institutions for raw materials, purchases, machinery and bank charges) themselves become payments to individuals, who then spend in the marketplace? No, Douglas replied, the problem here is *time*: before "B" payments become "A" payments time elapses, allowing a backlog of unconsumed inventory to build up; the economy never catches up with its own production.

Why then had the economy not collapsed completely long ago? Douglas replied that capitalism postponed its collapse by: (1) securing bank loans, the end result of which had to be the foreclosure of old debts, pyramiding individual and corporate debt, and the takeover of the economy by the banks; (2) the deliberate sabotage and destruction of produce – burning wheat, killing hogs, and so forth; and (3) the expansion of foreign trade and exports, the continuous competition for which inevitably leads to a struggle for colonies, and war. (The overtones of Hobson's and Lenin's theory of imperialism here are fascinating.)

Why was there a shortage of purchasing power (money and credit)? Because the creation and supply of it had historically been allowed to fall into the hands of a private monopoly, the chartered banking system; and the banks created purchasing power, not in response to social need or the need to consume full production, but in response to their own interests. Credit, he argued, was the bloodstream of commerce, but the banks were inducing an attack of anemia.

It was not that the bankers were necessarily evil men; they simply operated an intrinsically wicked system:

> It is doubtless a misconception to accuse financiers of deliberately planning wars, suicide waves, bankruptcies and the other tragedies associated with the existing state of affairs. They are much in the position of the immoderate drinker, whom it would be absurd to suppose desires delirium tremens. He will do everything possible to avoid delirium tremens – except stop drinking.*

Douglas's theory was hotly debated in many Western countries, particularly in the 1920s. In 1923 he was called to testify before the House of Commons Banking Committee, at the request of members of the Progressive Party's Western "ginger group". There were Douglasite study groups in many countries in the Commonwealth; there were several in Alberta, and they were later to cause Aberhart grief.

Douglas's theories were pooh-poohed by the banking establishment and by most academic economists. Douglas always had several strikes against him in the role he sought to play. He was an engineer and cost-accountant, not an economist by training. He was a turbid writer. In later years he became increasingly paranoid concerning the role of the Jews in the banking system; by the mid-forties he was an almost forgotten figure, even in Alberta.

But, in the mid-twenties and thirties, Douglas clearly had put his finger on a real problem of the capitalist system: the key role of monetary policy as a basic regulator of economic activity. And Douglas's influence was aided considerably by the fact that the bank establishment and the so-called academic economists (at least until Keynes) were themselves baffled by the Depression and quite unable to explain it or prescribe a remedy for it. By the mid-thirties the bankers, and most of their academic allies, were intellectually bankrupt.

Douglas had an answer for the Depression. The solution, he wrote, was government control of credit and prices. A government could break the banks' anti-social private monopoly on credit creation and

* *The Monopoly of Credit* (Belfast: K.R.P. Publications Ltd., 1958), third edition, pp. 13-14.

then create *social* credit. Social credit would be a supply of credit based on a realistic inventory of the real wealth of the economy, which was its ability to produce goods and services at maximum capacity. The government would issue to its citizens enough purchasing power to buy this production of goods and services. Through the office of a National Credit Authority, a kind of all-encompassing state bank, the government would issue "national dividends" to the citizens to augment their purchasing power. This would be a guaranteed income. The dividend would not be in the form of printing-press money; it would be an entry in each citizen's account at the National Credit Authority. Cheques could be written against this account but they would not be negotiable for currency. As the credit was used up in cheque purchases, it would be retired.

The second pillar of Douglas's theory was the *just price*. This was to be a nationwide system of automatic price control in order to guarantee that goods were marketed at their true cost of production plus profit, but excluding banking charges and interest. The National Credit Authority (which would also have broad statistical-analysis and economic forecasting functions) would write a formula relating total production in the economy to total consumption. This formula would determine a price discount which the National Credit Authority would pay to businesses willing to participate in the operation of the system, which entailed some regulation of profit. This discount would compensate the businessman for reduced profits; once production was brought into parity with consumption, the discount would be retired, foreign trade solely to get rid of surpluses would disappear, and the nation would be able to buy back its own production. Merchants would be allowed to sell at their own prices if they were willing to forego the discount refund. As one Social Credit text put it:

> If the merchant rejects this offer and sells a portion of his goods at whatever price they will fetch, he runs the risk of having a large portion of his goods remaining, for they will be in competition with goods benefiting from the discount. Here it must be observed that there is no compulsion involved. The producer makes his own choice.*

Douglas believed that all men were entitled to share in the wealth of the modern economy. Much of the wealth of the modern economy, he thought, depended upon the "cultural inheritance" of the twen-

* E.S. Holter, *The A.B.C. of Social Credit* (Toronto: Longmans, Green, 1944) p. 50

tieth century – the rich invisible capital of ideas, inventions, techniques and concepts that made large-scale production possible – and this inheritance belonged to *all* men; it was "owned" by no one. The national dividend was therefore not a hand-out; it was something every person had a right to as an equal inheritor of a common tradition.

Although he was opposed to state socialism, and remained a firm believer in the basic rectitude of private ownership of the means of production, Douglas shared with the socialists a profound belief in man's right to the good life in the industrial age. He saw nothing wrong with paying people for not working – in fact, he saw the liberation of man from the *necessity* of working as a positive good. Unemployment, he thought, was a natural and desirable product of technological improvement and automation; people should become unemployed, in order that (with the aid of the national dividend) they could become freer, more creative human beings. "Unrestrained by the financial system," he wrote, "the resources of modern production would be sufficient to provide for the material desires of the whole population of the world at the expense of a small and decreasing amount of human labour."*

> A small impetus from a body of men who know what to do and how to do it may make the difference between yet one more retreat into the Dark Ages or the emergence into the full light of a day of such splendor as we can at present only envisage dimly.

Douglas also dealt with certain questions of political philosophy, and his theories in this area give a clue to his own political ineffectiveness.

Douglas was convinced that he had found the way to make it possible to abolish poverty and guarantee security with freedom.

The people, he reasoned, could be trusted to know what their interests and general objectives were. There was a *general will* for more abundance and an end to poverty. Therefore,

1) There is enough potential wealth, properly organized, to bring about plenty and end poverty,

2) The precise method whereby this potential wealth may be converted to real wealth, and consumed, is a complicated matter which only specialists and technicians are equipped to understand; given the power of government, they could bring it about,

* Anyone familiar with the writings of Saint-Simon, some of the anarchists, and the young Karl Marx, will detect broad similarities with the underlying humanist concern of Douglas and a common dislike of the puritan ethic as a dehumanizing force.

3) The people have a right to demand that their will be followed, therefore they should

4) Unite, express their will in powerful and unmistakable terms, and demand *results* from their government.

It was by this circuitous route that Douglas reached the conclusion that political parties are wrong because they get people talking about *methods* of reaching reform, as well as many other matters, which the people are incompetent to understand; parties therefore served only to divide the people, dilute popular demand for *results,* and distract the people from the real issue. One of Douglas's lieutenants, who later got into a lot of trouble for his views, put it this way:

> It is this wrangling among electors as to why things are wrong and about METHODS of putting them right which enables groups of unscrupulous men to exploit THE PEOPLE. Politicians are hired to set them quarrelling as to whether the trouble is due to this political party, or that, being in power, or whether the trouble is distribution, administration or constitutional, and the party politicians are experts at introducing questions which will divide the electors into evenly balanced antagonists. . . . Thus, whilst THE PEOPLE argue, the unscrupulous ones get together to press unitedly for RESULTS which they know well enough they definitely want.*

The result? "The people are quite unable to govern; are unfitted in every way to say how things should be rightly ordered. Such matters are for technicians of all kinds."

The winning of elections and implementation of theory, however, was of little concern to the phlegmatic Douglas; what mattered to him (and to most of his suspicious and pedantic successors) was maintaining the purity of the faith.

It is not hard to see how such an elitist doctrine of political action found few supporters in Alberta for the Douglasite movement itself; it awaited a man of action – a broker, organizer, a manager of men – to translate Douglas's attractive but fuzzy creed into a "fighting faith." It awaited, in a word, Aberhart.

2. *The Crisis of the* U.F.A.

It was a bitter cold night in December 1929, but 2,000 Edmontonians were out at the C.N.R. station waiting to cheer him on his arrival back from Ottawa.

* George F. Powell, *A Sovereign People Demand Results* (Edmonton: Democracy House, n.d.) p. 4.

Big bonfires had been lit, and when the train rolled into the station the Newsboys' Band struck up a march. John Edward Brownlee, Premier of the United Farmers of Alberta government, had returned home from a federal-provincial meeting with the deed to Alberta's natural resources clutched in his hand.

It was Brownlee's finest hour, in a lifetime of success. For the first forty-six years of his life, he was one of those rare men on whose behalf the very fates seem to conspire. A handsome six-footer, Brownlee came West from his native Ontario and settled in Calgary, where he articled in the distinguished legal firm of Lougheed and Bennett (Richard B. Bennett, later to become Prime Minister and Sir James Lougheed, later Conservative Senate leader and grandfather of the man who overthrew Social Credit in 1971).

In 1917 Brownlee had joined the U.F.A. and the United Grain Growers as counsel. He met the great man of the U.F.A., Henry Wise Wood, and Wood evidently took a liking to him.

In 1921 the U.F.A. rejected Wood's advice (he was opposed to the organization becoming a political party) and entered the provincial election. It swept the corrupt Liberals from power and, at thirty-seven years of age, Brownlee was offered the portfolio of Attorney-General.

The first U.F.A. government was led by Herbert Greenfield, a well-meaning but politically colourless and ineffective man who gradually lost support from the U.F.A. rank and file.

In 1925 Greenfield resigned and Brownlee was nominated to take his place. In 1926 Brownlee led the U.F.A. to its second election victory with a substantial majority. He then piloted the negotiations that led to the long-overdue sale to private interests of the near-bankrupt Alberta Great Waterways and the Edmonton, Dunvegan and British Columbia railway. And, in 1929, he led the successful negotiations with Ottawa that turned over to the provinces control over their natural resources.

The 1920s were the salad years of the U.F.A., and of Brownlee, the years when the people were solidly behind both of them and nothing could go wrong.

There were strains within the U.F.A., but in good times this highly democratic grass-roots populist organization was able to hold together a rough consensus. This consensus was a left-of-centre position built around Henry Wise Wood's core ideology of agrarian democracy and social and economic co-operation, not competition. There was strong support in the U.F.A. for "direct democracy" (recall votes for unpopular officials, plebescites on contentious issues), state medicine, tight control of alcohol, and the teaching of "social co-operation" in the schools. Resolutions concerning all these matters were brought to the 1934 convention of the U.F.A. and passed – along with a resolution against the "munitions makers", "immoral magazines" on newsstands and in the mails, and a resolution in favour of maintaining the sabbath.

The Depression confronted this social movement with a challenge it could not surmount. In the 1920s the U.F.A. had already developed at least two distinct wings, a monetary-reform wing influenced by Major Douglas and led by William Irvine (who was behind the invitation to Douglas to testify before the Commons Banking Committee in 1923) and Norman Smith, editor of the U.F.A. magazine; and an agrarian-socialist wing led by men like Norman Priestly and Henry Young.

By the early 1930s there was enough monetary-reform sentiment in the U.F.A. to support a resolution favouring a provincial bank. And, by 1932, there was enough socialist opinion to cause the convention to instruct Brownlee to call a conference of farm and labour leaders in Calgary to consider solutions to the Depression. This Calgary meeting led to the Regina conference of 1933 that drafted the Regina Manifesto and founded the C.C.F.

As the thirties wore on, it became increasingly obvious that while the U.F.A. government was doing everything it could to stave off the worst effects of the Depression – it passed moratoria to try to prevent mortgage foreclosures, distributed relief and free seed, tried to provide basic medical and social services – the effects of its policies were not enough to satisfy the people. And as the government staggered from one piece of economic bad news to the next, the U.F.A. movement came more and more under the influence of the C.C.F. An excess of ideological enthusiasm over common sense led the 1932 U.F.A. convention to endorse nationalization "of all the means of production and distribution, including land." In a province with an economy based on the holdings of small farmers, the political effect of this can be imagined. There were shocked attempts to remove the phrase "including land" at the 1933 convention, but they were beaten down; only in the 1934 convention did the movement agree to substitute the phrase "all unalienated land and land that may revert from time to time to the Crown." By then the damage had been done.

By 1933 and 1934 it was becoming obvious to many that the U.F.A. had run out of answers. The people wanted satisfaction, not complicated explanations of why critical measures were not within the constitutional jurisdiction of the province.

And then, to top it off, the Brownlee scandal broke.

32

The complete story of the Brownlee scandal will probably never be told. Most of the participants have died, left the province or drawn the gentle curtain of forgetfulness across their memories. A substantial group of older Albertans, many of them Social Crediters, continues to believe that John Brownlee was the victim of a rather cloudy political plot, the details of which they are hard-pressed to explain. Here is what the record says:

In 1930 Brownlee was invited to tour the Edson district, one hundred miles west of Edmonton in the foothills, and go on a fishing trip on the McLeod River. During the tour, Brownlee had occasion to meet the mayor of Edson, A.C. MacMillan and his family. The MacMillans accompanied him back to his train when the weekend ended. Brownlee thanked them for their hospitality and told them that if there was anything he could do in return, just to ask.

Some time later MacMillan's pretty daughter Vivian decided to come to Edmonton to look for work. She looked up Brownlee and he found her a secretarial job in the Attorney-General's Department.

In 1934, at a time when popular discontent with the U.F.A. was growing ominously, and the government had to reveal that its financial position was precarious, Vivian MacMillan and her father took John Brownlee into an Edmonton court, accused him of seduction, and claimed civil damages.

The girl alleged that Brownlee had had a sexual affair with her that lasted two and a half to three years. During that period, she said, he had made love to her regularly, on the average of between two and three times a week. Often he had taken her on after-dinner drives in his official car and made love to her in the back. She said he had given her pills to avoid becoming pregnant, and her reaction to these, and his love-making, was so violent that her health had seriously suffered. And she had been forced to confess the affair to a young medical student whom she wanted to marry.

The province's conventional oppostion parties – particularly the Liberals, who smelled blood – had a field day with the trial revelations.

The Liberal *Edmonton Bulletin* printed thousands of extra copies each day during the trial, with the trial highlights in red headlines, and they were distributed around the province. The Liberals printed thousands of leaflets containing the juicier parts and distributed them free, especially in Brownlee's home riding of Ponoka.*

On June 30, 1934, the jury brought in its verdict. It found for

---

* At one point in the trial, the publisher of *The Bulletin* was convicted of contempt of court, and fined three hundred dollars.

Vivian MacMillan and her father and awarded them damages of $10,000 and $5,000 each. The corridors of the courthouse rang with spectators' cheers. But the trial judge, Mr. Justice Ives, said the jury's verdict was not consonant with the law or the facts, threw out its verdict, and ordered the MacMillans to pay all court costs.

The MacMillans appealed to the Alberta Supreme Court, which upheld Mr. Justice Ives' opinion. Said Chief Justice Harvey:

> It is necessary to consider the evidence for the plaintiffs in the case. It is of such a nauseating character that I shall deal with it in the most general way possible. In the first place, apart from the daughter's own evidence there is not a tittle of evidence that she is not still a virgin. In every reported case which counsel has been able to find in which the plaintiff has succeeded, with the exception of one nearly 100 years ago . . . which some of the courts have described as of doubtful authority, there has been the birth of a child or at least pregnancy furnishing indisputable evidence of sexual intercourse. There is nothing of that sort here, notwithstanding the fact that the witness swears that for between two and a half and three years sexual intercourse took place on the average of two to three times a week.
>
> She says that to prevent conception the defendant, not however till after the seduction found by the jury took place, furnished her with pills to take which she describes by a name unknown both to the physician whom she called and to the dictionaries, and of which no specimen is produced.

The Chief Justice was openly sceptical of the MacMillan story and said that it was "quite unsupported by other evidence in all material respects" and was "of such an improbable, not to say incredible, character, that it seems impossible that any reasonable person would believe it in its entirety." From his written judgment:

> She admits that that influence [Brownlee's influence over her, which she testified was the only reason she carried on with the relationship] was effective only when she was in his presence, yet after the relationship had existed for nearly two years and she had been at home during an illness for several weeks and her parents urged her to remain at home and not to return to Edmonton, she, against their wishes, returned and would have had no other expectation than that the former relationship with she says existed would be resumed.

Both Ives and the superior court refused to award the girl or her father damages because neither was able to demonstrate to the courts' satisfaction that they had suffered any real injury.

Public sympathy, however, was on the girl's side. A public fund to help defray the family's expenses was set up and generously subscribed. On March 1, 1937, long after the case had ceased to have political significance, the Supreme Court of Canada handed down its decision on the appeal. Some of the justices were sceptical about the Macmillan case. Said Mr. Justice Davis:

> During the summer of 1932 she consulted a physician as she had lost weight during the two prior years. She says she had 'stomach trouble brought on by nerves' and she felt 'very tired all the time' and that the pills she had been taking to avoid pregnancy upset her. The physician, who was called by her counsel . . . described her then condition as 'irritable colon.' . . . He said that there was no doubt that she was suffering from constipation.

Focusing on a clause in Alberta's Seduction Act, the Supreme Court overruled the decisions of the lower courts and awarded Vivian MacMillan $10,000, but her father nothing.

In 1934 Alberta was still, like the rest of Canada, a puritanical province. Public men were judged by very strict standards. The 1934 budget had shown the U.F.A. government to be close to financial bankruptcy; the Brownlee case – and another slightly later case involving a U.F.A. cabinet minister* – seemed to show that it was morally bankrupt as well. Brownlee resigned and left public life, a capable man caught up in a personal tragedy. And the U.F.A's stock fell still further.

Did the Brownlee scandal cause the ruin of the U.F.A.? That would seem unlikely. The U.F.A. was in deep political trouble by 1934 anyway. The government was on the ropes, the movement was splintering, and U.F.A. membership, which had reached 37,721 in 1921, had fallen to 9,838 by 1935. Brownlee was replaced by R.G. (Dick) Reid, his provincial treasurer – an honest and able man, but lacking in Brownlee's platform presence and stature. Brownlee might have been at least a focusing-point in the coming debate with Social Credit.

William Aberhart did not exploit the Brownlee scandal, nor did he have to. The Liberals, whose hunger for spoils was palpable, did

---

* The minister, who had six children, had gotten a quiet divorce, which *The Bulletin* had gotten ahold of and publicized. Before being forced to resign from cabinet, the minister cornered the publisher of *The Bulletin* at the Legislature one day and knocked him down the front steps.

the job only too well – destroying, in the process, not only Brownlee but themselves. It was not lost on people that the Liberals were the main ones trying to make mileage out of the Brownlee affair, that they were behind much of the newspaper publicity and the whispering. Their own efforts boomeranged on the provincial Liberals and gave them a stamp for cynicism.

The political vacuum into which Social Credit would rush was now complete.

CHAPTER FOUR

Aberhart and the Young Manning

1. *The Mentor.*

The man who brought Social Credit out of the realm of abstractions and into the realm of politics was William Aberhart, a powerful, volatile and inflexible teacher and religious organizer.

Aberhart was born, of a German father and English mother, on a small dairy farm near Egmondville, Ontario, on December 30th, 1879. In his youth he was a big, strong boy who worked hard scholastically and was a brilliant loner on the soccer team. His parents were retiring people with a healthy respect for hard work and study and a love of local revival meetings, to which they frequently took their son. In later years, Aberhart confided to friends that he had been so impressed by the way the evangelists had pounded the pulpit that he used to practise doing it himself, in the farmyard, on a pine stump.

Aberhart became a school teacher, and received an extramural B.A. from Queen's. In 1910 he came West to Calgary, and in 1915 he was made principal of the city's newest public school, Crescent Heights High School.

As an educator, he soon distinguished himself as a profoundly effective organizer of men and activities. Crescent Heights ran like a well-oiled machine: tasks were neatly assigned, accountability was strictly to the front office, and there were written procedures for nearly everything. Aberhart was an incessant organizer; his head was crammed with diagrams, flowcharts, organizational tables. He believed in rote teaching and precise, logical organization of subject matter. All the subjects he taught had charts (which he drew himself).

He was a born showman. He secured the school reams of publicity in the local newspapers and permeated the classrooms with a spirit of bustle. Although a forceful, even domineering personality, he fell short of being any autocrat. He had a good sense of humour and was willing to listen to argument from his staff. Teachers found that he would generally support them in disagreements with parents. He intensely disliked the Darwinian theory of evolution; but when he advanced his argument to the Crescent Heights biology teacher and was told, "*I'm* teaching biology", he left the subject alone. In 1922 when the idea was new in Calgary, he pushed through the organization of an elected students union at Crescent Heights.

A big man, six feet tall and weighing about 260 pounds (he liked to tell people that he weighed an eighth of a ton),* he radiated an aura of power and confidence. His bald head, deep voice and pince-nez reinforced the image. At home he was a strict father who got around little socially, frowned on dancing and cards (the first time his younger daughter danced, it was with her husband-to-be), seldom attended movies. Neither daughter was allowed to attend the movies until she was fifteen. Breaches of discipline at home were handled as they were in school: if either daughter broke the rules, she was quietly asked to come up to his study after dinner, at which time she would be lectured, then strapped.

The consequence of Aberhart's hard-driving leadership at Crescent Heights was that, by the mid-1920s, he had a wide reputation in Calgary as an efficient and effective educator. Crescent Heights was the kind of school most Calgary parents wanted their children to attend. Many parents and teachers would have echoed the sentiment of the teacher who described him as "a great noise and a great light. In his presence, one felt as if one were near a magnesium flare."

Although some were put off by his drive (he customarily rose at 6:00 a.m. for pre-breakfast study, took a bag lunch to school and worked through the noon hour, returned home for dinner, and then spent the evening working at the Prophetic Bible Institute until about 2:00 a.m.) and by his strong beliefs (he gave little encouragement to school dances and forbade smoking in the staff room), Aberhart generally had the respect and admiration of a broad following of parents, teachers and students.

The story of his religious activities is somewhat stormier.

In many ways religion was the real passion of his life. When he first arrived in Calgary he initiated Bible-study classes at Grace

---

* Aberhart had a robust appetite. His favourite dish at home was called "heavenly hash". Mrs. Aberhart made it from graham-cracker crumbs, evaporated milk, walnuts, marshmallows and icing sugar.

Presbyterian Church. By 1925 he was a controversial lay religious leader with a weekly two-hour radio program reaching over 350,000 listeners every Sunday. At a time when there was less atmospheric static and interference, the signal from the CFCN transmitter on the north bank of the Bow River reached as far west as the Okanagan valley, south into the mountain States and eastward far across the prairies. According to CFCN he had the largest radio following of any religious broadcast in the country, and easily outdrew the Jack Benny program which came on immediately after him.

Between 1911 and 1925, however, lay a trail of bitter church feuds and schisms. Aberhart quarreled with church officials at Grace Presbyterian, went to Wesley Methodist and quarreled there, and finally came to Westbourne Baptist Church, a somewhat run-down and declining congregation in Calgary's east end. In each earlier church Aberhart's strict doctrinal views and unwillingness to compromise had led to clashes. At Westbourne, however, he was more at home. Here, he built his base.

All his life, Aberhart's religious activities were punctuated by controversy and criticism. He was a strong leader but a poor follower, a confident pilot but a fractious, quarrelsome and sometimes rebellious crew-member. Even his takeover of Westbourne Baptist Church was bracketed by charges from members of Westbourne's parent church, First Baptist, that Aberhart has misled them on the question of his support for Baptist missionary activities.

Here is the context in which Aberhart must be seen as a religionist:

With the Protestant reformation, many Christians began to rely on the authority of conscience and Scripture as a counterpoise to the authority of the Church. Protestants denied infallability to the Pope and his Councils and attributed it to the Bible.

Beginning in the eighteenth century, the methods and findings of scientific and historical scholarship were brought to bear on the authority of the Bible itself. The effect of this "Higher Criticism", as it came to be called, on the minds, confidence and faith of many Protestants was devastating. By calling into question the historical validity of literal Biblical passages, the Higher Critics seemed to some believers to be calling into question the authority of Christianity itself. Theological debates within the churches took on a more strident and bitter note; it was the storm from this debate that washed up, on the shores of church work in the West, Aberhart himself.

Aberhart was a fundamentalist and traditionalist. He rejected the argument that Scripture should be re-interpreted in light of new knowledge; such a re-interpretation, he held, threatened the very

39

basis of belief. By the 1920s this debate was waning somewhat in Europe but in many parts of North America, Alberta included, it was still going strong.

Aberhart believed that the Bible was an unerring and infallible authority and that it was verbally inspired in all details. He made the fight against modernism and liberalism a main thrust of his life's work. Scholars who sought to re-translate the King James Version of the Bible, he said, were "rushing in where angels fear to tread":

> Conditions are fast becoming as they were in France just previous to her horrible infidelity and Revolutionary period. . . . Can you estimate the effect upon the rising generation to have nothing settled? Will our children not soon begin to think that Holy Scripture is a nose of wax to be twisted hither and thither? Would to God I could use a dispeller that would roll back this fog in every direction, for I believe God has spoken: "If the foundations are destroyed, what can the righteous do?" (*Psalms* 11:3)

Aberhart wanted to turn back the clock to an earlier time in theology and religious belief. In that sense, he was a theological reactionary.* He devoted his life to an almost Talmudic analysis and memorization of Scripture so that he could recall, verbatim, literally thousands of passages from memory.

It was in this vein that Aberhart's furious energy turned Westbourne into a beehive of activity and organization. Overnight, large Bible study classes and a whole slate of through-the-week activities were instituted. The congregation picked up; new members flowed in. In 1922 a full-time pastor, E.G. Hansell, was brought in. In this way was the basis of Aberhart's formidable religious organization created.

In 1925, without realizing the significance of his act, Aberhart agreed to try some experimental radio broadcasts from Westbourne over CFCN, the radio station owned by W.W. Grant, a free-wheeling radio promoter. After he got over his initial nervousness, Aberhart proved to be a "natural" for radio; in hundreds of farm communities he was an overnight success.

2. *The Pupil.*

The first seventeen years of Ernest Manning's life were shaped in an

---

* There is no automatic correlation between religious conservatism and political conservatism. The leading exponent of the left-wing social gospel in the early twentieth century was Walter Rausenbusch, a Baptist. Another such Baptist was Tommy Douglas.

isolated Saskatchewan frontier community where the wind always blew, and the water tasted of iron. They were fairly uneventful years that shaped many aspects of Manning's character: his modesty, his reserve, his shyness, his earnestness.

George Henry Manning, Ernest's father, was a short, taciturn Englishman who came to Canada around the turn of the century, several years ahead of the great flood of immigration. An orphan and the youngest of thirteen children, he was raised by his oldest brother and his wife. He joined the merchant marine and was on the verge of sailing when it was found he had lied about his age, so he came to Canada instead. He worked as a hired hand for a time, then staked a homestead near Carnduff, Saskatchewan, a hamlet nestling the Manitoba border. In 1903 he sent for his old country sweetheart, Elizabeth Mara Dickson. She was a slim wan girl who had been a "ladies maid" in London in the home of an Austrian noblewoman who lived near Picadilly; before she came, she used to join the eleven other servants on the roof to watch Boer War parades below. In one parade, Kaiser Wilhelm waved at her. She had been diagnosed with tuberculosis in England but it disappeared in the dry Canadian climate. They were married in the Carnduff Baptist Church.

At Carnduff the Mannings were plagued with bad luck. Three years they were hailed out.

On September 20, 1908, their second son, Ernest Charles, was born; the next spring, the old man hitched a team of oxen and went west to find a new homestead for his family. On his second "draw" at the Saskatoon land office he got rights to a quarter-section of rich loam four miles south and west of Rosetown, a nice piece of land straddling a shallow valley and looking west. Rosetown lay twenty-two miles past the end of the railway at Zealandia and was a typical small frontier town and not much more: a collection of clapboard shacks, a dirt main street, some supply stores and two brand-new grain elevators.

It was a hard land, but often a good one. In winter the only sound was the drone of the ceaseless wind; in summer the wind was joined by the cheerful whistling of the gophers and meadowlarks. They built a sod house on a rise overlooking the land; later, Manning Sr. planted a stout caragana hedge around the yard to break the wind.

Life was a serious affair, mainly of hard work. The Mannings had only a few close friends. Manning's father was not an outgoing man. Manning's mother was a vivacious woman, bothered by loneliness. The basis for life was work, duty, respect for one's elders. The Manning boys knew what was expected of them and did it.

In 1912 the last Manning child, Roy, was born, and the same year

41

the Saskatchewan Department of Education opened a local school, Glen Payne. In 1914 Ernest Manning went there.

It was a stereotype one-room schoolhouse. The walls, high roller blinds and steel water cooler were all painted in Official Dark Green. There was a cloakroom and a square heating register in the middle of the room, directly above the coal-and-wood furnace in the basement. Every winter day, there was a race to see who could get the precious spaces around the register to leave their lunches; left in the cloakroom, lunches froze solid.

The learning resources of the Manning household were not bountiful, but were probably average for the time. There was a Bible, a well-read Eaton's catalogue, and a dog-eared collection of Victorian boys' fiction including Manning's favourite, *The Shepherd of the Hills* by Harold Bell Wright (a predecessor of Zane Grey) and *The Lamplighter, or, An Orphan Girl's Struggles and Triumphs,* by "Miss Cummins". And there was a thick, one-volume copy of the *Peoples' Home Library,* a kind of farm almanac which Mrs. Manning purchased from a travelling salesman.

Rosetown was controlled by the "drys" and was a quiet prairie town. Young Ernest took violin lessons and was a competent if somewhat unenthusiastic performer.

He tended to be shy, and had a boyish sense of humour. He used to throw a girl from a neighbouring farm into a panic by picking up her pet rabbits and starting to carry them off, threatening to "clip" them. Once he took a pair of pliers and pinched the neck of a woman teacher who boarded at the Manning house; when people expressed curiosity about her bruise, he told them his brother Bill had bitten her.

In the winter, the Manning boys went to occasional skating parties and church socials. Ernie played his violin at a few chivarees – those wild community noise-fests aimed at disturbing the first-night attentions of young honeymooners.

He finished grade eight at Glen Payne, doing well in mathematics and literature (he had an excellent visual memory) but decided to go no further.* He was not an enthusiastic scholar. He entered a rather restless and aimless period of his life. He worked half-heartedly around the farm, did chores, read the occasional book, hired out to a neighbour's threshing crew at harvest time. He liked to tinker, and bought a decrepit old Model T for fifty dollars which he stripped down (at its prime it lacked muffler, headlights, brakes, windshield

---

* This was not uncommon in the community, apparently; his brother Bill was the first Glen Payne student to go past grade eight and on to higher education, eventually getting an M.ED. from the University of Saskatchewan.

and speedometer) and called "The Bazoo".

Then he got the radio bug. In the autumn of 1924, when he was sixteen, he put aside his harvest earnings and sent a hundred dollars to Montgomery-Ward for a radio, complete with headset, gooseneck speaker and dry cell batteries. It finally came and, on Christmas Day, Mrs. Manning had to wait inside, her repast growing cold, while father and the boys struggled on the roof, in freezing winds, to erect a one-hundred-foot antenna.

Overnight, radio bridged the frontier and brought in the outside world. On cold winter nights around a kerosene lantern or hissing Coleman light, the Manning boys "logged" stations as far away as Pittsburgh, Denver, New Orleans. There was less electronic interference (Rosetown, four miles away, turned off its municipal AC power system at midnight) and signals could be picked up from incredible distances with considerable clarity.

It isn't recorded when the Mannings heard their first Aberhart radio broadcast. We do know that Aberhart's electronic confrontation with the restless young farm boy was a turning point in both their lives. The Mannings had rather loose denominational ties and had attended the United Church as well as the local Baptist and Methodist churches. In summers young Ernie went to the community Sunday School organized at Glen Payne School by young United Church ministers on summer mission.

Underneath, however, the young farm boy was obviously looking for something. Hard work and good fortune had enabled the family to do well; they had six bumper crops between 1919 and 1927 and enough money in the bank for Ernie to manage to persuade his cautious father to buy a McCormick-Deering tractor.*

But farm work was repetitive drudgery, school was boring, the family had no political interest,** they never travelled and he was, after all, an energetic young man. To such a young man, Aberhart had a radio message: come to Calgary and learn more about Christ. In the winter of 1927, Manning came.

3. *Staff College for Christian Soldiers.*

For some time now, it has been felt by many lovers of THE TRUTH ONCE DELIVERED that there is a great need, in this Western country of ours, of an uptodate Bible Institute or School

---

* It was one of the first in the area and the neighbours used to complain about the noise it made.

** His father was a nominal Tory who had once voted for the Progressive party. But he was politically inactive and politics was almost never discussed in the home.

43

of Learning where our young people especially, and any others who wish it, can secure a good training in Bible Knowledge without having their faith undermined by atheistic and modernistic teaching, too often found in many of our present day theological colleges and universities. The cry of young people, who have had their faith shipwrecked, is to be heard on every side. Has it reached you where you live yet?

– Prophetic Bible Institute prospectus, 1927

In early 1926 Aberhart and his colleagues began to realize that dependence on Westbourne alone was cramping their style. Westbourne now had a very large congregation. A correspondence course in Bible studies had been created for rural listeners of Aberhart's Sunday broadcasts and other activities were burgeoning. What they needed was a large, central building of their own in downtown Calgary, a building that could become the campus of a full scale Bible college of their own design and conception. So the idea of the Prophetic Bible Institute was born.

Aberhart planned extensive publicity and fund-raising. He plugged the project each Sunday on the radio. Groups were urged to purchase foundation "sods" at a hundred dollars each and "bricks" at five dollars each. Competitions were held between locales to see which group could raise the most money. Literature was sent out far and wide. The purpose of the Institute, it said, was to train leadership "for this great fight for truth against infidelity." "We are facing a condition of spiritual things that is very detrimental to the higher life of men and women everywhere . . . "

Young Manning came to Calgary on the C.P.R. on February 17, 1927, to meet Aberhart and inquire how plans were coming for the Institute, due to open that fall. His arrival was somewhat inauspicious: the sleeves on his mail-order suit were too short for his long arms, he was a shy and awkward 118 pounds, and the day he arrived Aberhart's younger daughter was married and Manning got lost in the shuffle.

He did get to speak to Aberhart briefly and went down from his room at the Y.M.C.A. to look in on the youth group at Westbourne – a group that included young Muriel Preston, whom he later married. He was evidently impressed by the Aberhart organization; he returned home to Rosetown anxious to enroll in classes in the fall, and when the doors opened at the Prophetic Bible Institute he was the first student registered.

The institution in which he was to spend the next eight years of his life bore the stamp of Aberhart on every brick and shingle. For full-time students the academic term was a full six months. The routine was rigorous. Students were boarded out in homes with a good "moral atmosphere" and were required to be present for pre-breakfast worship each morning, regular prayer meetings, special prayer meetings, and classes (8:30 a.m. to 9:45 p.m. weekdays, 8:30 a.m. to 8:45 p.m. Saturdays). Students were asked to lead a life

> of separation from all harmful and spiritually degrading pursuits and worldly affairs such as the moving picture show, the theatre, the dance, and any similar carnal institution which tends to lower moral standards and destroy the Christian influence of a pure life.

Aberhart recommended to his followers that their children be sent to the Institute before entering university.

Aberhart hand-picked the staff, mainly from the ranks of those who had taken Bible study courses from him at Westbourne. Apart from Aberhart himself, the Institute staff had only one professionally certified teacher (Miss Mabel Giles, who taught at Crescent Heights) and no one with theological training from a recognized academic institution. The instructors included an insurance agent, an accountant, a dentist, and several housewives. All were volunteers serving without pay and all held their posts at the pleasure of Aberhart.

There were no problems with student discipline. Students were allowed very little free time of their own. Because attendance was tuition-free, it was regarded as a privilege. Manning enrolled in what the Institute called its "graduate specialist" program, a full three-year course of studies designed for "those who are entering the Ministry or the Institute Lectureship." Manning took some high school courses by correspondence and the Institute offered options in motor-mechanics, English, shorthand and typing; but the core curriculum was taken up with Apologetics ("the Great Evidence and Proofs of the Bible"), Systematic Theology ("when a student has completed this course he . . . will not be easily side-tracked by the many heresies on every hand"), Sacred History, Bible Geography, Missionary Work, Bible Interpretation, Personal Evangelism, Public Speaking and Sunday School Teaching. The directors of the Institute set out the "doctrinal basis" for teaching, which included, in addition to conventional Christian theology, divine verbal inspiration of Scripture and the "absolute supremacy, infallability and efficiency" of the Bible "in all matters of faith and creation." And as well:

> 5. The creation of man in holiness, by the direct act of God and not by an evolutionary process: the historicity and terrible reality of the fall of man and the resulting total and universal depravity of human nature . . .
>
> 9. The everlasting happiness of the righteous and the awful and

everlasting misery of the unbelieving wicked, in a literal lake of fire, prepared for a real, personal Devil and his angels . . .

10. The resurrection of the dead, both of the unjust and the just, the Christians at the Lord's appearing, the Israelites at his coming, and the unbelieving dead at the end of the millenium.

Several themes recurred throughout the Institute's textbooks. One was criticism of the Revised Standard Version of the Bible ("it is characterised throughout by a false basis, by inherent error, and by deceit and fraud"). One was criticism of the Theory of Evolution ("no true science can deal with the question of the origin of life since it cannot acquire knowledge of events preceding the existence of a trained observer"). One was concentration on popular arguments about Biblical literality: did the "great fish" actually swallow Jonah? Did Joshua actually cause the sun to stand still? Is the world eons old – or was it created, as Bishop Usher calculated from *Genesis,* on October 23rd, 4,004 B.C., at 9 a.m. (Eastern Standard Time)?

Today much of this seems quaint and unreal. In the 1920s, however, it reflected the real emotional and spiritual crisis many Christians were passing through in response to the impact of a new way of thinking about the world.

The ecumenical spirit was not well-developed at the Institute. One Institute text described Roman Catholic missionary work as "characterized by false doctrines, unscrupulous methods and . . . not frequently . . . shocking immoralities and grievous scandals." The other major world faiths were treated even more critically.

Running through much of the Institute's teaching was the fundamentalist doctrine of Original Sin, which was administered straight: the Institute text taught that Man was "intellectually, spiritually, morally and physically" depraved, sinful, alienated from God, deceitful and wicked," "vile and detestable and lustful."*

Contrary to Social Crediters' later claim that their political faith was "applied Christianity", the Christianity taught at the Prophetic Bible Institute was devoid of any social teachings. Aberhart's evangelical Christianity was a personal, not a social, faith: its aim was the radical transformation of the individual, and the individual only. Men made right with God would presumably take care of social problems in due course. The only political movement which evangelical Christians ever backed enthusiastically in North America was Prohibition – prompting the criticism that blue laws were the highest stage of evangelical social thought.

* Manning was not without a sense of humour about all this; for years, when vexed by another driver cutting him off in traffic, he would say dryly, "there goes the accumulated consequence of 6,000 years of human depravity."

Manning's years at the Institute did give him an indissoluble grounding in evangelical Christianity, a grounding upon which he built a formidable following as a lay evangelist. But nothing he learned in his classes at the Institute made him into a Social Creditor. *That* grew out of his personal association with Aberhart.

In his three years as an Institute student, and his subsequent years as an Institute employee, Manning made only one lifelong friend – Aberhart. Apart from this friendship, Manning was caught up in the swirl of Institute activities. In summers he returned home to Rosetown to do farm work and harvesting. Sometimes he slept in dirty mobile cook-shacks while doing custom combining. Several times he practised writing sermons by the light of a kerosene lantern in an empty granary.

His first few years at the Institute did nothing to broaden him socially. A Calgary newspaperman once dropped in at the Institute to interview Aberhart and was let in by Manning. The newspaperman mistook the thin, shy young man for the janitor.

Manning and Aberhart were unquestionably attracted to one another. Aberhart was thirty-two years Manning's senior, and a powerful, fatherly figure. Manning was an ideal pupil – attentive, respectful, clever, sober and dedicated. During Manning's second term, Aberhart began to befriend him; when the Aberharts went away to the coast for holidays, they asked young Ernest to mind the house for them. Finally, in 1930, after his graduation, Aberhart appointed Manning secretary of the Institute main office. And that same year, Manning moved in to live permanently in the Aberhart home. He was given a small desk in Aberhart's upstairs study, and often the two would stay up late, talking and writing sermons, almost until the sunrise.

It was during this time that Manning's speaking voice began to develop an uncanny resemblance to Aberhart's. Radio listeners found it harder and harder to tell the difference between them – except that Aberhart's voice was somewhat deeper. Why did it happen? There are many theories. Two plausible explanations might be that Manning learned public speaking from a textbook Aberhart had written; and the close association between them developed an almost father-son quality which probably led to a certain amount of unconscious emulation.

Manning had no serious rivals for Aberhart's favour. The only one who came close was Cyril Hutchinson, a tall, good looking young man four years Manning's senior who had been a student of Aberhart's at Westbourne Baptist. Hutchinson taught part-time at the Institute but had an outside job with the C.P.R., later with the city of Calgary. Much more than Manning, the courtly Hutchinson had an outside life of his own. The two were close friends and often travelled together; when Aberhart picked up the Social Credit standard in 1932 and took Manning with him, Hutchinson remained behind to become Institute secretary. The Institute carried on even after Aberhart went to Edmonton to become premier.*

4. *The Conversion.*

It cannot be said that Aberhart's response to the crisis of the Depression was very rapid. By 1931 it was obvious to most people that something had gone horrifyingly wrong with the economy. Aberhart, however, was deeply caught up in his church work and never had been very concerned about current affairs. Manning was busy learning from Aberhart. As a single-minded religious activist and school principal on secure tenure and salary, Aberhart was slow to personally feel the Depression's pinch.

Gradually the pressure began to grow. Aberhart began to find it harder to raise money to finance the Institute and his radio series. Then the Calgary newspapers, with the backing of the city's business elite, began a massive campaign to retrench teachers' salaries, and Aberhart began to ponder what was happening. He made his opposition to the campaign privately known.

Students and former students began to come to him and tell him about their troubles at home, and their difficulty finding work. Many out-of-work men came to Aberhart for personal loans. Several children fainted in class at Crescent Heights; they admitted to Aberhart it was from hunger. Just before Aberhart left Calgary for Edmonton in early July 1932, to mark examination papers, one of his young grade twelve pupils became despondent and committed suicide.

---

* The Institute continued to run smoothly for five years after Aberhart's death, until 1948. Then an internal quarrel over doctrine – the old curse of the evangelical sects – split it down the middle. Manning (who was by this time Institute president) and Cyril Hutchinson disagreed over the role of foreign missions. Hutchinson wanted more emphasis on them, Manning wanted more emphasis on the needs of the prairie communities. The argument came to a head and Manning and the Board suggested to Hutchinson that he take three months "leave of absence" to think about his position. Hutchinson said this was tantamount to coercion and resigned, taking five of the Institute's six teachers with him. Eventually they established a new institution, the Berean Bible College, on the north hill just a few blocks from, of all places, Crescent Heights High School.

The Prophetic Bible Institute went downhill all the way. A few die-hard staff tried to resuscitate it, but to no avail. Fewer and fewer students came, and finally it was closed. In 1968 the building was leased as a discotheque.

When Aberhart arrived in Edmonton, he met an Edmonton teacher friend of several years' acquaintance, Charles M. Scarborough. Scarborough had once met a friend of Major Douglas's on a boat trip, and the man had sold Scarborough on the Douglas theory of Social Credit. Scarborough began to spread the word at home, and when he heard Aberhart over the radio one Sunday, decided that he would be the perfect man to sell the Douglas system to the masses.

Scarborough had marked examination papers with Aberhart during two previous summers, and had worked on him earnestly, outlining the Douglas theory and how it applied to the needs of the times. Aberhart had shown interest but avoided committment.

When Aberhart arrived in Edmonton, Scarborough again met him to mark papers and decided on one last attempt at persuasion. He came to Aberhart's room at St. Steven's College on the university campus one evening and spent hours pleading the Douglas case with all the fervour he could muster. Aberhart was interested, and promised to immediately read a primer on Social Credit by British actor Maurice Colbourne, which Scarborough left him.

Aberhart sat up with the book the rest of the night. When the morning sun finally splashed over the sleepy campus (or so the story goes), Aberhart snapped the book shut, convinced at last of Douglas's theory.

Thus began the most spectacular political crusade in the history of the Canadian West.

CHAPTER FIVE

Prairie Fire

Scarcely realizing where it would lead him, William Aberhart took his first, hesitant step into Depression politics in the autumn of 1932. He asked for, and received, the permission of the Institute's Board of Managers to begin interjecting "plugs" for Social Credit into his regular Sunday broadcasts.

He began with this hope: that if he could spread the good news about Social Credit far enough and quickly enough, the people would recognize it as their economic salvation and somehow – he was not clear how – bring pressure to bear on government to implement it.

Only when it later became obvious to Aberhart that his secular evangelism was not going to yield government action did he take a second step and organize the Alberta Social Credit League as a pressure group to force government action. And only when that plan failed (it took more than three years to discover this) did Aberhart take the movement into politics itself and launch a drive for office. Once in politics, it took Social Credit less than a year to break the back of the once-unbeatable United Farmers of Alberta.

It was an immense tribute to the dynamism and fervour of Aberhart – and to the political opportunities open in a tumultuous time – that he was able, as a raw amateur starting from scratch, to bring down the most popular and powerful political machine Alberta had known until that time.*

* The 1932 to 1935 years were the epic years of Social Credit, the years of romance and mythology; when old-timers got together to reminisce in later years, it was always to the prairie-fire triumph of 1935 that they returned. For Socreds, the ordeal by fire from 1932 to 1935 was their psychological equivalent of Mao's Long March.

Aberhart's first plugs for Social Credit in his Sunday broadcasts in the autumn of 1932 were in the nature of intellectual probes, attempts to get people thinking and give focus to their grievances.

He began at a fairly innocuous level. What's wrong with our system that we are poor, and yet potential riches lie all around us? he asked. Is it God's will that we should have to suffer? Isn't there anything men of goodwill can do about our plight?

The transition from spiritual to secular prophecy was so subtle in Aberhart's broadcasts that people were a while catching on. But gradually, their ears began to prick up.

The new year came, 1933; and Aberhart thought it was time to put the spreading of the word on a more rational and organized basis. The term "social credit" had by that time been used over the air several times and a number of listeners had written in, curious, wanting to know more. The idea of monetary reform – as we noted earlier – had roots in Alberta, and under Aberhart's public prompting, began to send up new growth. Aberhart then went on the air to announce the organization of week-night lectures and classes on Social Credit theory.

Almost at the same time, he privately organized a Social Credit study group with about thirty students. They were subjected to a thorough course in Social Credit theory, as interpreted by Aberhart. Mimeographed study lessons were handed out, readings were assigned, and Aberhart brought into play all his effective paraphernalia of charts and diagrams. Many of the members of this first study-group – which included Manning – were destined to become a part of the hard core of the Social Credit movement in months to come.

Through the winter and early spring of 1933 Aberhart's young movement slowly coalesced. It was, at this stage, an "educational" venture, designed to propagate Social Credit doctrines at the wheat-roots level, in Calgary, and soon throughout southern Alberta. But as events soon showed, its structure – set up to facilitate education and propaganda – was easily adaptable to direct political action.

During the winter and spring, the movement built up a supply of pamphlets and circulars, most of them written by Aberhart, and sent out speakers to service clubs and voluntary groups throughout Calgary. A few study groups were established across the city, but the centre of study remained the Institute. As Aberhart's activities became more common knowledge, and as he bore down a little harder each Sunday on questions of economic reform, requests to hear him speak began to trickle in, both from groups in Calgary, and from groups without; and Aberhart met as many of these as he could.

The first great public campaign of Social Credit began in the summer of 1933, when Aberhart and Manning, freed at last from routine and moving in response to ever-increasing requests, made a speech-making tour throughout southern Alberta. In the space of about one month the pair visited more than forty centres and held two meetings a day. They spoke to people in churches and community halls, in stores and arenas, in farm backyards and on small-town main streets. Manning chauffered the older man, and handled all appointments. Five days a week, they were on the road; on the weekends they came back to Calgary to handle the Sunday services.

The net impact of these two men, travelling at their own expense, can hardly be exaggerated. Their energy and obvious dedication was apparent to everyone. Aberhart's broadcasts had always had their largest audience in the south; now his listeners, many of them, were getting an opportunity to see the great man in person.

The thirties were a time of great turmoil and energy in the propagation of proposals for reform. But it was obvious to many, from the summer of 1933 on, that among all the theories, only Social Credit claimed disciples eager and sincere and motivated enough to come out into the countryside in the white heat of summer and across bone-jarring country roads, to bring their message to the people. Even those unimpressed by Aberhart's speeches had to be impressed by that.

The other importance of that first tour in 1933 was that it indissolubly cemented Aberhart and Manning together in the eyes of the public. In 1933 and in years later other Social Credit workers were out in the countryside in other parts of the province, spreading the word – workers every bit as dedicated, hard-working and effective as Manning. But Manning was with Aberhart. For the better part of a summer, the two were together almost constantly. It took any remaining formality out of their relationship and made them, at least for the moment, something like equals.

Aberhart returned to the Institute in the autumn to confront a veritable mountain of public requests for further speakers, for Social Credit literature and for study groups. He turned to the thirty odd members of his original personal study group, and put the problem to them: would they go out as his representatives and spread the word themselves?

They would; and did. New study groups were organized all over Calgary, and a few outside the city. Speakers were sent out to local communities beyond. Some canvassed communities door-to-door, others offered their own living rooms as meeting-places. By the spring of 1935 there were sixty-three study groups organized in Calgary alone.

From the very beginning, all the groups in Alberta that should have known better – the ruling United Farmers government, the opposition Liberals and Conservatives, the moguls of business and finance, the newspapers – consistently under-estimated the growing power and strength of the Social Credit movement. The movement was a going concern, an immense popular force, before Aberhart's political activities even began to receive adequate journalistic attention; and as for the political parties, they awoke to the potential of Social Credit far too late.

The period from the fall of 1933 until the spring of 1934 witnessed a near-disastrous internal rupture in Aberhart's new movement. Precisely at the time when the movement was attempting to sink roots across the province, there developed a vicious dog-fight for organizational control and ideological purity; and the movement nearly collapsed before it got off the ground.

The fight was between Aberhart's group and a group of Social Credit ideologues of longer standing, men who regarded themselves as superior and accredited students of Douglas's theories, and the Aberhart men as half-baked interlopers.

The problem had interesting roots. Years before Aberhart was converted to Douglas's view of things, there were, in various Alberta communities and movements, a number of quiet but convinced Douglas students – men like Herbert Boyd of Egerton, A.J. Logan and Larkham Collins, of Calgary. All the Douglasites, as they came to be called, were fervent students of economics who could quote chapter and verse on virtually everything Douglas ever wrote. All were intensely proud of their mastery of Douglas's theories. Many of them were well-educated and well-read. Most of them were superlative theoriests, but politically inept.

Aberhart's Social Credit movement had never really established any control over them, in a strict sense; as a result, the movement's inner councils were frequently dominated by arguments over theory. The Douglasites made no great effort to conceal their belief that Aberhart was a disorganized thinker who was muddying the waters and distorting some of the clarity in Douglas's thoughts. They were probably right. But Aberhart did not take well to their suggestions.

In the summer of 1933, when Aberhart and Manning were on tour, the Douglasites got together with a college-trained businessman, Charles G. Palmer, and set up the New Age Club, which they then affiliated, not with Aberhart's organization, but with Douglas's Social Credit Secretariat in London.

From its office in the Board of Trade Building, the New Age Club carried on a second Social Credit crusade, as it were, independent of Aberhart's efforts, with its own finances, organization, interpretation of the Douglas doctrine, and view of the constitutional application of Social Credit policy. People representing the club refused to submit in any way to Aberhart's control or direction, and openly criticized his version of doctrine.

Aberhart's great appeal in Alberta was to the common people, the farmers and their families, people in small towns, shopkeepers and blue-collar workers, minor officials. His flamboyant delivery and earthy language spoke a political language they understood. The New Age Club message was pitched at a higher, cooler, more analytical level; while it lacked popular appeal, it had a certain attraction for the better-off and the better-educated. The New Age Club had some of the best analytical minds in the movement; Aberhart had the following of the people. The struggle for power that soon developed between the two was a struggle for ideological leadership, a struggle to see who would interpret doctrine. It was the men of words of the New Age Club against Aberhart, the man of action.

The Douglasites launched a frank and undisguised attack on Aberhart's ideological reliability. Larkham Collins, in an interview with the *Vancouver Sun,* said Aberhart's understanding of Douglas's ideas was inadequate and faulty. Over the winter, the attacks mounted. C.V. Kerslake, of the Toronto-based Douglas Credit League of Canada, tried to rally the Douglasites together against Aberhart. Kerslake spread the word that Social Credit was not, contrary to what Aberhart urged, applicable in a Canadian province; it was *ultra vires* of the British North America Act. (Douglas himself, ironically, was reluctant to disagree with Aberhart on this point, especially after 1935; to quarrel with the constitutionality of provincial Social Credit reforms at such a time would have been tantamount to saying that Social Credit's spectacular victory was all for naught.)

In February Douglas's London Secretariat intervened directly in the controversy, on the side of the Douglasites. The secretariat sent a letter to Aberhart (with a copy to Palmer, secretary of the New Age Club) informing him (1) that Douglas could not officially endorse the Alberta Social Credit movement, and (2) that Aberhart should remove Douglas's name from the pamphlet Aberhart had written, *The Douglas System of Economics.*

The pamphlet was virtually the textbook of the Aberhart movement. Aberhart, in effect, was asked to say publicly that the pamphlet – hence his theories – were not *bona fide* Social Credit at all.

There had been a failure of communication, it now seems. A copy of *The Douglas System of Economics* had been shown Douglas in England, and Douglas, without fully reading it, had autographed the cover. The pamphlet found its way back to Aberhart, who took Douglas's signature as representing an endorsation. When the validity of its contents was called into question by the London Secretariat, that was the argument upon which Aberhart fell back.

The letter from the secretariat was received on February 23. Aberhart, who never responded well to bitter criticism, and who was heavily burdened with work, decided to lay down his tools. The next day, an advertisement appeared on the church pages of the *The Albertan,* and the *Calgary Herald,* announcing that on February 27, Aberhart would give "his last address" on the Douglas system, at the Prophetic Bible Institute.

It was a moving address. Aberhart had the audience on the verge of tears. He recounted his "persecution" at the hands of the New Agers, and announced his resignation.

The history of the Alberta Social Credit movement in the 1930s turned upon a handful of critical accidents. One of them was the fact that Aberhart and Douglas actually spoke to each other face to face only two or three times. Because both of them generally acted with polite restraint, the personal hostility between them seldom burst into the open. But there can be no doubt that an undercurrent of it was always there. Part of it no doubt was rooted in the fact that both men were dogmatic and intolerant of criticism or competition for control. But perhaps an even larger part of it grew out of Aberhart's bitter memories of how Douglas connived with his Alberta followers to topple Aberhart from the movement's leadership in 1934. The fact that, after 1935, Douglas never returned to Alberta, that he quarrelled with Aberhart, and that the formal relationship between the two finally chilled to the freezing point, cannot be understood without harkening back to Douglas's role in the abortive *coup d'etat* of February 27, 1934.

While the Douglasites were able to topple Aberhart from the leadership and replace him with one of their own, they were not able long to resist his return. The Central Council of the movement, shortly after Aberhart's resignation, elected in his place as president one Gilbert McGregor, while Charles Palmer of the New Age Club stayed on as vice-president.

What were Aberhart and the Douglasites fighting about? The question is worth answering briefly, for two reasons. A peek at how Aberhart modified Douglas's thinking serves to illustrate how Aberhart tried to adapt Douglasism to Alberta's situation, and how Aberhart's mind worked.

Aberhart's version of Social Credit naturally evolved over the years. The mature version was contained in the "blue book" – or, as its formal title ran, *The Social Credit Manual: Puzzling Questions and Their Answers.* Unlike *The Douglas System of Economics,* the "blue book" admitted Aberhart's authorship. It was published in Calgary in 1935 and, in sixty-four pages, sandwiched in among advertisements for artificial legs, chiropracters, "Henry's Yeast Donuts", and the Leyden Funeral Home ("THE MODERN MORTUARY, Where Lowest Prices Prevail"), were Aberhart's prescriptions for a sick age.

"Intended to give a comprehensive, general outline," the Blue Book advanced this "basic premise":

> It is the duty of the State through its Government to organize its economic structure in such a way that no bona fide citizen, man, woman or child, shall be allowed to suffer for lack of the bare necessities of food, clothing, and shelter, in the midst of plenty or abundance.

Up to a point, the text reads like orthodox Douglasism. The total market value of Alberta products ($152,878,863) is computed from official sources and listed. So is the province's immense potential wealth (although how one computes "potential" wealth is an interesting question). Aberhart insisted that the cause of distress is not over-production (people can use everything being produced); nor is it unemployment. Unemployment, rather, is a symptom of "our real trouble"; unemployment is "a permanent disability of the modern state."

Still along the lines of orthodoxy, Aberhart stressed that Social Credit was "not based on any confiscation scheme by which we take the wealth of the rich or well-to-do to give to the poor."

> Social Credit recognizes individual enterprise and individual ownership, but it prevents wildcat exploitation of the consumer through the medium of enormously excessive spreads in price for the purpose of giving exorbitant profits or paying high dividends on pyramids of watered stock. . . .

Here, the differences began subtly to creep in. And one can understand how they might have caused the Douglasites to choke on their late-night sherry.

Aberhart's definition of the cultural heritage was fairly orthodox ("each consumer has a right to a share in the production from the natural resources of the province"), but then Aberhart introduced his famous notion of the "Fifty Big Shots":

> At the present time, this great wealth is being selfishly manipulated and controlled by one or more men known as the 'Fifty Big Shots of Canada.'

Douglas, in talking about the National Dividend, had always been deliberately vague as to its amount; the precise amount, he maintained, would be determined by the economy's need for extra purchasing-power to buy up unbought production.

Aberhart was less cautious. Although he said the figures "are merely suggested for illustration purposes", he put forth the famous slogan of "$25 a Month." He foresaw a system wherein each citizen would be issued with a pass-book in which the State Credit House, at the start of each month, would make an entry (with a corresponding entry in the person's account) of twenty-five dollars. Each person could then write twenty-five dollars worth of "non-negotiable certificates" (in effect, cheques) on that account each month. Who ever they were made out to would have that amount credited to his account; at no time would the credit entries be redeemable in cash money or currency. The credit was to be a supplement to cash income. And Aberhart envisaged a descending scale of payments for families: Adults over twenty-one would receive twenty-five dollars a month, people twenty years of age twenty dollars, people nineteen fifteen dollars, people seventeen and eighteen ten dollars, and those sixteen and under, five dollars a month.

The social effects of a political offer of this kind in a time of acute unemployment and low wages can be vividly imagined. At a time when eggs sold for a nickel a dozen and good roasts for seventy-five cents, good dwellings rented for nine dollars a month, and the standard, made-to-measure suit in the catalogue of Tip-Top Tailors sold for $24.50 (vest included), the prospect of a second income of at least twenty-five dollars a month was irresistible.

The writer has heard it said by those who should know that the major reason Social Credit swept the Communist-dominated Crowsnest Pass in 1935 was the appeal of the twenty-five dollars a-month slogan to the mothers of families – not to the tough miners – who thought in terms of what such money could buy for their children.

Aberhart promoted the idea that only a relatively small amount of purchasing power would be necessary to do the trick: the velocity of circulation he said, employing the analogy of the human bloodstream, would multiply by many times each injection of new purchasing-power. When queried about this, he never failed to mention the case of a town in Alberta in which an unsuspected bad cheque had done $8,000 worth of business before the error was discovered.

(The only trouble with the analogy is that people only do business with bad cheques when they have confidence that they are good cheques, that is, cheques redeemable in currency; what would happen after the introduction of "non-negotiable certificates" *un*redeemable in currency is at best unanswerable.)

The other aspect of Douglas reform, of course, was the Just Price – and this one Aberhart misunderstood badly. This passage in the "blue book" is almost impossible to follow. Aberhart talks about a "just price" – aimed at "excessive profits" – which is really a sort of "fair price," to be decided by "a commission of our best experts from every sphere of life." He also talks about a "compensating price" which is closer to what Douglas meant by a "just price": that is, a discount on prices sufficient to hold them down and prevent them simply rising to keep pace with increases in purchasing power arising from the distribution of the Dividend. Aberhart, it seems, confused economically justifiable prices with morally justifiable ones.

In practical application, Aberhart's muddy just price proposals were aimed centrally at producers and farmers; what he tried to promise them was some kind of price-control, to guarantee them a fair return for their work, a return sufficient to compensate them for expenses plus a fair profit. The farmers certainly understood their problem – prices were so low they failed to pay back even the cost of production. Whether they understood Aberhart's proposed solution of course is another matter.

But the best way to sample the flavour of Aberhart's hybrid version of Social Credit is to sift through the blue book's "questions and answers". Only there does the quality of Aberhart's thought come out.

In response to a question, where will the credit come from to pay dividends?, Aberhart answered: "The credit issued will be a charge against the Natural Resources of the Province much in the same way as the present Government Bonds are."

The problem with this, of course, is that bonds are negotiable for money; moreover, they are *not* a charge against the natural resources of a country – raw natural resources have no specific worth – but rather against developed, taxable resources; that is, against fixed, measurable, existing assets.

Where would the money for dividends come from? Douglas would have answered that it came literally from the end of a pen; that it was created by the state as a figure in a ledger, against the overall assets of the economy – just as a bank creates credit in a ledger by creating a drawing-account in return for a claim on real assets.

That was all Aberhart had to say. But he went farther. The credit, he said, would come from a "levy" on production and processing.

It would not, he argued, be a tax, but rather payment for a service. But this argument fooled no one, least of all the Douglasites, who zeroed in on it right at the beginning. Such a levy, they charged, would be nothing but a form of sales or processing tax. It was not only a gratuitous graft on Douglas's proposals, it was a socially regressive form of revenue-collection.

Aberhart seemed to think a "levy" necessary to recover the credit issued by the state. But credit is recovered or cancelled out as it is spent, i.e., translated into goods and services purchased.

Would there be any conditions attached to the issuance of the dividend to all citizens? Aberhart said frankly, "the only requirement necessary would be that all bills for food, clothing and shelter must be met before the luxuries can be bought." This, seemingly, would imply some system of state inspectors, to keep tabs on how the dividends were being spent – a fairly large limitation on the freedom of the individual, one would think.

On the question of work, Aberhart turned Douglas on his head. Douglas was rigidly opposed to the puritan work-ethic; Aberhart was not. What would happen, Aberhart was asked, if a citizen, after receipt of his dividend, refused to go to work, when work became offered and available? Aberhart answered:

> Immediately after such conduct was called to the attention of the State Credit House Inspector, the offender would be warned that if he persisted in refusing work, his dividends would be cut off or temporarily suspended. Then, as there is no relief or dole under a social credit system he would be compelled to work.

It may have been, of course, that in taking that position, Aberhart was much closer to the realities of a still under-mechanized and labour-oriented farm economy than Douglas; nonetheless, it is an interesting index of the difference between the approaches of the two men.

What would the introduction of Social Credit into Alberta do to the foreign investor, then? Aberhart's answer is interesting, in light of Manning's later friendliness to outside capital:

> By the issuance of interest-free loans [by the Alberta government] foreign capital will find it very difficult to compete. . . . Capital that is already invested in Alberta will be protected for its owners provided they co-operate in every way possible. Foreign capital that supplies our people with goods will be required to pay the unearned increment levy [the form of "sales tax" referred to earlier] to enable our people to purchase their goods.

The introduction of Social Credit would also mean greater equity in income-distribution. Asked if it was his intention, under Social Credit, to "limit the income of the citizens to a certain maximum?", he answered:

Yes, it is, for no one should be allowed to have an income that is greater than he himself and his loved ones can possibly enjoy, to the privation of his fellow citizens.

Social Credit, in addition to all of this, would usher in a new age in the moral conduct of Mankind. The consumption of alcohol would decline (both because government would not allow dividends all to be spent on liquor, and because economic unhappiness would decline, thus driving fewer fathers to drink); and crime – which Aberhart saw rooted in poverty – would taper off.

The final question was perhaps the most important, and it was a question that exercised Aberhart, the Douglasites, the banking and financial interests, the federal government, courts and the opposition parties for the better part of a decade: would it be constitutionally within the terms of the B.N.A. Act for a Canadian province to implement Social Credit reforms? We will return to this question later. It is sufficient to say here that Aberhart always maintained publicly (and as far as this writer can determine, privately) that Social Credit reforms *did* lie within the aegis of the province. That was the position he took in the "blue book", and in his debates with opponents both inside and outside the party.

All in all, it seems clear, a rather confused melange of proposals, almost devoid of internal consistency and organization; a blend of half-truths and hopes. No one believed it, apparently, but the people.

On the level of logic and intellectual analysis, the critics were right. Aberhart's theories were confused and confusing, particularly his own interpretations and additions.

But to make this criticism – and it was often made – was in a sense to miss the political point. First of all, very few ordinary Albertans took the trouble or had the training to subject every jot and tittle of Aberhart's writings to a searching analysis. Nor did Aberhart fall back heavily on his own interpretations; pushed to the point of admitting his own inconsistencies and contradictions, he would always insist that he was not an expert on Social Credit; that he understood only the fundamentals; and that his first move as head of a Social Credit government would be to import the social credit "experts", who alone had a sufficient mastery of detail and technique to implement a workable scheme.

There was, in such a course, a large element of obfuscation; in effect, Aberhart tried to conceal his inner doubts and confusions by contending that the details of Social Credit were beyond the understanding of ordinary people, himself included; in asking for the vote of the people on such a basis he was asking, in effect, for a popular act of faith. The election of 1935 showed conclusively that the people of Alberta wanted to believe that Aberhart was right and that his critics were wrong. And in the face of an overwhelming will to believe, intellectual counter-arguments and criticisms were foredoomed.

Aberhart resigned, and the Douglasites took control of the movement. They were able to hold power less than ten weeks. In that time, Major Douglas visited Alberta and had a furious altercation with Aberhart, both men testified before a special committee of the provincial government in Edmonton, and there was a wave of popular demands for Aberhart's return as head of the movement.

The sequence of events may be recalled briefly. The movement had been active throughout the southern part of the province circulating petitions calling on the United Farmers to study Douglas's theories; and in response to this, the government (with, it is said, grave misgivings) announced on February 22, 1934, that it would hold hearings on Social Credit before the House Agriculture Committee, and ask Douglas to come and testify.

Come and testify (at government expense) he did; and the net effect of his visit was to destroy his reputation and power in Alberta and help re-establish Aberhart in the driver's seat.

Douglas arrived in the province from Britain about the beginning of April. Aberhart had already led off in the testimony before the Agriculture Committee on March 19, for even though he was no longer formally the head of the Social Credit movement, he was still the movement's leading provincial spokesman.

An anecdote reveals that Aberhart was unsure of himself as a public figure. On his arrival in Edmonton to testify, he went to see the Clerk of the Legislature to inquire what his "fee" for testifying was to be. The clerk informed him that it was five dollars, plus travel. Aberhart was aghast to discover that it was so little, and he refused to leave until he got the cheque for five dollars and his trainfare. "What if the school board deducts me more than that for my time missed?", he said.

Aberhart got a good working over by various members of the Agriculture Committee, many of whom had long itched for a chance to shoot holes in his proposals. The hearings carried on for many days, before a packed gallery; others called to testify included spokesmen for the Douglasites, who wasted no time in telling the committee what they thought of Aberhart as a theoretician.

But Douglas, the big star of the hearings, was yet to come; and just before his arrival, several members of Calgary's Open Mind Club thought, as a project, that it would be interesting to have Douglas address a public gathering in Calgary in the course of his stay. Douglas's people were contacted, and readily agreed. The Douglasites leaped at an opportunity to bring their biggest gun to bear on Aberhart publicly; and so the Calgary Armouries were reserved for the big event, April 8.

The Douglasites began by trying to exclude Aberhart from the meeting altogether – a direct and unmistakable snub that was immediately felt by Aberhart's large following in Calgary. Strong protests were lodged by Aberhart's people, and only shortly before the meeting did the Douglasites agree to sit Aberhart on the platform as guest of honour. The personal friction between Douglas and Aberhart was already rumoured: some days earlier Douglas refused an Aberhart offer to take the Sunday Bible broadcast, and when Aberhart met Douglas on his arrival at the train station, Douglas cut him dead.

Thousands of people were present at the Armoury that cool Spring night, and the presence of a fine brass band and a good part of Calgary's civic administration turned it into a large affair. The massively pro-Aberhart crowd was pacified by the chairman when they kept chanting. "We Want Aberhart". The chairman implied that Aberhart would be heard from later. Then Douglas was introduced by the mayor of Calgary.

Douglas's speech – which was received in a waiting province as a major historical event – was extraordinary. He began by presumptuously announcing that he had taken steps to help the Alberta movement secure good leadership, and had invited an old friend, Charles Bowman of the *Ottawa Citizen,* to preside over a Social Credit organizing conference, to be held elsewhere. The effect of such an announcement on the pro-Aberhart crowd – almost all of whom had first been drawn to the movement by Aberhart, who had organized it from the ground up – can be imagined. There was a ripple of puzzlement in the hall.

But Douglas went on. He proceeded, for nearly two hours, to drone out a routine and entirely unoriginal account of Social Credit doctrine, and a description of the battle Albertans faced in its implementation; and he went so far as to imply that Social Credit could best be put into effect by bringing pressure to bear on the federal government!

Douglas concluded, not having made a single reference to Aberhart, who sat directly behind him. A city official rose to ask for a vote of thanks; it became apparent to the now-enraged crowd that Aberhart was not only going to be insulted, he was not even going to be allowed to say his piece. The "We Want Aberhart" chant took on a more frantic note; a large mob of people broke into the aisles and began to stream toward the centre and front of the hall. There was bedlam. The band was signalled to play "God Save the King", and the meeting disintegrated into chaos.

Aberhart, who suffered through Douglas's indignities in silence, had reached the breaking point; his temper exploded. He stormed after Douglas into a cloakroom, and began to shout charges at him. Douglas was imperturbable, which only made it worse. The two men broke into a violent quarrel, in which Aberhart apparently called Douglas several very rude names. Douglas replied in kind and both huffed away. Thus ended one of the very few face-to-face meetings the two men ever had. Its bearing on Douglas's influence with the movement was obvious. From that time forward, as far as Aberhart and most of his followers were concerned, Douglas ceased to be an inspiration and guide, and became, instead, an unwelcome intruder.

Douglas's visit to the province had long been awaited, and his every word and move, upon arrival was amply chronicled in the province's newspapers. Yet his effect was anticlimactic. His manner of speech was stolid and unemotional and uninspiring; his speeches were utterly predictable, and devoid of concrete suggestions or new proposals. He said, roughly, about what Aberhart had said over the past eighteen months, only less imaginatively. The province's political establishment – which no doubt hoped Douglas would undercut Aberhart's following, or, alternatively, provide some miraculous new suggestions for attacking the Depression – was much disappointed; Douglas did neither. The average Albertan found him a cold fish; civic officials and provincial representatives (particularly the cabinet) found him woolly and unconvincing. However, the abundant publicity Douglas received did help spread the general reputation of the Social Credit movement across the province.

The Douglasites were still riding high, in full control of the movement's Central Council in Calgary; but the end was in sight. Aberhart's successor, McGregor, a man who favored the Douglas line that Social Credit was a federal question was a pariah to the rank and file. The Legislative hearings, which ended early in April, only succeeded in publicizing Aberhart yet more widely; and the only reaction to Douglas's abortive stop-Aberhart speech at the Armouries was a definite hardening of opinion throughout the movement against the "disloyal" Douglasites, and in favour of Aberhart's return.

In May, McGregor resigned; and a short time later, Aberhart

returned as president of the Central Council. A purge began; Aberhart fired Palmer and Logan as vice-president and secretary of the Council, sent the word out to all study-groups to isolate the Douglasites, and demanded of McGregor that he submit his public speeches to Aberhart for personal censorship. McGregor refused, and resigned from the movement altogether. Douglas, by this time, had gone back to England; and the Douglasites, at least for the moment, were smashed. Aberhart cleaned out all elements disloyal to him, and surrounded himself with personal followers, most of them people that he had brought into the movement himself. To fill Logan's position on the Central Council, he reached into his pool of lieutenants and appointed Manning.

It was about seven years since the young man had first come to Calgary to meet the master; and now, at the age of twenty-five, Ernest Manning was given a key position in the top council of the new movement.

The Social Credit movement was slowly maturing. Aberhart, through a network of lieutenants, had created doctrinal study-groups all across the province – chiefly in the south, but gradually expanding northward. Once again, the movement was firmly united under an undivided leadership. For the first time, silence descended over internal sniping at Aberhart's ideological reliability; from the spring of 1934 on, Aberhart became the chief arbiter of ideological purity.

In May the movement, awaiting the Agriculture Committee's report on the Social Credit hearings, began to popularize the slogan "Social Credit for Alberta". For a period of some weeks the leadership waited quietly, biding its time, concentrating on internal organization. Aberhart's position was that he was not interested in personal power; nor was the movement interested in gaining office. What he wanted to do was put pressure on existing governments – and particularly on the Alberta government – to bring Social Credit reforms into existence. That done, presumably, his mission would be complete. The key to the future of the movement would lie in the response of the United Farmers government to Aberhart's proposals.

In June the government finally released the Agriculture Committee's Report – and the noose began to tighten around the U.F.A.

The whole 127-page document reprinted accounts of the testimony of various witnesses at great length, but devoted only two paragraphs to the government's summation and conclusion:

> Your Committee is of the opinion that while the evidence disclosed the weakness of the present system and the necessity for controlled Social Credit, it did not offer any practicable plan for adoption in Alberta under the existing constitutional condition.

Major Douglas recognized this and urged that a thorough study be made, first to arrive at a definitive objective, and second, to get a clear idea of the obstacles to be overcome and the limitations to be removed in order to clear the way, and the best method of procedure to secure results.

Popular reaction to a conclusion at once so meagre and waffling, was bitter. The testimony headlined once again the split between Aberhart and the Douglasites on the constitutionality of Social Credit at the provincial level. Neither Douglas nor Aberhart nor any of their disciples had had any startlingly fresh proposals to put forward. Douglas himself waffled somewhat as to whether Social Credit was feasible at the provincial level; Aberhart, when driven to the wall by the committee's critics and forced to admit his own theoretical shortcomings, kept reiterating that his first recommendation would be to turn the implementation of Social Credit over to Douglas.

But in Alberta, the people, driven to desperation by four consecutive catastrophic years of Depression, were in no mood for abstruse arguments over constitutionality. The net import of the Agriculture Committee's Report was that the United Farmers were not going to do anything about Social Credit. And so a great wave of enthusiasm for direct political action began to sweep through the ranks and beat upon Aberhart's door.

We will never know whether it was fear, reticence, a canny tactical cautiousness or a genuine dislike for power that held Aberhart back from a quick commitment. But in any case, for several weeks he held back from even turning the movement to more active political participation. Yet before the publication of the report of the Agriculture Committee, he published and circulated a small pamphlet called *The B.N.A. Act and Social Credit*, in which he pooh-poohed the constitutional strict-constructionists and maintained that a reasonable interpretation of both the B.N.A. Act and the Bank Act would not preclude Social Credit at the provincial level. It is hard to see his promotion of this pamphlet as anything but a prelude to throwing his large hat into the ring.

He talked with the Liberal and Conservative leaders, but they offered very little in the way of real encouragement; the Tories were openly hostile to Social Credit, while the Liberals seemed torn between an opportunistic desire to cash in on the Social Credit fervour, and their traditional opposition to soft money as such.

Aberhart concluded he could expect no help from either of them.

The United Farmers were suddenly in real trouble. Both the traditional opposition parties, the Liberals and the Tories, excoriated the U.F.A. for its failure to reduce government overhead and taxation.

The representatives of the Eastern commercial establishment made regular tours throughout the province, smiting at the U.F.A.'s debt-moratorium legislation and calling for the full collection of all over-due debts in both the city and countryside. Like the Bourbon kings, who learned nothing and forgot nothing, the spokesmen for the finance establishment took their cue from the Hon. Mr. R.B. Bennett's Minister of Finance, who intoned in 1932 in his budget speech that "The preservation of the national credit is a prerequisite of the return of prosperity."

It now seems incredible, but many Albertans, in a perversely human way, blamed the U.F.A., not for starting the Depression, but for failing to end it – as if the powers of any single province were adequate to that task. With its debt legislation and its work in public relief, the U.F.A. did about as much as any provincial authority could, except offer plausible hope; it trimmed expenses, provided a dole, forecast an upturn around the corner, and waited.

Social Credit, by contrast, seemed to have an answer. It was an answer that every Albertan was capable of understanding, and that seemed to make sense. It was an answer that damned economic orthodoxy as a kind of black magic – but since the province was brimful of bankrupt farmers and businessmen who had watched the theories of orthodox economics send their wages and savings down the drain, that was no disadvantage.

The Social Credit crusade began to pick up momentum. A number of cars labelled, simply, "Social Credit" appeared in the Calgary Stampede parade, surprising Prime Minister Bennett.

Gradually, almost imperceptibly, the U.F.A. at the local level began to disintegrate. Long a farmers' movement with an ideological split personality, the U.F.A. began to become internally polarized into two factions: monetary reformers, and agrarian socialists. The agrarian socialists would have nothing to do with Social Credit and considered it a panacea and a delusion, capable only of diverting the peoples' attention from the real evils in society: the profit motive, and private ownership of property. Aberhart sent his lieutenants out to woo the monetary reformers.

The attraction Social Credit had for many rank-and-file U.F.A.-ers is hard to realize, and was even harder for the beleaguered U.F.A. leadership to combat. What began to happen in 1934, and gathered steam until the election in the summer of 1935, was the takeover of the U.F.A.'s base of support. The Social Crediters burrowed into the U.F.A. foundation like termites; the process was not unlike that employed by certain undersea predators, which drill into a victim's shell and eat the contents, leaving only the empty carapace.

The problem was that the U.F.A. was not a monolithic organization with strict controls over the beliefs of its members. It began its life in 1909 as a farm pressure-group, and did its earliest and best work in the area of organizing co-operatives and wheat pools and in pressuring governments to court its favour. A highly democratic movement, it was long famed for the extent to which its executive (and the provincial cabinet, after it entered politics) listened to the demands of its members, expressed at the annual convention each January. A movement of this kind necessarily tied together a diverse group of people, and the U.F.A. had representatives of many groups in its membership, from the far left – in July 1935, one U.F.A. local seriously contemplated a United Front with the Communists in the ridings of Sturgeon and Wetaskiwin – to the centre-right. The U.F.A. cabinet, after 1921, was almost always more conservative than the movement proper, and was not above telling the annual convention that its demands were unreasonable, impractical or impolitic.

The internal factions within the U.F.A. were in danger of tearing the movement to pieces.

The monetary-reform faction, led by William Irvine and Norman Smith, editor of the U.F.A. magazine, were all in favour of the movement embracing Douglasism, or some variant upon Social Credit.

The agrarian socialists would have none of it; it must be remembered, amidst all this, that Alberta was in a sense the original birthplace of agrarian socialism in Canada.

By 1933 the internal debate in the U.F.A. was noticeable to those who had their ears to the ground. One delegate to the 1933 convention in Calgary recalls that going down on the train from Edmonton, only two things were talked about: Social Credit, and technocracy.

This internal friction helped to prevent the U.F.A. from coming to grips with the Aberhart challenge. There just was no internal consensus on the merits of the Aberhart proposals.

Aberhart, meanwhile, worked at organizing for a fight. No overt committment to active participation in any election had been made; but the preparations went on nonetheless.

The movement held outdoor rallies, the bigger the better, with entertainment, political skits, good food, and of course Aberhart. Small businessmen, long alienated from the farmer-dominated U.F.A., were actively courted; business contributions were solicited, and the names of the contributors given prominence. (The "blue manual," printed in 1935, carried 137 advertisements in sixty-four pages.)

In an attempt to secure a more friendly press – for relations between Aberhart and the *Calgary Herald* particularly had always fluctuated between icy and frigid – Aberhart appointed three enthusiastic Socreds, Charles Underwood, Frank Hollingworth and Eva Reid, to organize and promote a party newspaper, the *Alberta Social Credit Chronicle*. It had tough going for some months, but suddenly it caught on. (For the first several weeks, most of the copies had to be given away, and the first edition secured only forty-three dollars worth of advertising.) But, by autumn, its weekly paid circulation was nearly 14,000 and about 6,000 more were sold at party meetings.

Aberhart didn't overlook anyone in his organizational zeal. The movement organized special groups for labour unionists, women, young people and businessmen; strong in the south at the beginning, the movement worked hard to build up support in central and northern Alberta, where Aberhart's radio audience had never been as large.

And Manning joined him for another tour, this one much farther north. In July alone the two travelled 2,500 miles and gave thirty-nine talks to some 30,000 people, and the response was perhaps even more enthusiastic than the previous year. The pattern again was the same: Manning drove the car, arranged the itinerary, and supplemented Aberhart on the platform.

Each time, Aberhart appealed to his audiences to organize Social Credit study groups, which he would help supply with teaching materials and literature. And, almost invariably, the people responded. Often the U.F.A. local simply became a Social Credit study cell. This fact was well known to the U.F.A. leaders, but there was precisely nothing they could do about it.

Both men continued to maintain that their purposes were absolutely "non-political". Aberhart always maintained that he was speaking only for Social Credit and not for himself. From time to time the Douglasites would have a heckler in the crowd, but their effect was negligible. And when the Douglasites appealed to Aberhart's followers, they often found that Aberhart's "extreme" suggestions were more in tune with the times than theirs were.

When C.V. Kerslake, the Douglasite leader from Toronto, wrote the editor of the *Consort Enterprise* in July and suggested that the editor was soft on Aberhart's "secessionary" views, the editor replied to Kerslake in his columns:

A drowning man will grasp at a straw. If people here are so deluded, so obtuse, unreasonable and foolish as one might conclude (from your letter) may we attribute it to malnutrition, to the disconcerting influence of standing helpless while women and children suffer for food and clothing; with the knowledge that granarics are bursting with grain, factories packed full of clothing, and wealthy, influential men standing pat for sound money in order that their bonds and dividends may not be affected? . . . Do those who promise Dominion-wide Social Credit, or improvement in conditions in five years, eight years of thirteen years from now realize that this does not appeal to people with empty stomachs?

But Aberhart had not yet committed the movement to action. Reid, the U.F.A. premier, at this point was going through hell in cabinet. Many advisors urged Reid to call an election, hoping perhaps that if one were held, the government could be returned before Aberhart's movement "peaked". But Reid was reluctant to call an election before the U.F.A.'s entire term was up. And this delay of about one year gave Aberhart just the space he needed to whip the movement into shape.

The moment of truth was not far from hand. As soon as the autumn started, Aberhart inaugurated mid-week radio broadcasts to step up the pressure and issued countless appeals for "one hundred honest men" to represent the interests of the people. A number of Aberhart followers – no doubt with his acquiescence, but without his official approval – went ahead and organized provincial constituency organizations in their districts, quietly, but effectively. And from Calgary, the famous "Man From Mars" series began over radio in October. Aberhart auditioned a number of followers until he discovered Charles Wilmott, a Calgary C.P.R. employee, whose voice could improvise precisely the kind of unidentifiable foreign accent Aberhart wanted. Wilmott became the "Man From Mars", and they went on the radio together – Aberhart and Manning explaining what economic life on earth was like, and the Man From Mars explaining, in his halting way, how puzzled he was by the sight of poverty in the midst of plenty. It was highly imaginative political showmanship and Alberta audiences loved it.

As the weeks went on, Aberhart began to hint, subtly at first, but more and more openly, that in the next election, the people should vote for Social Credit. At the same time, he excoriated the rottenness of all political parties, and told the people that political parties – as opposed to honest movements of the people – were simply crooked and dishonest holdovers from the past, a means of preventing the ordinary folk from getting their will. All politicians like to put on that garb, of course, but some wear it more comfortably than others. Aberhart spoke as a man with a firm reputation as an educator and a religionist; when he said he was a well-meaning amateur out only for the people, the people tended to believe him.

In response to his challenge, the names of "honest men"

flooded into the Prophetic Bible Institute office daily. Many of them were later to become Social Credit candidates.

The United Farmers could no longer ignore the looming power of Aberhart's movement. In response to tremendous pressure, both from their own ranks and from the province at large, the U.F.A. agreed to allow a thorough discussion of Social Credit principles at the upcoming convention scheduled to begin January 16. For the U.F.A. and for Aberhart, this was the moment of truth: if the U.F.A. accepted and endorsed Social Credit for the province, the steam would have been taken out of Aberhart's burgeoning young movement; on the other hand, if the U.F.A. rejected Social Credit, a direct political collision would be inevitable.

There was plenty of tension in the air as the U.F.A. delegates poured into Calgary for the meeting. The night before the scheduled debate on the floor of the U.F.A. convention between Aberhart and the farm leaders, the Socred leader sponsored a reception for the U.F.A. delegates over at the Institute building.

Aberhart and his team gave them the full psychological treatment. Aberhart was genial and grandfatherly, and in abundant good spirits. He appealed to their sense of nonpartisanship. Manning was in the chair, and directed the ceremonies. The Man From Mars put in an appearance, as did that perennial sceptic, Mr. Kant B. Dunn. (The other Social Credit skit-member for such occasions, Mr. C.C. Heifer, was notable by his absence.) Aberhart concluded with a rousing speech, and the delegates, it is said, went home much impressed.

The next night, in the large auditorium at Central United Church, Aberhart threw down the gauntlet at the feet of the leaders of the U.F.A.

He opened his long speech by poking the U.F.A. leadership for its non-co-operative attitude in past, and hinted that genuine mutual help between the Social Credit movement and the U.F.A. might be unlikely. Then he provided, with charts, an exposition of his doctrine. He moved not a jot nor a tittle from his position in the *Blue Manual*. He stressed the advantages that farmers would reap from the just price and the dividend, and concluded with his analogy between the circulation of credit in the economy and the circulation of blood in the human body – the moral being, a little goes a long way.

For two hours he was cross-examined by the delegates. Then the debaters in the U.F.A. leadership took over, and went over Aberhart's proposals with a rhetorical fine-toothed comb. Finally, late in the evening, the debate was closed by the chair, and the resolution of the Hilda local of the U.F.A. was moved for the vote:

Whereas, the present financial system has failed to meet the requirements of modern civilization;

Therefore, be it resolved, that a system of Social Credit as outlined by Mr. William Aberhart, of Calgary, be put as a plank in the U.F.A. provincial platform, to be brought before the electorate at the next provincial election.

The minutes do not record the exact vote. Social Credit lost.

The leaders of the U.F.A. had fought their case well, and no doubt they thought that they had finally vanquished Aberhart and his infernal movement for monetary reform. But, of course, the opposite was true. It took Aberhart only seven months to show that, in rejecting his proposals, the United Farmers of Alberta had signed their death warrant.

It would be naive, of course, to think that the Social Credit move into politics began only with the formal rejection of Social Credit reform by the U.F.A. Aberhart had built an educational machine that was heavy with political potential, and some weeks prior to the U.F.A. convention, he began to hint broadly that the time for direct action was drawing near. The vote on the floor of the U.F.A. convention on the night of January 16 marked the point beyond which Aberhart's commitment became irrevocable.

A matter of weeks after the U.F.A. convention, Aberhart began to apply his masterful organizational talents to the problem of organizing the Social Credit movement for an electoral slugging match in the summer contest upcoming. He began by sending out his local organizations a mock ballot to test the "straw vote". Voters in each constituency were asked to indicate (1) if they had a vote in the upcoming election, (2) if they favored the introduction of Social Credit, and (3) if they would vote for "a 100% Social Credit Candidate". The local Social Credit groups, whether study groups or constituency organizations, canvassed each district thoroughly, and the results, which were kept secret, indicated an overwhelming wave of public opinion in favor of Social Credit – about ninety three per cent of the people polled.

By early April, the movement had constituency organizations across the province. The speed with which the movement changed gears was a tribute to Aberhart's delegation of authority, his rational organization of everything and to the overwhelming support that Social Credit had by this time cultivated. Aberhart had done his three years of radio propaganda effectively; between that, his tours with Manning, the tours of the lesser figures and the large play the movement had received in the newspapers since 1934, the good word had penetrated into every cranny of the province. In horror, the opposition began to realize what was transpiring before them. But by this time it was too late.

The organization Aberhart laid out was masterfully conceived; Aberhart was at least twenty years ahead of his time in techniques of political organization. Every constituency was divided up into zones on a giant map at the Bible Institute, and each zone was put in the charge of subordinates, all with their own organizations. The central office at the Institute began sending out campaign and platform material in very early March and constituency conventions were ordered. These appointed all formal officers, including district directors for each zone. Also, delegates to the forthcoming provincial conventions (there were to be two, one in the south and one in the north) were chosen, and the party – for now it surely was a party – was to begin discussion of platform planks for the election.

The first party convention was held at the Institute in Calgary on April 4. Manning was appointed chairman of the meeting. The newspapers reported that the young lieutenant kept the meetings well in hand, and handled proceedings with impartiality and dispatch. The convention was permeated by an unmistakable feeling of confidence and *esprit de corps*. The Social Crediters were on the march, and knew it.

The convention formalized Aberhart's control and authority in two clear-cut resolutions (of which there can be little doubt Aberhart was at least part author). The first clearly established that he was unquestioned leader of the movement:

> . . . Whereas, William Aberhart, despite the fact that he has repeatedly declared his personal aversion to political office and has constantly refused to enter the field of political office, is, nevertheless, recognized as the one responsible for the social credit movement in Alberta, and the individual best qualified to lead (it) to victory . . . Be it therefore resolved that this convention, as representative of the thousands of social crediters in Southern Alberta, demand that Mr. Aberhart complete the work that he has begun by assuming the active leadership of the social credit forces of the province . . . .

The same resolution also authorized Aberhart to head the movement in the forthcoming campaign *without standing for election in a specific seat* – a provision, critics later credibly charged, that freed Aberhart from any chance of personal embarrassment lest he should stand for a seat and lose.

The second resolution indelibly expressed the spirit and character of the new movement, its commitment to radical change and its fear of compromise, backroom deals, or any possibility of "political" betrayal. It took note of the Douglasite principle that "it is a fundamental under true democracy that the people directly, or indirectly, through representation are qualified to indicate the general course of their desires but that execution of them must be left to experts,"and authorized local constituency organizations only to nominate three or four alternative nominees, from whom Aberhart, sitting on a special "advisory committee" and consulting with the constituency convention delegates, would choose the representative of the party in that constituency. This in effect gave Aberhart ironclad control over the selection of the party's candidates.

Social Credit was to be more than an ordinary political party, made of up assorted cause-followers, axe-grinders, and office-seekers; the party was to be, instead, an instrument of radical change, and such an instrument must be made up of men who are loyal to strong leaders committed to strong principles. Aberhart strongly believed that such a party could only be created by a strong leader, and he so told the Calgary convention: "If you are not going to let me have any say in the choice of my supporters, you will not have me as your leader."*

The convention also passed a resolution that reflected its belief that some employers were attempting to intimidate pro-Social Credit employees from expressing their political views; the resolution called on the province to pass a law banning such intimidation. (This recalls the experience of many C.C.F people in Saskatchewan, and it is interesting to note that the big business and commercial establishment in Alberta thought Social Credit was almost as subversive as its rivals on the socialist-left.

Aberhart gave the closing address, and warned the delegates of the task they faced:

> You have your chance at the next election, and if you have ever cast your ballot you will cast it at that time, or you will never need to cast another. . . . Soldiers are not afraid. We will not run. When the day comes, when they say, now cast your ballot, what do you want, are you going to support the old parties in power?

---

* A scheme – and statement – of this kind had an ominously totalitarian ring, as any number of Social Credit critics have hastened to point out. In point of fact, Aberhart seldom violated the consensus of local constituencies in his choice of candidates; and all the broad paper powers the Calgary convention conveyed upon him were not sufficient to prevent a backbenchers revolt that nearly unseated him as leader in 1937. More about that in the next chapter.

In early May, the northern half of the province held its convention in Edmonton. Essentially the same things were ratified. That done, the party got down to the hard work of fighting the election.

The U.F.A. was not lacking in spirit. In the late winter and spring, they threw into the contest against Aberhart their incisive vice-president and best debator, Norman Priestly, a highly-articulate former United Church Minister who went on radio to analyze Aberhart's proposals and poke his finger into the loopholes.

But for the vast majority of Albertans, Priestly's tightly-reasoned onslaughts might as well have been in a foreign tongue. Priestly was aiming at their heads: he demonstrated, time and again, that Social Credit was unworkable at the provincial level, that Aberhart's grasp of the theory itself was questionable, that the theory had been put before the best economists of the world, and found wanting. But no one seemed to listen.

Aberhart's absolute support in the movement was illustrated by an incident after the Calgary convention, when the head of the Drumheller constituency organization, A.F. Keys, criticized Aberhart's powers and publicly accused the leader of "dictatorship". Within days, study-groups and zone organizations throughout the constituency assembled to consider the charges. Unanimously, they reaffirmed the stand of the Calgary convention, reaffirmed their loyalty to Aberhart, and called for Keys' resignation. Keys was drummed out of the movement.

Through May and June Aberhart's Advisory Committee travelled throughout the province, interviewing and screening, and finally selecting, the party's candidates for the upcoming election. It is an index of the stature Manning held in the high councils of the party that, along with Aberhart, he was the only permanent member of the committee; it picked its others members afresh from each region it visited.

This meant, simply, that Manning, in the crucial days of the formation of the party itself, was in a central position of power: apart from Aberhart, he was the only Social Credit official with an opportunity to interrogate all the party's nominees, learn about their strengths and weaknesses and background, familiarize himself with the local party personnel in all areas, and ingratiate himself with them. Moreover, there was a reciprocal effect: if Manning profitted in those days from learning about the future M.L.A.s and the non-public officials of the party, he also profited by their learning about him; for it could hardly have escaped anyone's attention that the serious, quiet young man always at Aberhart's side was marked out for a large future role in the party's plans.

The practice of the Advisory Committee is worth noting. Each constituency association held a convention and nominated a slate of nominees to stand as candidates. The constituency's representatives to the party convention then interviewed each nominee thoroughly, using a questionnaire Manning drew up and provided.

On the basis of their findings, the delegates chose one nominee and presented him to the Advisory Committee, which interrogated him afresh, and then almost always reaffirmed the delegates' decision and chose that person to stand for election. Only in four instances did the Advisory Committee override the decision of the local delegates in this matter.

Only in Calgary (in 1935, a multi-candidate single riding) did the Advisory Committee send people into a tizzy; the Advisory Committee picked only three of the party's six representatives for the city from the list forwarded by the constituency organization; it reached into its own bag to find the other three. One of them was Fred Anderson, an upper-class Anglican whom Aberhart wanted brought in, it is said, to broaden the party's base of respectability.

The opposition began to panic. The U.F.A. for some time had realized how much trouble the movement was in at the local level, and Reid, on the hustings, had to drag the Brownlee scandal behind him everywhere, like Jacob Marley's chain and cashbox.

The more panicky the Liberals, the Conservatives and the U.F.A. became, the more extreme their charges and improvisations grew. In a sudden burst of enthusiasm for Social Credit, the U.F.A. announced in March that it had arranged to bring Major Douglas back to Alberta to serve as a high-paid "Reconstruction Adviser", a ploy that fooled no one. The critics charged Aberhart with making his hybrid blend of politics and religion a substitute for real reform; the *Calgary Herald* in particular, the oldest of Aberhart's critics, said his religious fanaticism was a blind for the fact that he hadn't the faintest idea how to go about organizing Social Credit policies – a charge to which Aberhart retaliated by calling on his followers to boycott the *Herald*.

The opposition, eagerly awaiting Douglas's arrival, did their best to widen the split between him and Aberhart, and time and again tried to manoeuvre Douglas into an irrevocable denunciation of Aberhart's competence – but Douglas, who may have been a tactical neophyte, was no fool, and was cautious in his replies. The U.F.A. cabinet played up to Douglas and involved him in the social and golfing life of the capital, and it is reliably reported that Douglas responded to this by once admitting in private that he was dismayed to find all the intelligent men in the province opposed to him, and all the dunces on his side (or words to that effect). At the same time, Douglas was not about to repudiate the only Social Credit movement in the world that had a ghost of a chance of winning power – not even one led by a man that he profoundly distrusted. And so in early June, Douglas sent Aberhart a letter – which Aberhart's followers gleefully publicized far and wide – denying that there was a split between them and pointing out that "no statement in regard to matters in Alberta which is not a written statement signed by me, has any authority from me."

On June 5th, Douglas's *First Interim Report on the Possibilities of the Application of Social Credit Principles to the Province of Alberta* was released to the press by Premier Reid. The report had two parts; the first was an orthodox Douglasite analysis of the economy and banking system, and the second was a consideration, not of a detailed plan for Social Credit itself, but of how the power to implement Social Credit could be gotten by the province. Douglas maintained – in contradiction of what his followers in Alberta had always charged, and perhaps in contradiction of what he himself had earlier hinted – that the province *did* have enough residual power under the B.N.A. Act to implement Social Credit. The power, he maintained, lay not in the power to issue money (which patently is a federal responsibility), but in the "property and civil rights" clause of the Constitution and in the power of the province to raise money upon its "sole credit". The utilization of these powers, he pointed out, would be strongly and bitterly resisted by the financial establishment, and possibly by the federal government as well, and great care would have to be taken not to overstep constitutional boundaries. He therefore concluded with three recommendations: (1) that the province set up a "news circulation system" – primarily a radio network – to put its point of view before the people when the financiers began their inevitable campaign of lies and calumny; (2) that the province organize a "credit institution" to provide credit – either a chartered bank or "otherwise" [?], and (3) that the province begin accumulating "foreign exchange", in cash and credit, to lay away for the storm ahead.

The report, of course, did absolutely nothing to help the U.F.A., and merely served to give a measure of government sanction to what Aberhart was proposing all across the province already.

The response to the campaigns of the Liberals and Conservatives was dismal. The Conservatives, never really much of a force in Alberta, were badly hamstrung by their identification with the hated R.B. Bennett regime in Ottawa. The Liberals, out of power since 1921, wanted back in so badly they could taste it – but unfortunately, so could everyone else.

76

The Liberal campaign was too clever by half. On the hustings, Liberal speakers went even beyond Aberhart and the C.C.F. in their attempts to stir up class hatred and hostility; Howson, the Liberal leader, tried to make mileage by telling the voters that the common people mattered less to the "Big Shots" than their own "boudoirs".*
And the Liberals hinted that, should they be elected, they would listen with a sympathetic ear to authentic Social Credit "experts".

But it was too painfully obvious to everyone that the Liberals were simply would-be hangers-on to the Social Credit movement; moreover, the Liberals in Ottawa, under Mackenzie King, had hardly distinguished themselves by their resolute concern to end the Depression and dispell poverty at any cost.

But the biggest burden the Liberals carried was their identification, in the eyes of thousands of Alberta little people, as "politicians". Social Credit's use of the term "old line parties" has become something of a joke in current times, but in 1935, when Aberhart promised to bring to government a non-partisan spirit unblemished by desire for personal gain and ties with hated Eastern interests, he touched a very deep and responsive chord in many Albertans. No matter how hard they protested their concern for the common man, the Liberals simply could not compete with a "citizen statesman" genuinely regarded as such by the little man.

Two days after he announced the election on July 22, Premier Reid issued the U.F.A.'s platform, entitled *Manifesto of the Alberta Government.* The *Manifesto* harkened back to the U.F.A.'s achievements in social welfare and debt relief, and promised action to secure old-age pensions at a lower age, lower interest rates, greater federal aid for welfare measures, attacks on excessive price spreads, reforms in the court system and new policies for dealing with youth and juvenile delinquency, highways, lower tariffs, and an investigation into the desirability of expropriating the oil industry. It was a highly "progressive" document that reflected the U.F.A.'s traditional concern with breaking new political ground – but it had little relevance to the crying emotional needs of Albertans.

The U.F.A. found this out in the most disconcerting ways – as when, for example, Norman Priestly lectured an audience on the impracticality of Aberhart's proposals, only to be interrupted by a weeping farm woman who stood up in the crowd and cried: "This is the first time since I've been in Alberta that I've had hopes of getting some of the things I've wanted, and I don't want to lose the chance of getting them!"

---

* Not long after the election Howson became a "big" shot. He was made a judge when the Liberals returned to power in Ottawa.

The leaders of the U.F.A. were anything but fools, and in their campaign tours they soon realized the futility of their task. Their own membership figures told a grim story: in 1921, at the peak of its power, the U.F.A. – which then represented the New Wave – had 37,721 members; but in 1935 the rolls listed barely a quarter of that number. In areas where the U.F.A. leaders could even gain a hearing (and in some, they could not: hecklers drowned them out and unidentified hooligans sugared the gasoline in their cars), the hearing was at best a polite concession to a movement whose name had once been great, a formality only. Premier Reid recalled that during his travels even old-time U.F.A. supporters would come up to the platform after his speech and say, apologetically but firmly, "sorry, but we're still voting Social Credit."

Perhaps it was because of this growing feeling of impotence in the face of Aberhart's impending landslide that critics of Social Credit went to such ends to try and discredit the Dean of the Bible Institute – and why irate Social Crediters went so far in replying to those attempts. One speaker on the radio in July – he was a Conservative – charged:

> Aberhart used the pulpit to spread his incendiarism of hate, to set class against class, to foment the fires of revolution, to stir up fountains of bigotry and intolerance amongst a suffering people and to crucify them upon his political ambitions.

The speaker later claimed that within a day of his broadcast he was anonymously threatened with shooting and beating, and with a telephone call telling him "gangs would gang up on you and make you crawl and plug you full of holes."

On the other side, the representatives of commerce and banking went to great lengths to describe in lurid terms what would happen to the province should Aberhart win. Vancouver mayor Gerry McGeer attempted to land his private plane in a field near Three Hills, in order to address a Liberal meeting there; but the farmer came out and when he found out who McGeer was, he ordered him to take off and land elsewhere. And on August 6, only weeks before election, the traditionally-noncommittal Edmonton Chamber of Commerce issued to the public a leaflet entitled *The Dangers of Aberhart's Social Credit Proposals*, which after paying tribute to Aberhart's sincerity and energy, said:

> . . . we cannot remain silent when, to a distressed people, glowing promises are being made which far surpass the power of any government to fulfil. . . . We venture to think that the hope of creating something out of nothing, which is the essence of the

whole plan, rests on a fundamental fallacy as to the nature of banking credit. . . . We fear Mr. Aberhart's scheme for Alberta because it threatens the ultimate mortgaging or confiscation of all private property. . . . We fear Mr. Aberhart's plan as simply a huge debt-making scheme – a further mortgaging of our future. . . . Alternatively, we fear Mr. Aberhart's plan as a colossal scheme of fresh taxation. . . . We fear Mr. Aberhart's plan of a crushing sales tax. . . . We fear Mr. Aberhart's attempt to fix Just Prices on thousands and thousands of articles and services, many changing almost daily. . . . We fear his attempt to pay "dividends" out of such intangible assets as "cultural heritage" and undeveloped natural resources. . . . We fear his issue of certificates – an irredeemable paper currency. . . . We fear his seizure of all "good money" to be replaced by these depreciating certificates. . . . We fear his seizure of all good Dominion money received for "exports" from the province. . . . We fear his attempt to put Alberta on a different monetary basis to the rest of Canada. . . . Finally, we fear the attempt to isolate Alberta for this experiments. . . .

Eleven times, the use of the pregnant term, "we fear" . . . a striking unconscious testimony to the mood of the business establishment a few weeks before the 1935 election.

The oratory was fierce. The critics questioned Aberhart's intelligence and good faith, and blamed him with splitting the Alberta community, stirring up rancour and hatred, destroying the province's credit, and leading the people down dead ends. Aberhart replied in kind, calling the critics, at various times, "grafters, crooks, scheming politicians, insincere office seekers", "henchmen of the financial interests", "worshippers of the Golden Calf", "fornicators, grafters and hypocrites", their statements "splutterings, ramblings, prattlings, and . . . baloney", and their principles as "like those of the man who betrayed the Christ."

The only thing the people listened to, or wanted to hear, was the good news of the new deal to come. A U.F.A. cabinet minister who toured the province came back and said that directing intellectual criticisms at Social Credit was "like shooting peas at a warship."

The boards of trade and chambers of commerce of the province banded together and formed the Economic Safety League, to propagandize against Social Credit and point up its economic fallacies. The league circulated thousands of anti-Social Credit pamphlets and provided Aberhart with an unlimited supply of political straw men and sitting ducks. If Aberhart wanted to demonstrate to his audiences who it was that was against him, all he had to do was point to the Economic Safety League, and enough was said. In 1935, with enemies like the chambers of commerce, Aberhart didn't need any friends.

The election itself was a foregone conclusion. The U.F.A. leaders admitted among themselves that they were going to lose, and hoped only that they could salvage some vestiges of support.

On August 12 the Advisory Board announced the party's six candidates-at-large for Calgary: Manning headed the slate, along with Fred Anderson and John Hugill (both of whom were included by the board as representatives of social respectability), O.G. Devenish, Walter Little and the omnipresent Mrs. Frank Gostick.

Election day dawned, August 23. The day was clear and hot, and the voters flooded the polls in unprecedented numbers – 301,752 as against 182,219 in 1930.

The rout was complete. Social Credit had so infiltrated the machinery of the other parties that many U.F.A., Liberal and Conservative workers failed to turn up at the polls or campaign offices. One Liberal candidate found later that his "party workers", even the paid ones, had voted Social Credit.

By 10:00 p.m., Premier Reid conceded the election, and there was little else he could do as the returns mounted in. Social Credit took fifty-six of the province's sixty-three seats. The Liberals took five, the Conservatives, two. The U.F.A. was totally wiped out, signalling its death as a political force in the province.

It was a victory that shocked a good part of the already-jittery western world. Half the journalists in Fleet Street spent the next day frantically trying to reach Major Douglas for comment, but he was away yachting off the south coast of England. In London's City, John Hargreaves's pro-Social Credit "Greenshirts", flags waving and drums beating, marched down the streets and around the Bank of England. Very Rev. Hewlett Johnson, the "Red Dean" of Canterbury and a Douglas supporter, met the news with acclaim; London's conservative newspapers were less sympathetic. Banner headlines and bold type featured the news in Canadian newspapers from coast to coast, and Britain's *Sunday Express* said: "The vagueness of the plan did not hinder the party from getting votes, but it is hampering the opposition because they do not know what to attack."

Manning headed the polls in Calgary. At the Institute, the assembled were jubilant. When Aberhart, at 10:30 p.m., was handed a Canadian Press telegram informing him that Reid had conceded the election, it is said that the old man turned white and had to lean against his pulpit for support. The crowd then came to his moral support, rose and sang "Oh God, Our Help In Ages Past".

The first battle was over. The war was about to begin.

Part Two

The Years of Power

CHAPTER SIX

The Alberta Experiment

Between 1935 and 1939, the Social Credit movement and its leaders learned their first bitter lessons about the difference between aspiration and feasability.

Aberhart held power. The question was, what would he do with it? Social Credit had gained a small beachhead on the Canadian power structure – one province, and in 1935 a rather poor province at that. Arrayed against Alberta was the might and majesty of Canada's economic establishment, the banks, insurance companies, the large Eastern corporations, the mortgage-holders and the trust companies. That, plus the political apparatus of economic conservatism: the B.N.A. Act, the courts that interpreted it, the old-line federal political parties who enforced it.

His beachhead was surrounded by a ring of steel.

Because Social Credit gave no thought to anything other than a peaceful and democratic change (for reasons moral and practical) the battle was fought in the legislatures, the courts, the media, and around conference tables. By 1939 another War had broken out in Europe, and a domestic truce was called which became an uneasy peace. Social Credit's undeniable mandate for change was frustrated, but the struggle to put it into effect was valiant and colourful.

On August 29th Aberhart drove up to Edmonton, together with Manning and John Hugill, another of the party's successful Calgary candidates.

Two days later Aberhart announced his cabinet. Aberhart (who still did not hold a seat) was to be Premier and Minister of Education. Hugill, the reserved little K.C. who wore spats and had once been secretary to R.B. Bennett, became Attorney-General. For Provincial Treasurer, Aberhart named Charles Cockcroft, an accountant and successful country merchant with several small stores. William N. Chant, a Camrose farmer, was named Minister of Agriculture and Minister of Trade and Commerce; C.C. Ross, a former federal civil servant, Liberal, and mining engineer, was named Minister of Lands and Mines (on the proviso that he did not necessarily subscribe to Socred monetary theory). W.W. Cross, a crusty country doctor, was made Minister of Health. W.A. Fallow, a C.N.R. station agent, was made Minister of Public Works, Railways and Telephones.

And, at the age of twenty-six, Ernest Manning was made Provincial Secretary and Acting Premier. (At the time, he was the youngest man ever to be appointed to a Canadian cabinet.)

In terms of *provincial* experience, the new government was raw indeed: not one sitting Social Crediter had ever been an M.L.A. On the other hand, the M.L.A.s were no gaggle of wide-eyed hicks, either: of the fifty-six Social Credit members, twenty-four had university or normal school degrees, and the twenty-four included eleven teachers, four lawyers, three clergymen, two doctors of medicine, two engineers, a dentist, a druggist and a professional agronomist. Those without degrees included butchers, farmers, hardware merchants, a chiropractor and an undertaker. Many had been on local school boards and municipal councils.

On September 3 Lieutenant-Governor William L. Walsh swore in the informally-dressed cabinet and the new administration began work.

The immediate situation was desperate. Before the election, Aberhart had cautioned voters that the implementation of Social Credit dividends would take at least eighteen months. He had said:

> You don't have to know all about Social Credit before you vote for it. You don't have to understand electricity to make use of it, for you know that experts have put the system in and all you have to do is push the button and you get light. So all you have to do about Social Credit is to cast your ballot for it, and we'll get the experts to put the system in . . . if you are not satisfied with it, you can put the recall into operation.

Aberhart told the press that the new government would do nothing "rash" and wasn't interested in confiscating wealth. The bondholders needn't have worried: the new government was less concerned about revolutionizing the world than about surviving in it. Some

52,000 Albertans were on relief, 10,000 of them heads of families. Fifty per cent of current provincial revenue was earmarked for debt charges. The Treasurer, Cockcroft, telephoned Aberhart and told him there was doubt whether the civil servants could even be paid. Payments on Provincial Savings Certificates had been suspended "temporarily".

Notwithstanding Aberhart's statements, a number of people thought the Millenium had arrived and telephoned to ask where they could pick up their dividend cheques. In several instances, men changed or quit jobs in the expectation of new income; steamship companies reported an increased number of inquiries about reservations from people who were counting expected dividends into their income. A Calgary alderman advised the city to tighten up relief regulations to anticipate and prevent a flood of people from outside the province, looking for dividends.

Confused and feeling the strain, Aberhart left for Ottawa to try and negotiate a Dominion loan of $18,000,000. He returned with a loan of $2,500,000, exacted (it was said) partly on the promise that Social Credit would not contest the West Calgary federal seat held by R.B. Bennett, the Prime Minister.

The new cabinet began to hold strategy sessions. It was agreed that, pending the drafting of distinctly Social Credit legislation, the immediate task at hand was the re-organization of the civil service and the cutting of costs by the trimming of administrative fat. This was begun in earnest, with Aberhart taking the lead in the re-organization of the province's school system into a smaller number of larger school divisions. The senior ranks of the civil service were purged, and vacant offices were filled with Social Crediters. The first incumbent to go was Alex Ross, chairman of the Workman's Compensation Board, who was asked for his resignation a bare two weeks after the Socred victory.*

Manning's immediate tasks were not great – the Provincial Secretary did not carry the heaviest load in the cabinet – and he had time to be interviewed by a reporter from *The Edmonton Journal*, who

---

* Within its first twenty months of office the new government had replaced thirty-four middle and upper-echelon civil servants. Of this number, twelve were police magistrates and eleven were staff members of the Liquor Control Board; the remainder included the provincial auditor, three deputy ministers, the president of the University of Alberta, the King's Printer (customarily a patronage appointment), the Superintendent of Child Welfare and the Superintendent of the Ponoka Mental Hospital. Not all of these men left under duress, of course; even in the 1930s there was some normal staff turnover. Some were victims of the economy drive.

recorded that the young minister was "a pleasant unassuming chap with his feet planted firmly in his native soil . . . neither flippant nor insincere . . . a slim man of average height [who] looks slightly older than he really is. His sandy hair lies rather carelessly, and he wears light horn-rimmed glasses. When he laughs, which is frequently, it is with gusto."

In the course of the interview Manning told the reporter:

> I wasn't looking for it [a cabinet position] at all. I had no interest in this from the point of view of a job, although probably no one would believe it. I'd just as soon be busy with my Bible work. . . . We will be making adjustments as we go along. We will go ahead with our aggressive ideas as soon as possible, but we won't do anything rash . . . all of us entered into this in the spirit of a crusade. We're not politicians. We've always opened our meetings with our hymn and there has been an atmosphere wholly different from that of a political campaign. . . .

To assist him in retrenching, Aberhart brought in Robert J. Magor, a well-heeled Montreal philanthropist and financial adviser who had earlier acted in a similar capacity in the Crown Colony of Newfoundland. As financial czar of Newfoundland, Magor had carried out shrewd cost-efficiency studies into government costs and had slashed many expenditures. He had also attracted the attention of the Douglasites, who labelled him as a typical front-man for the Eastern banking interests. Magor's appointment occasioned raised eyebrows and anxious questioning within the Social Credit movement.

Perhaps more important, it provoked the displeasure of Major Douglas himself. On the night of the election victory, Aberhart had cabled Douglas: VICTORIOUS WHEN COULD YOU COME? Douglas, who was technically still in the employ of the province as "Reconstruction Advisor", was irked by the Magor appointment. The early communications between Douglas and Aberhart failed to yield a concrete plan to bring Douglas to Alberta, and on October 29 Douglas wrote Aberhart:

> A policy which apparently aims at defeating the banks with the assistance of the banks themselves, under the supervision of an agent of the banks, seems to be so dangerous that I do not feel it has a reasonable chance of success. . . . Under these circumstances, and in view of the situation created by the acceptance of Mr. Magor as adviser in connection with the Debt of Alberta, which is, of course, an integral feature of the plan to modify the Alberta financial system I feel that it would be desirable that the

contract I have with the Alberta Government should be terminated by mutual consent. . . .

On November 27 Aberhart wrote Douglas a long reply, pleading that the affairs of the province first had to be stabilized, that there was no collusion with the banks, that the local situation was desperate and complex, and that Magor was "not the nominee of a group of Montreal bankers; you have been wrongly informed about this. . . . I trust that you will give us a little confidence in this matter. We are trying to be honest and sensible in it all." He went on:

Surely you will allow us the right to use our best judgement in all these affairs, and you will fulfil your engagement as our reconstruction adviser to the best of your ability. Nothing can be gained by your assuming the position of dictation rather than that of advice. . . . You have asked us to approach the banks for a credit of five to ten million dollars, with no promise to return same or pay interest on it. Our Executive Council feels that it cannot approach any bank with such a suggestion at the present time. You have evidently misunderstood our letters when you say that we prefer to work in co-operation with the banks. This is hardly true. We are not trying to stir up opposition and conflict with them, however.

In one sense, of course, Douglas was right: Aberhart was in collusion with no one, but he was confused and unsteady, and unsure of where to turn. He had already discovered that it is one thing to make a promise and outline to the voters a "plan" that gains in apparent ease of application every time it is repeated; it is quite another to implement it, once in office and under the barrage of all the influences and demands that impinge on a government.

Aberhart revealed this in his letter: "What we are anxious to have from you as our adviser is the definite outline of some course in more or less detail, showing what steps you feel we ought to take when we begin to establish social credit. . . . " In September, Aberhart *had* said that if the banks would co-operate, it could become possible to pay dividends through the banks, and had approached the banks to sound them out. The Dean of Canterbury, Hewlett Johnson, had made a speaking tour of Canada at about this time and conferred with Aberhart; Johnson was a friend and confidante of Major Douglas's and had no doubt relayed to the Major, on his return to Britain, his impression that Aberhart was vacillating and unsteady.

Everything was in a state of flux and no one was really sure what was going to happen or what should happen. The press, never friendly to the movement, was stepping up its attacks. (Prior to the election, *Maclean's* set the tone for this by referring to Aberhart as "the Hitler of Social Credit.")* A wave of stories swept the province that people were transferring their savings to Vancouver and that at least two large Eastern companies, previously contemplating expansion in Alberta, had changed their minds and decided to locate elsewhere.

The enthusiasm of some Social Crediters caused Aberhart difficult moments. In October the Social Credit League decided to run candidates in the federal election and sent out form letters to businessmen requesting contributions. Many refused, and wrote to say so. Herbert A. Webster, Secretary of the League, sent them this reply:

> Dear Sir: Yours of. . . . to hand. Referring to our letter of October 1st, we beg to draw your attention that we have not circulated that letter excepting to those who have had the privilege of doing business with our government in the past. We trust that you will reconsider the matter in this case.

There were howls of outrage from the business community and the League formally repudiated the letter. But the episode added to a climate of anxiety.

The incident did the movement little harm politically. Seventeen Social Credit candidates were elected in the federal election in November.

On November 1 Aberhart appointed Manning Minister of Trade and Industry. The young disciple was put in control of Aberta's newest department of government, a department created by the U.F.A. in 1934 to regulate the province's small but growing industrial base and oversee trade. Because the U.F.A. left office not long after the department's creation, Manning was really the first cabinet minister to gain a chance to see what the department could be made to do.

The department's powers were broad. It was charged with bringing regulation of provincial trades and industries into the twentieth century – in particular, with creating codes to govern wages, working conditions and hours of work, and with the promotion of new investment and the development of natural resources.

Like Roosevelt's National Industrial Recovery Administration, (NRA), the department was empowered to arrange conferences between employers and employees for the purpose of rationalizing, stabilizing and humanizing the commercial and industrial sector of the economy.

* Issue of April 1st, 1935.

The Act gave the minister the power to open round-table negotiations to hammer out regulatory codes for prices, wages and hours, and provided for the licensing of skilled trades, the setting of floor prices on commodities, the regulation of "loss leader" advertising and the promotion of schemes for central marketing of goods.

The new appointment drew Manning out of the cloisters and into the marketplace. He was required to meet with businessmen, labour leaders, chambers of commerce and boards of trade, and to handle a wide variety of industrial grievances. It taxed the young minister's tact and diplomatic skill to the limit, and because he had almost no prior experience in this area, it forced him to learn quickly the intricacies and fine points of commerce. While Aberhart and the rest bore down on establishing the province's credit and re-organizing the civil service – and drawing up plans for the implementation of dividends and just prices – Manning came to increasingly oversee the "New Deal" aspect of the new government. What Manning was entrusted with had little to do with orthodox Social Credit, and a good deal to do with pragmatic social reform.

While Manning was settling into his new post, the central concern of the cabinet continued to be financial survival. On November 4 Aberhart, through the courtesy of an elected follower who stepped aside, was elected by acclamation in a by-election in the riding of Okotoks-High River. Thus safely ensconced, he continued to reassure the business and financial world that changes in policy were proceeding prudently and again cautioned his followers that the monetization of the province's credit would take time. He went to the federal government for more support, and got it; on November 19 Alberta received a second loan, this one for $1,000,000. Tightening up across the board, in an effort to gain fresh revenue before budget time, the government moved to take over beer distribution, and increased farm telephone rates by thirty-five per cent, abolishing the rebate.

In December as Acting Premier, Manning sent out a letter to all major bond dealers in the country. In it, he advanced tentative suggestions as to how the province could come to terms with its creditors. On behalf of the government, he offered to reduce expenses, "apply the maximum of economy and efficiency" to operations, and seek new revenues – provided the bondholders would agree to reducing fixed charges. The essence of the province's offer was a re-funding of the debt, half of it with perpetual securities at low interest, the other half with serial bonds paying two and three-quarters per cent. The province offered to earmark the whole of its Dominion subsidy to debt payments provided the bondholders would agree to reduce interest.

The bondholders met the offer with a stony silence.

At the turn of the New Year, it was announced that Ottawa had loaned a further $3,000,000; and on January 6 Aberhart advanced the suggestion that he might need – and should thus be given – a four to six-month extension on his original eighteen month deadline.

Around the middle of the month, the elected members began to arrive in the city, and tension began to grow in anticipation of the opening of the world's first Social Credit legislative session. Aberhart announced only that "empowering" legislation would be introduced at the Session, but what this meant was a subject of great conjecture.

On February 6 a packed crowd of 2,000 people jammed the legislature as a guard of honour escorted in the Lieutenant-Governor to open the first Social Credit session. Only those with advance invitations got in the gallery; 1,000 others had to wait outside in the corridors. It was thirty below zero outside, but inside fresh flowers had been put out and it was sweet and humid, an atmosphere of expectation. Speaker Nathan Tanner's borrowed uniform didn't fit and he had to sit on an ordinary wooden office chair because the U.F.A. had given away the Speaker's chair to the previous Speaker. The Clerk, Robert Andison, had to guide the shaky and inexperienced Tanner through the intricacies of procedure. The members of the new government banged their desks lustily when the Speech from the Throne was read.

The speech was couched in general terms. It promised action to stablize agriculture and prices, a recall bill, a plan for the reorganization of rural schools, the improvement of civil service efficiency, the introduction of a bill "leading to the formulation and adoption of a plan based upon the principles of Social Credit", but, above all, "to deal with the affairs of the province in such a manner that no illconsidered action of today will jeopardize the welfare of the future."

As *The Edmonton Journal* commented, mystified, "not much light is thrown on the actual measures that the members will be asked to deal with."

After the opening, the Lieutenant-Governor put Government House at the disposal of the elected members of the administration for the traditional post-opening party. Because of the premier's known dislike of alcohol, the Lieutenant-Governor instructed the clerk to forego the usual wine with dinner. They agreed between themselves, however, that the known tastes of government imbibers also merited consideration and the Lieutenant-Governor agreed to leave a few bottles of liquor in his study, where the clerk could surreptitiously escort those who wished to indulge. This compromise seemed to please everyone.

After dinner, some of the members retired to play bridge and billiards. Aberhart and Mrs. Edith Gostick did not want to take part, however, and so the Clerk was able to find an old checkers set stored behind the furnace in the basement. They played checkers instead.

Manning's baptism into power politics was not long coming. The proposed industrial codes of Manning's department were unpopular with many businessmen, larger businessmen especially. Manning met their criticism squarely. On January 13 the provincial Manufacturer's Association advised Aberhart of its opposition to the codes; but Aberhart backed Manning unflinchingly.

It soon became obvious that Manning enjoyed Aberhart's full confidence as no other minister did.

The early days of the first Socred session were dominated by a debate over Major Douglas, in particular by argument over a statement made by Douglas in London to the effect that the proposed Dominion-Provincial Loan Council was a bank-inspired device to "filch away" the provinces' fiscal autonomy. The opposition demanded to know by what right Douglas, still formally a provincial civil servant, could make such a statement; and while Aberhart defended Douglas, the incident served to dramatize the increasing distance between the two men. The prospects of Douglas coming to Alberta were becoming dimmer.

As the weeks ground on, it began to dawn on the financial community and the critics that nothing radical was likely to come from the first sitting of the government. In establishment quarters there was a collective sigh of relief. In grass-roots Social Credit organizations there were murmurs of growing puzzlement and impatience.

The first Social Credit budget was an exercise in orthodox, pre-Keynesian economics. It pared many expenses, effected economies by re-organization, increased expenditures in several fields (relief, tuberculosis care, mother's allowances), and boosted government income by increased taxation. The price of liquor was hiked, as were taxes on land, personal income, and corporations. A tax on fuel oil was instituted, as well as a new two per cent provincial sales tax.

On the question of striking out at debt – the curse of the province – little was done. An act was passed giving the government the power to compulsorily reduce its own interest payments, but apart from that, little. The Social Credit Measures Act, the only bill overtly pertaining to Social Credit itself, was passed, but all it did was empower an investigation into the possibilities of insituting reform. It was simply enabling legislation.

A Recall Act, empowering 66 2/3 per cent of the electors of any riding to recall their representative, provided 66 and two-thirds per cent of those registered affirmed this view, was brought in, in fulfillment of a campaign promise. It was to have a fascinating history a few months hence, when it was turned on Aberhart himself. But it was immediately attacked by critics on the grounds that it demanded a much higher percentage of dissident voters than recall acts elsewhere. (The common figure at the time was between twenty and thirty per cent.)

Manning piloted through changes in the Trade and Industry Act, empowering the industrial codes to set both "minimum and maximum" prices for commodities and services; the original act had simply envisaged minimum prices. This was clearly a step in the direction of authorizing price control. The Act amendments also made it possible to bring a code into effect with only a "majority" of the workers or employers concerned consenting, and not, as before, sixty-six per cent. The amendments authorized codes to cover virtually all groups in the provincial economy, and authorized Manning to initiate his own investigations into industrial abuses that might call for codes. Manning also piloted through the House an act to authorize the issuance of efficiency certificates to skilled workmen – an attempt to introduce a note of rationalization to industrial work, and to protect the livelihood of skilled tradesmen.

One of the great influences on Manning's development in this period was his Deputy Minister, W.D. King. A Social Credit appointee, King was, ironically, an ex-manager of the Bank of Nova Scotia in Calgary, who came to the government from the Alberta Bankers' Association. The kind-hearted King personally disagreed with many banking practices and he gave Manning the practical business and commercial back-up he badly needed.

It's interesting to reflect, in light of Social Credit's later reputation for defending big business, that Manning's main role in the 1930s was to spearhead Social Credit's attempt to stop cut-throat competition in industry, introduce humane working conditions, and create "floor prices" that would prevent the crowding-out of small businesses. Between 1935 and 1938, Manning's "new deal" department set up codes regulating hours of work, advertising, wages, pricing and labelling in the automotive industry, barbering, cleaning and dyeing, commercial printing, photo finishing, retailing and wholesaling. Eventually many of the codes collided with wartime price controls and were scrapped; but the essence of the codes was retained in permanent legislation that remained on the books. At no time was Social Credit a "laissez-faire" government.

In the first session of 1936 Manning introduced more legislation than any minister save Aberhart and Cockcroft, the Treasurer.

On April 17 the House prorogued. It had made little progress toward implementing Social Credit and Aberhart's magic was beginning to wear a little thin with a hungry, impatient people.

On March 12 the St. Paul Social Credit group passed a resolution denouncing Aberhart for his "miserable failure to set up a new system."

Spring came, and to many the government seemed to be marking time. Relations with Major Douglas continued to deteriorate. The tone of the correspondence between Aberhart and Douglas took on an increasingly harsh tone. Aberhart was struggling, still, with the problem of keeping the province solvent – meeting bills, paying civil servants and teachers, maintaining essential services, postponing the day of reckoning with the creditors. Douglas, on the other hand, kept insisting the first priority of business was an attack on the power of Finance. In particular, Douglas viewed the increased taxation in Aberhart's first budget with something bordering on detestation. Douglas advised Aberhart by confidential letter in late February that the two problems – implementing new credit and meeting the bills of the creditors – might be solved with a single solution. He proposed that

> . . . within three months of the due date of redemption, all bonds which are raised upon the credit of Alberta should be presented in Edmonton for stamping together with the names and addresses of their owners (which will, in all probability, be found to be chiefly financial institutions). . . . All holders of more than five hundred dollars of the issue falling due, and such holders of smaller amounts electing to be dealt with in this manner should be informed that a credit in Alberta of the amount of the face value of the bonds, plus 15 per cent, has been opened with the State Treasury in their favour, and that this credit will be available for the purchase of any product, whether wheat or otherwise available for sale in Alberta. . . .

Aberhart could not or would not agree and nothing was done to implement the proposal. (In 1938, after the creation of the Treasury Branches, a hybrid system of "consumers' bonuses" supplied in the form of "non-negotiable transfer vouchers" was implemented and remained in effect until 1945.)

In late March, realizing that Douglas was not going to come to Alberta, Aberhart cabled him asking how much it would cost for a Social Credit adviser. Douglas replied on March 21: NO CONTRACT STOP TERMS PLAN TWO LETTER FEBRUARY EIGHTEENTH OFFER OF

COLLEAGUE FOR ACCEPTANCE TUESDAY LATEST OTHERWISE DO BEST LOCALLY – DOUGLAS. And, to end the important correspondence, Douglas sent a letter, dated March 24, which ended on this note:

> I can only assume that you must have in mind the pursuit of some policy which does not require the assistance of those who are familiar with the advice already given. . . . Should you feel that you can proceed without further advice from outside Alberta, I am confident that it is desirable that you should obtain the co-operation of Mr. Spenser, the late M.P. for Battle River, Mr. Herbert C. Boyd, M.A., of Edgerton, and Mr. Larkham Collins, F.C.A., of Calgary. I trust that you will feel as I do, that the issues involved are much too serious to allow any question of Party affiliation to influence the action taken. Yours faithfully, C.H. Douglas.*

The government, under opposition pressure to table the Aberhart-Douglas correspondence, at first held fast. A few days before the session ended, it gave in, under considerable pressure from both the public and the party rank and file. And the revelation of bitter feuding at the top did Aberhart's prestige – and the morale of the party – no good. A further indication of growing restiveness among the back-benchers was a picayune party revolt on March 28th, which killed a bill to have all pet-owners in the province taxed one dollar a year to pay for damage to livestock and other animals caused by pets.

Meanwhile, a provincial financial crisis was again looming. Aberhart had refused to subscribe to a Dominion-Provincial Loan Council to regulate provincial borrowing, and in retaliation Ottawa had refused to accede to his request for a further loan to meet an upcoming bond issue of $3,250,000. On April 1, in a move that sent the province's credit plummeting in financial markets around the world, Alberta defaulted on her bond issue. A motion debated before caucus, to institute a tax lottery to help the province out of her squeeze, was defeated. The next day, Ottawa announced a fifteen per cent cut in the grant to provinces for relief, and Aberhart was forced to announce a similar cut in the province's grant to the cities. On April 7, on a note of disappointment and frustration, the session prorogued.

One of the themes successfully employed by Social Credit in the landslide 1935 election had been: you don't have to understand

---

* This, as Douglas probably knew, was the cruelest cut of all: in their testimony before the Legislature's Agriculture Committee in 1934, Collins and Boyd had strongly implied that, when it came to Social Credit theory, Aberhart didn't know what he was talking about.

Social Credit in order to vote for it – the first task of government will be to bring in "experts" and "technicians" to design ways and means of implementing the Dividend and the Just Price. The public's responsibility – and the legislature's responsibility – was not to question methods, but to *demand results.* Now Aberhart had been unable to deliver results. This failure, the failure to bring in anyone who *could* deliver results, and the publication of Douglas correspondence began to eat into Aberhart's public credibility.

Government supporters were becoming divided into roughly three groups: (1) those thought, whatever his actions, that Aberhart could do no wrong; (2) those who attributed Aberhart's vacillation to intellectual confusion or ignorance, and (3) those who were convinced Aberhart had sold out – that he never intended to bring in Social Credit. The latter could point, and did, to an article in *The New York Times* of September 1, 1935, in which Aberhart was reported as saying, "seventy-five per cent of those who voted for me don't expect any dividend, but hope for a just and honest government."

Pressure on Aberhart continued to grow. One M.L.A., S.A.G. Barnes of Edmonton, was read out of caucus – and his seat in the House surrepticiously edged farther and farther away from the government side – for his criticisms of Aberhart's delaying. Aberhart had ignited and fanned embers of hope in the hearts of Albertans; he had told them that the milennium was just around the corner. Such passions once aroused, would not be easily extinguished.

> The *Douglas Social Credit Advocate* wrote: "Back east, they thought the Social Credit gun was loaded. It now turns out to be a pop-gun with a cork in it. Every now and again the Premier shoots it off, and his followers, hearing the noise, still believe he is a very bold man."

On May 1 the new provincial sales tax went into effect, and was bitterly and universally resented. On May 27 the province acting on legislative authority granted at the session months before, slashed the interest rate on provincial bonds to two and one-half per cent. Days later the bondholders – which included a number of churches and pension funds, as well as life insurance and trust companies, and banks – issued yet another protest. On June 3 Alberta bonds were barred from the London Stock Exchange.

Press criticism increased. Aberhart, never able to face criticism well, reacted strongly. He told friends he hoped to be able to repair the situation of the province in about five years, and then return to teaching; he also said he couldn't understand press and other opposition. On June 1, he charged the province's newspapers "coloured" stories about the government, and said he favoured a move to license the press. On June 2 Aberhart announced the province intended to issue $200,000 worth of "prosperity certificates", or scrip, which it intended to use, in part, to pay men doing highway construction, and in grants to muncipalities.

The plan was not a success. Merchants were reluctant to accept the certificates, the province itself refused to accept them in payment of taxes, and in order for each certificate to retain its value, the holder had to affix to it each week a special one-cent stamp. The government threatened sanctions against merchants who refused to accept scrip, but to little avail. To help inspire confidence, the government offered to have cabinet ministers and M.L.A.s accept a part of their indeminities in scrip. The offer had little impact. Boards of Trade and Chambers of Commerce in Calgary, Medicine Hat, Lethbridge and Drumheller officially refused to co-operate.

There can be little doubt that the government fell back on the use of scrip in order to buy time for the preparation of genuine Social Credit legislation. Scrip never commanded much public enthusiasm, and over the months less and less was said about it. But it cost the government little to issue, and it was a useful tool at the time, both as a device to fight off attacks and to meet needs for current expenditure.

In late July, with an August Session planned, the caucus gathered in Edmonton and approved the registration of all Alberta citizens, in anticipation of the issuance of dividends. A few days later, Manning predicted that six months would decide whether or not dividends would be issued, and urged all citizens to join in the registration campaign. And in a speech at Vermilion, Mr. Fallow, the Minister of Public Works, injected a still more ominous note into attacks on the press: "They are giving us a rough ride now, but that is nothing like the ride they are going to get before we are through."

Plans began for the drafting of "citizens' covenants," which were, in effect, contracts, made between each citizen and the government, in which the government undertook to pay a dividend each month, provided the citizen undertook to abide by Credit House regulations, accept dividends as currency, and so forth. Similar covenants were drafted for submission to merchants, wholesalers, and corporations. This went forward in spite of the limited acceptance of scrip.

On August 12 Aberhart announced a Social Credit bill was being drafted for the upcoming special session of the legislature. At the same time, he attempted to shift the onus for action onto his critics, by charging that if too many people failed to co-operate in the plan to register the population and distribute scrip, the government could make no headway. "If you fail us, I'll be sorry, because I will not be able to fulfill my promises."

This, however, had something of a boomerang effect, for many people registered and signed the covenants in the expectation that nothing more stood in the way of their receiving dividends. Aberhart's attempt to buy time and take the heat off the administration, only succeeded in looking like the last step before the implementation of his mandate. That step completed, he could no longer claim that any unfulfilled business forestalled action to produce the dividend.

On August 25, just three days after the first anniversary of the new government, the Legislature met in special session in Edmonton to consider Aberhart's long-promised Social Credit legislation.

Two acts were passed that seemed to promise the fulfillment of the Social Credit mandate. The first was the Alberta Credit House Act, which promised to issue to all covenanted, registered Albertans "Alberta credit", a dividend not negotiable for currency or payable for taxes. On August 29 the second phase of the Social Credit attack on impoverishment began, with the introduction of the Debt Adjustment Act, and the Reduction and Settlement of Land Debts Act. The first bill gave the Debt Adjustment Board power to hand down decisions which could not be questioned in the courts, and the power to declare a debt moratorium. The second act provided that for private debts in Alberta, interest on loans made before July 1, 1932, was uncollectable. It also limited payable interest on all other private debts – regardless of the initial terms of the loan – to five per cent.

This was radical legislation – at last – and the economic interests at whom the bills were aimed were quick to make their anguish heard. *The Financial Post* spoke for them all, when, on September 19, it characterized the Social Credit debt legislation as

a social and economic revolution commonly known as Communism. Recent debt legislation is akin to confiscation of private property. It strikes at the very roots of commerce, business and finance in a way which characterized the early stages of the Russian Revolution.

The government was at last beginning to change the rules of the commercial game by legislative fiat; in particular, it was making them more humane, and more in tune with the tragic realities of the Alberta economy.

The implementation of Social Credit and the attack on private and public debt were two sides of the same political coin.

The first was an attempt to get the province's economy moving again by creating new purchasing power. The second was an attempt to lighten the heavy burden of debt – debt acquired in good times and unbearable in bad. By 1936 the public and private indebtedness of Alberta was about $395,000,000. This represented an average annual cost of about $40,000,000, a herculean obligation for a depressed economy. Aberhart's aim, an aim for which he unquestionably had broad popular support, was to renegotiate the terms on which Alberta dealt with the world economy, and gain the province control over its own economic destiny.

What was obvious about such an objective was that it would be fought to the end by those institutions and individuals who stood to lose by its attainment. For the people of Alberta to gain, other interests had to lose. It was as simple as that. But those same firms, institutions and individuals whose interests Social Credit placed in jeopardy were actors with great influence in national politics, with great leverage over those who controlled the federal power. Alberta was a mere province, and was venturing onto constitutional thin ice; Article 91 of the British North America Act made that quite clear.*

A confrontation between Aberhart's government and the federal power was inevitable; that much is certain. What was also certain was that Alberta had few weapons it could bring to the contest. It was not a powerful province, economically or politically. Social Credit had few allies in the House of Commons, none in the other provinces. The courts were largely manned by men whose politics, class background and prevailing views Social Credit had chosen to villify. To top it off, Aberhart and his lieutenants were politically inexperienced and dangerously unsure of themselves, and the government had very few friends among the media.

Perhaps most important, the time was not yet ripe for national acceptance of the key beliefs of Social Credit economic doctrine.

Like socialist economic theory, Social Credit theory collided with the conventional economic wisdom of the time. Today it is possible to find theorists – even banking theorists – who will admit that while Douglas's theory was technically deficient, he did succeed in putting his finger on a neglected problem: the role of monetary policy in regulating the economy. But in the 1930s in Canada both governments and the banks were still doggedly committed to the platitudes of tight budgeting and "sound money". This conventional wisdom had become embedded in the very constitutional and legal frame-

* " . . . the exclusive Legislative Authority of the Parliament of Canada extends to all Matters coming within the Classes of Subjects next hereinafter enumerated; that is to say, . . . (15) Banking, Incorporation of Banks, and the Issue of Paper Money . . . (19) Interest . . . (20) Legal Tender. . . .

work of Canada: to challenge the conventional wisdom meant challenging the power structure itself. And, unlike the socialists, the Social Crediters had no allies in the university community to spread their doctrine and interpret and develop their views.

The contest between Aberhart's movement and the political and economic system went on for four years. When the contest adjourned in September 1939, it was conceded that Social Credit had fought the good fight, and lost. An uninterrupted series of political and judicial set backs, combined with the onset of the war, closed the books on Alberta's assault on the money power. When the war elapsed, six hectic years later, the movement had matured; the economic backdrop of politics had been repainted, and a new crop of leaders, headed by Manning, were in control. The radical era of Social Credit was over.

But none of this was evident in the autumn of 1936, as the administration went back to its offices armed with a whole new arsenal of political weapons.

In early September, Manning, speaking for the cabinet, said the necessary machinery for providing dividends was being established, and that the day was drawing near when the government could begin the circulation of "Alberta Credit". Aberhart promised the people on September 10 that dividends would be paid in three months time.*

He later forecast that the dividends would be between five dollars and ten dollars monthly. He also lashed out at the press in a fresh attack, calling for the licensing of newspapers "for the protection of the public" and referred to the "mad dog tactics" of "certain financial newspapers" which should be "curbed". Blasts at the newspapers, in response to the harsh and unremitting critisicm the government continued to receive from most of the daily newspapers of the province (the *Calgary Herald* in particular) soon became *de rigueur;* no Social Credit meeting was complete without at least one.

On October 16, 1936, the Alberta Credit House Act was officially proclaimed. Six days later, application was made in an Edmonton court to test the legal validity of the Debt Reduction Act. Six days later again, the Bank of Canada refused Alberta a loan of $3,500,000 to meet debt charges and on October 31st, Aberhart announced that Alberta would default on a further $1,250,000 bond issue. (In retaliation, Edmonton City Council cut in half the interest payable on its

---

* Progress was a little slower than that. On March 4, 1937, the government had to admit in the House that premises obtained for Credit House locations had been disposed of, and none were held in readiness. The next day Manning, who had been appointed by cabinet to supervise the preparations, tabled a reply indicating only that a survey of possible locations had been made.

own bonds, many of which were held by the provincial government; later it learned that it did not have the legal authority to do this.)

Establishment political opposition to Social Credit began to coalesce. The dormant opposition political parties began to come back to life; the Conservatives threw their weight behind an anti-Social Credit united front called the Peoples' League, a province-wide "non-partisan" organization ostensibly dedicated to "good government".

On November 19 Manning, who had literally worked himself to a frazzle, was ordered to bed by doctors for an "extended rest". He was suffering from tuberculosis in one lung, and stayed at his home on the city's south side to be nursed back to health by his wife. He was not to return as a full-time minister of the Crown until June 30, 1937. And not long after his temporary departure from the scene, Aberhart was to face a full-scale revolt from his own followers.

For a time, things seemed to be cooling off for Aberhart and the party. Popular pressure for dividends had been mollified somewhat by the government's action at the August session. Then, in late December, there arrived in Edmonton, unannounced and uninvited, British writer and Social Credit organizer John Hargrave – the deep-voiced, confident, charismatic leader of Britain's "Greenshirts," or, as they were earlier and more romantically known, "the Kindred of the Kibbo Kift."

Hargrave's was a figure of moment in Britain; he had transformed the Kift from an association of young unemployed men dedicated to returning to nature and studying woodlore – a kind of grown-up Boy Scouts – into a tight-knit political machine that became the organizational backbone of the British Social Credit movement.

Hargrave's arrival was timely, from the standpoint of Aberhart's critics, for Hargrave was very distinctly his own man, and had made it clear he couldn't understand what was holding Aberhart up: he offered Aberhart an eleven point plan for the implementation of dividends and a just price, but the cabinet gave him the run-around from one office to another. Finally, the message got through. He left Edmonton in a huff – though not before discussing his frustrations with local reporters, over a bottle in his hotel-room – and issued the following statement:

> I still feel that the first Social Credit government in the world is not yet publicly committed to the principles of Social Credit . . . it lacks technical knowledge and as a consequence has, over the past sixteen months, groped its way like a man stumbling along on a pitch-black night.

Not only was it necessary for me to deal with a preacher-schoolmaster personality, abnormally resentful of criticism, but one that could not accept and act upon any proposition without taking it to pieces and putting it together wrongly. Having done my utmost to help, I am leaving Alberta because I find it impossible to co-operate with a Government which I consider a mere vacillating machine which operates in starts, stops, and reversals.

The rejection of Aberhart's leadership by virtually all the leaders of British Social Credit was now complete. For Aberhart, Hargrave's attack could not have come at a worse time. At the end of the year C.C. Ross, the able Minister of Lands and Mines, resigned over differences on oil policy. In the middle of January, the annual party convention passed a resolution underlining the "imperative necessity" of putting the dividend into effect "as rapidly as possible". At the end of January, Charles C. Cockcroft, the Treasurer, also resigned – because, it is said, he had favoured a Federal-Provincial Loan Council, and Aberhart stood rock-stubborn against it. Cockroft had led some delicate negotiations with the federal authorities; to some extent, it seems, he felt Aberhart was continually undercutting his position.

Three days after his departure, J.F. Perceval, Deputy Provincial Treasurer, also resigned. Perceval had been a member of the board of management Aberhart created to set up provincial Credit Houses.

When Solon Low was sworn in as new provincial Treasurer on February 2, he became the second Mormon to join the cabinet; the first was E. Nathan Tanner, who replaced C.C. Ross as Minister of Mines and Minerals.

On February 10, P.J. Rowe, one of the party's federal M.P.'s, was expelled from caucus for his undisguised criticism of Aberhart's vacillation. And rumours began to circulate that two of the four remaining cabinet ministers, John Hugill, Attorney-General, and William Chant, Minister of Agriculture, would be asked for their resignations.

On February 25 the history-making third session of the legislature convened in Edmonton. Six days earlier, the Alberta Supreme Court had declared unconstitutional the six-month old Reduction and Settlement of Land Debts Act, the chief weapon in the government's debt arsenal. Pending an appeal, Aberhart signed a six-month debt moratorium. Mr. Justice Ives of the Alberta Supreme Court also struck down the 1936 Act reducing the rate of interest on the province's bonds.

Aberhart was clearly in hot water. Local Social Credit groups from Rabbit Hill to Red Deer began to issue calls for his resignation.

For the first time, there emerged an organized movement to remove Aberhart from the leadership. At first, there were twenty-two identified "insurgents" who muttered that Aberhart was going too slow, that the time for moderation and delaying was over. They began meeting every night, behind locked doors, in the basement of the Corona Hotel, where many M.L.A.'s stayed while in Edmonton for the session.

As the session swept into March, the insurgents began to rise in the House and denounce Aberhart openly – an extraordinary occurrence in the parliamentary system. A civil suit in Vancouver, by people suing Aberhart for back wages, heard testimony from one employee that Aberhart told her the public has "the mentality of a 13-year old."* That rankled. On March 11 a return in the House revealed that no cabinet ministers had taken any part of their pay in scrip, after all. The next day, the lid blew off.

The government, which had made a vague commitment in the Throne Speech to take final action on dividends, brought down a budget. It contained no mention of Social Credit: taxation was increased on banks, corporations, railways, insurance, gas and power companies and a total deficit of $1,227,885 was forecast – but this was to be reduced by the province reducing the interest rate on its debentures.

The opposition angrily labelled it "the default budget". The Social Credit militants were even angrier: Aberhart's self-imposed eighteen months were up, and he had brought down another conventional budget. As the budget debate began the Social Credit "insurgents", as they came to be called, rose one after another to denounce the budget and its author.

Aberhart sat on the front bench, his head down, his neck and face flushed. There were several calls for his immediate resignation. Aberhart's shock and shame were intensified by the fact that virtually all were from men whom he had attracted to Social Credit in the first place, men whom he had approved for nomination as candidates for the party. They were ordinary men, for the most part, and the challenge they were throwing at him had been fashioned from his own promises.

From that night on the Social Credit caucus split into "loyalist" and "insurgents" camps; both met behind closed doors and locked transoms. The insurgents met in the downstairs dining room of the Corona Hotel late every night. Their ranks included A.V. Bourcier, Alf Hooke, A.L. Blue and G.L. MacLachlan – between twenty and

* The case was later thrown out of Court.

twenty-five back-benchers in all, about half of Aberhart's total following. The insurgents had no formal leadership, but Dr. Harry Brown, the dentist, was usually their spokesman.

The hostilities between the two groups grew. Aberhart had a barricade erected across the corridor leading to the room where the loyalist caucus met. Both sides had "spies" in the other group. The insurgents even drew up their own plan of Social Credit, calling for consumer dividends and interest-free loans; but Aberhart rejected it, claiming in a radio broadcast that it proposed expropriation and confiscation of property.

Cabinet decided the fusillade had to be halted. The government was close to moral and political collapse. Aberhart seconded a motion by Solon Low to resolve the House into Committee on Supply, and thus choke off the budget debate, and silence the insurgency.

But twenty-one insurgents joined with the six Opposition members and defeated the motion. The government, humiliated, was forced to continue the debate.

The cabinet met round the clock, trying to hammer out a compromise. Finally, one was agreed upon, and submitted to the insurgents: the cabinet offered to draft legislation providing for a five-man commission to implement a Social Credit plan for Alberta, to set up Credit Houses, and to distribute the dividend – provided only that the insurgents would agree to pass an interim supply bill. On March 31, with several abstentions, the insurgents agreed; provisional estimates were passed,the budget was hoisted for ninety days, and the crisis cooled.

On April 8 the cabinet introduced a new omnibus bill, the Alberta Social Credit Act, which fulfilled its promises, and on April 13 the House adjourned to reassemble June 7 to receive the report of the newly created Social Credit Board, and to vote on the budget.

It is difficult to unscramble Aberhart's motives in agreeing to the compromise. From one standpoint, it did represent a capitulation to the insurgents' demands – or seemed to. It took the final step necessary for the implementation of the party's promises. On the other hand, the Social Credit Board was a queer hybrid: it was fully responsible for the implementation of Social Credit, yet it was still under the cabinet. If it failed, the cabinet could absolve itself of any blame. Moreover, the board, which was headed by G.L. MacLachlan, and which included Bourcier and Hooke, was staffed primarily by insurgents. If the board failed, the insurgents could be pinned with the blame. Finally, the cabinet was left with power to supplement or alter the provisions of the Alberta Social Credit Act, and to keep reign on the board. Very strange indeed.

From a tactical standpoint, the settlement was a victory for Aberhart. He was left secure as party leader; the adjournment dispersed and cooled off the insurgents; and he was given a break to go on radio and appeal directly to the now somewhat demoralized rank and file.

Some of the insurgents began to wonder if they had been out-manoeuvred. Dr. Harry Brown apparently thought so, for he began a speaking campaign around the province, putting his feelings about Aberhart on the line:

> Aberhart never did have any real and sincere intention of trying to implement Social Credit. . . . You have come to the point of choosing between principles and a man. . . . We have now sat in three sessions of the legislature since we were first elected to effect Social Credit. We have done a great deal of talking . . . and I was one of the talkers. We had faith then in our leader who said he could lead us. Well, 20 or 30 of us in the legislature have made up our minds to carry this thing through to get Social Credit. If anyone gets in our way, he's going to get into trouble . . . we must choose between principles and party, between Social Credit and Premier Aberhart.

The chairman of the Social Credit Board, MacLachlan, was ordered to sail to Europe and consult with Major Douglas; and to bring back either Major Douglas, or one of his top trusted aides, to serve as a policy advisor and technical expert. But while MacLachlan was en route – he stopped off in Ottawa to consult with the federal members – the battle raged on at home, although often at the conspiratorial level. A mysterious petition, calling for the resignation of Aberhart and the cabinet, was circulated among the sitting members. The petition gave every evidence of coming from an insurgent. Then it was learned the petition had really been circulated by the cabinet, as a means of finding out who was loyal and who was not.

It was a time of frayed tempers, broken trusts, injured egos. Aberhart called Bob Andison, the clerk of the legislature, on the mat and accused him of giving "disloyal" advice to certain insurgents; Andison reminded Aberhart that, as an employee of the whole house, he was bound to serve all members. The Aberhart – Andison feud had a comic climax when Aberhart got Andison out of bed one night after a long, grueling day to demand that he come down to the legislature and get some papers out of the vault for a late cabinet meeting. Andison did so and when he found Aberhart not in his office and the door locked, slid them under the door. But Aberhart had left the window open, and the top-secret documents blew all over the place, some of them out the window. Aberhart had to stamp around angrily picking them up himself.

The tide had turned. At the peak of the insurgency the rebels had Aberhart on the defensive. But Aberhart's tactical astuteness – and the indecision and naivete of the insurgents, who placed their ideals before their personal ambitions – turned things around. Now that results were within their grasp, the insurgents had no choice but to support Aberhart.

An interesting note, which few paid much attention to at the time, occured on April 9, when the Social Credit group in Aberhart's constituency of High River-Okotoks voted to demand his resignation, accusing Aberhart of inadequate interest in the constituency itself. But nothing was done about it . . . for the moment.

On April 30 William Chant was fired as Minister of Agriculture. His resignation was quietly asked for, at first; when he balked, he was axed publicly. This left W.W. Cross, John Hugill and Bill Fallow as the only members left of the original cabinet, apart from Manning. And two of them were soon to go, too.

The charges continued to fly, and lost none of their virility. In fact, if anything they grew in intensity as the insurgents realized they had been outflanked, and time was not on Aberhart's side. H.O. Haslam of Nanton charged Aberhart had held a secret meeting with the bankers, and since then had shown no interest in dividends. Aberhart retaliated by calling the insurgents the tools of the financial interests. Floyd Baker, a loyalist, went about as a spokesman for Aberhart, gamely standing up to the insurgents at their own meetings. At one such meeting of 4,000 people in Calgary, Baker was shouted down.

On June 10, his consultations with Major Douglas complete, Maclachlan arrived back in Edmonton, the first of two Douglas "experts," George Frederic Powell, in tow. Powell was ordained as Douglas's "political expert", and was, first, to look the situation over and report back to the Major, and second, do what he could to help the government close ranks and start work on a Social Credit plan. "I'm here to learn, not to teach," Powell said.

A few days later, Douglas announced his second appointee, L. Denis Byrne, an Irishman in the British insurance industry. Byrne was told he would be needed for about five weeks, and left on that assumption; while he was on the way, Powell directed negotiations with the insurgents to try and put the government back together again. A "Unity Pledge", meant to re-establish the government's unanimity, was drawn up; and Powell appealed to loyalists and insurgents alike to sign it as an act of good faith – to restore popular confidence in the government, and get reform on the road. The insurgents, convinced of Aberhart's good faith, and awed by the annointed emissary Powell, gave in; Dr. Harry Brown was one of the first to come forward and sign. The pledge, which was strictly secret and confidential (and which the press obtained within days), reiterated the government's mandate, pointed out that twenty-five dollars a month dividends were "physically possible and must therefore be financially possible", and pledged the signer to uphold the Social Credit Board and its technicians. and "avoid recriminations for the past and provocative utterances for the future". It also pledged each signer to "subscribe unreservedly" to the necessity for passing acts to "control all banking and financial institutions operating within this province until we achieve our immediate objective." It concluded with a final promise:

> So I promise for so long as a majority of my electors concur in my so doing, to vote consistently for a government which does give continuous and unremitting legislative priority to such procedure until our above declared immediate objective has been achieved; and I will vote consistently against any government which does not. I also realize that the government of which I am a member is virtually at war and that in war information which may appear unimportant is often vital. . . .

The insurgency was over. Provided he adhered to the terms of the pledge, more or less, Aberhart was assured of continued control. Likewise, the insurgents were bound to co-operation and silence.

A strange episode, indeed. In it, Manning played but a marginal role. He took to his sick-bed as the insurgency was beginning to take shape, and did not return to fully active and energetic participation in the cabinet until it was in full flower. His loyalty to Aberhart was never seriously questioned; yet he did not drastically alienate the insurgents themselves. He was too quiet, too tactful, too cool for that. The fact that he did not incur anyone's lasting enmity as a consequence of the insurgency of course strengthened his future standing. There are times in politics when the number of one's enemies is far more critical than the number of one's friends.

The lasting consequences of the insurgency are hard to measure. There was never again a serious threat to Aberhart's power. And to raise the issue today is to invoke hasty denials that any bad feelings whatever persisted – although in light of the stakes, the tempers then and the seriousness of the charges made, this is unlikely. But what happened for all practical purposes was that those insurgents who did not in some fashion ingratiate themselves thereafter as dependable loyalists, with either Aberhart or Manning, slowly faded away.

The radical era of Social Credit was fast nearing its climax. The government, freshly fuelled with high-octane ideology, moved to the attack. In late June Byrne, Douglas's "financial expert", arrived in Edmonton and immediately sat down with the Social Credit Board to begin plotting strategy for the upcoming session in August. In late July the board put out a statement warning all institutions operating in Alberta to "co-operate with the government". Days later, Aberhart said over the radio from the Prophetic Bible Institute, "I believe in the session of August 3, history will begin to be written."

The session opened, and two days later the new legislation was tabled. The bills – the Credit of Alberta Regulation Act, the Bank Employees Civil Rights Act, and the Judicature Act Amendment Act – struck at the power of the banks in a way more profound than any legislation ever drafted in a free nation. The new bills put the banks under virtual provincial control (it forbade them to operate without licences, and gave the province control over licence provisions), denied bank employees access to the courts, and forbade unlicenced bank employees from working.

There was no attempt to disguise the strategy, which was related to one suggested years before by Major Douglas himself, in his testimony before the Agriculture Committee, and in his Interim Report to the U.F.A., in which he wrote:

> It is important to realize that the sanctions [which the banks may attempt to bring against any government trying to introduce dividends] are not wholly upon one side . . . vindictive action by the financial authorities could be pilloried, through the agency of Press and broadcasting . . . .

This was radical legislation, and the Lieutenant-Governor, Mr. Bowen, asked the Attorney-General, Mr. Hugill – in the presence of Aberhart – if he would be prepared to say, as a lawyer, that the acts were constitutionally within the power of the province. Hugill was a forthright and principled man, long schooled in the law, and he was candid: he said he did not believe the acts were within the compass of the province. Aberhart said, "your resignation is accepted, Hugill."

On August 17 the federal government, responding to the protests of the banks, disallowed all three acts.

The government urged the voters to "bombard" Ottawa with protest telegrams; but some of the telegrams sent, for example one signed by the Edmonton Chamber of Commerce, instead protested Aberhart's claim that he represented the people.

Aberhart promised to keep up the fight in legal channels, but not all his followers were inclined to be so patient. When a follower, attending an Aberhart speech at South Cooking Lake, heard the news that Ottawa had struck down the legislation, he shouted, "give us a gun!"

In September the government returned to the offensive. This time it widened its range of fire to include a new target: the press. Social Credit had gotten a bad press in Alberta almost from its origins. Some of the small rural weeklies were either neutral or slightly pro-Social Credit, but the rest of the weeklies, and all of the large dailies, were government critics. From the dailies, and the "national" (i.e., Ontario and English Montreal) press, Aberhart received a continual bombardment. Of all the dailies, Aberhart was the most vexed by the *Calgary Herald:* the *Herald*'s omnipresent snoopers had many contacts within the civil service and, it would seem, within Aberhart's own government; Aberhart began to feel persecuted about the government's inability to keep its secrets from these prying scribblers. The Socreds began to develop a "siege mentality" that lasted long after the press campaign had trailed off.

But while the conventional newspapers' attacks were vexing, they were at least partly based on fact; for several years Aberhart also had to face the rantings of an incredibly anti-Social Credit broadsheet published bi-weekly in Calgary by a Tory, Mr. J.J. Zubick. This broadsheet, entitled *The Rebel,* was pure vituperation, and characteristically referred to Aberhart as "a disgusting, contemptible liar", "yellow", "spineless" and began lengthy attacks with rhetorical questions like, "Is Aberhart insincere or insane? Our view is that he is so morally depraved that he will not hesitate to lie, slander and deceive . . . ."*

Now, in one sense, this barrage of attacks did not harm Aberhart politically; in fact, it may have assisted him. With only a very small amount of exaggeration, Aberhart was able to depict the press as a mere tool of Eastern financial and commercial interests; to the extent that he succeeded in this argument, many Albertans came to regard the attacks from the big dailies as a form of left-handed compliment. On the other hand, Aberhart was a more sensitive soul than he sometimes seemed, and never was able to suffer much personal criticism. He revealed his growing bitterness in a radio broadcast September 20th: "Some of these days these creatures with mental hydrophobia will be taken in hand and their biting and barking will cease."

Four days later another special session was called. Aberhart laid before it a bundle of new legislation: acts which re-enacted the federally disallowed bills of the August session in new terms, and two new

* Vol. 1, No. 3, May 28, 1937.

bills, The Bank Taxation Act (which punished the banks by increasing the provincial tax on them by 2,230 per cent), and the Accurate News and Information Act . . . the government's long-threatened retribution against the newspapers.

The Bank Taxation bill forecast a $2,200,000 a year bank levy.

The Accurate News and Information Act was even headier stuff; it carried zeal for reform right into autocracy. The bill empowered the chairman of the Social Credit Board to require the editor or publisher of any newspaper to publish "any statement furnished by the Chairman which has for its object the correction or amplification of any statement relating to any policy or activity of the Government or Province." The statement would have to be equal in length, in the same type size, and displayed with the same prominence, as the statement to be "corrected". The principle of free government advertising made the newspapers angry enough; but the bill went even further. The chairman was also empowered to require any editor to supply to the board the source of any story and the name of the writer of any given article or editorial. Cabinet was empowered to prohibit the publication of an offending newspaper, the publication of any article by a given writer and the publication of an article based on information supplied by a given source.

This was a harsh blow at free speech, and the critics rightly lost no time in saying so. The protests were universal; the "press gag" bill was condemned by virtually every Canadian newspaper and newspapers abroad. One London paper called Aberhart "a little Hitler". The Opposition called it "legalized robbery".

The session ended October 6. Without seeking Ottawa's guidance (as he should have under proper protocol), the Lieutenant-Governor "reserved" all the major Social Credit acts for the approval of Ottawa. The Supreme Court was not to pronounce a verdict on them until the next January.

On the same day the session ended, George Frederic Powell, advisor to the Social Credit Board and Major Douglas's "political expert", was arrested by police and charged with criminal libel and counselling to murder.

Powell's troubles with the law began three days earlier when on the House objections of Mr. Duggan, the Conservative leader, police raided the Social Credit League office in Edmonton and seized 4,000 copies of a pamphlet called "The Bankers' Toadies".

One of the crude leaflets, printed on two sides of a single sheet, had gotten out, and Duggan had seen it. More particularly he had seen his name on it, and protested to police. The famous pamphlet read:

BANKERS' TOADIES. My child, you should NEVER say hard or

unkind things about Bankers' Toadies. God made snakes, slugs, snails and other creepy-crawly, treacherous and poisonous things. NEVER, therefore, abuse them – just exterminate them! And to prevent all evasion demand the RESULT you want – $25.00 a month and a lower cost to live.

On the opposite side was a list of the "toadies", which read:

Bankers' Toadies:
S.W. Field K.C., Lawyer for the MORTGAGE AND LOAN COMPANIES OF CANADA, President of the Peoples' (!) League.
H.H. Parlee, K.C., Lawyer, Canadian Bank of Commerce. President, Edmonton Liberal Association.
J.F. Lymburn, K.C., Lawyer, Bank of Montreal. Peoples' (!) League.
H.R. Milner, K.C., Lawyer, Royal Bank of Canada and Canadian Bankers' Association, President, Edmonton Conservative Association.
G.D. Hunt, Investment broker, United Canada Association.
L.Y. Cairns, K.C., Lawyer, Dominion Bank of Canada, Member, Conservative executive.
G.W. Auxier, Lawyer, National Trust Co., Secretary, Peoples' (!) League.
W.A. Griesbach, K.C., Lawyer, Represents several trust companies.
D.M. Duggan, Investment broker. Peoples' (!) League. Provincial Leader, Conservative Party.
Exterminate Them.
And to prevent all Evasion, Demand the Result You Want –
$25.00 a MONTH and a lower cost to live.

Powell's arrest provoked rumbles. In far-away London Douglas told reporters "trouble" was in store for those out to get Powell and there were mutterings from strange other quarters, too; in Toronto, a spokesman for the Canadian Communist Party protested Powell's arrest and urged a "united front" to fight the Peoples' League. On November 12 Joe Unwin, the Socred whip and Powell's accomplice (he had been arrested and charged with Powell) was tried and found guilty by an Edmonton jury and sentenced to three months of hard labour for publishing a defamatory libel. Three days later Powell, too, was found guilty and given a six-month sentence at hard labour, with deportation to follow.*

* A year later, the government got its revenge, A.H. Gibson, K.C., the magistrate who committed Powell and Unwin for trial, was sacked.

The government received a further setback to its image during the 1937 session. Cabinet sponsored a motion to repeal the 1936 Recall Act, just in time to save Aberhart from losing his High River-Okotoks seat to a recall petition. Forty-four hundred signatures were needed to unseat Aberhart, but the sponsors of the petition had somehow gotten them – in part, no doubt, because of popular impatience over the implementation of dividends. The government was able to show that some of the signatures were those of people who came into the constituency for the express intent of signing the petition; Aberhart called it a "low down trick", and the motion to repeal the act went through. Aberhart kept his seat but lost face.

On November 3 the session's contentious bills were referred to the Supreme Court of Canada for review and testing. While waiting for a decision in the new year the government occupied itself with other matters. One was a by-election in Lethbridge which quickly became a two-way race between J.A. Butnap, the Socred, and Dr. Peter Campbell, a "unity" candidate backed by the Peoples' League and the Liberals and Conservatives. On December 3 Campbell won handily. (Two years earlier the Socreds had taken the seat with a 2,000 vote majority).

A disturbing omen for the Socreds was the gradual, halting growth of a movement to unite the Liberals and Conservatives into a firm anti-Aberhart coalition. The negotiations several times ran aground on the Liberals' ambitions: they nourished a stubborn hope that they could beat the Socreds alone. The weak Conservatives had no false hopes, but they distrusted E.L. Gray, the Liberal leader. On more than one occasion, Gray had set back the alliance by his attacks on the Conservatives and their policies.

On December 10 Aberhart was disturbed to learn that the "fusionists", as they called themselves, had named a "Council of United Forces" and had appointed a Calgarian, John McFarland, as chairman. There continued to be petty feuding among the council, the Peoples' League and the two parties over who stood for what, but the trend toward an anti-Social Credit united front was clear.

The early opposition to Social Credit was opposition the average voters identified with unpopular vested interests. In this sense, "Bankers' Toadies" was a perceptive piece of political propaganda. Aberhart could still claim that only he represented the will of the common people. But now Social Credit had held power for twenty-seven months and much had changed. The voters had had an opportunity to witness Aberhart's indecisiveness. There had been an almost-successful revolt against him by his own backbenchers. It was easy to support Social Credit in the beginning; it had never been tried, and the Depression had served to detach scores of people from any affection for the status quo or the status quo parties. Their attitude was not unlike the slogan later used by Real Couette: "What have you got to lose?" But now the honeymoon was ending. Popular patience with the government was wearing thin. Aberhart's reasons for not delivering the goods were viewed more critically.

The new opposition coalition had a number of issues around which it could rally divergent people to the anti-Aberhart banner. Aberhart had catalyzed high hopes and ridden to power on great expectations; but he had not been able to fulfill those expectations and he had needlessly offended some sympathizers with rash acts like the Press Gag Bill. It was becoming evident that the skills Aberhart had in such abundance – magnificent oratory, a talent for organizing, a flair for the dramatic – were vital in the conquest of power, but not helpful in the formation of effective policy. An ineffective parliamentarian, Aberhart frequently yielded the floor direction of the government in the House to the younger, more tactful and restrained Manning.

When the 1938 session opened February 10, Aberhart turned to the second part of his mandate: new legislation on debt. (The first part, including the Press Gag Act, was being argued before the Supreme Court of Canada.) Aberhart brought in new bills to re-enact what the courts had undone in 1937: the bills prohibited foreclosures on farm homes mortgaged prior to March 1, 1938, and on urban homes unless the owner were paid an irrevocable deposit of $2,000 by the mortgage company.

The House was still debating these new bills when the news came in that the Supreme Court had disallowed all the major 1937 Social Credit statutes, including the Press Act, as *ultra vires* of a provincial government.

The ring of steel had held. Aberhart's beachhead was contained.

Three weeks later, government members took out some of their resentment and frustration on a newspaperman in the legislature press gallery.

On March 25, in a move headlined across the country, a House resolution ordered that Don Brown, legislative reporter for *The Edmonton Journal,* be detained in Lethbridge Jail "during the pleasure of the assembly".

Brown had stated in his column that Dr. J.L. Robinson, the Socred M.L.A. from Medicine Hat, and a chiropractor (the only one in the House) had opposed an effort to have chiropractors included in services provided under the Workman's Compensation Act. Brown's comment was partially true; Robinson did say he would support the finding of a committee that chiropractors not be included, but if the matter came to a vote and an amendment were offered to include chiropractors, he would support it. Robinson shouted that his rather woolly stand had been misrepresented and the House asked the Speaker to issue a warrant ordering the Sergeant-at-Arms to remove Brown for incarceration.

The whole picayune issue became comic opera. *Journal* officials were called to testify before the House and did so, gravely; extreme charges were flung about; the warrant was not even signed. Brown was never arrested (or even shadowed) and one day later, on a Liberal motion, the House solemnly resolved to "direct the release of Mr. Don C. Brown from custody".

The government was made to look less ominous than silly.

Stripped of his more sophisticated weapons by the courts and the federal government, Aberhart continued the debt fight with the only two weapons he had left: moratoria and default. By unilateral act, the government reduced the rate of interest it would pay on its debts; by August 1939, it was saving the people $3,400,000 a year in interest charges, and had defaulted on $12,000,000 worth of payments.

Nor was the 1938 debt legislation thrown out immediately by the federal government. Aberhart had made political mileage out of Mackenzie King's failure to abide by his promise to let the Socreds conduct their experiment without interference. In Saskatchewan, where the Liberals were still in power, the Socreds had launched a serious organizational drive for the June 9 provincial election; Mackenzie King and his colleagues bided their time and awaited the Saskatchewan results as a barometer of Social Credit's wider appeal and popularity.

When the results came in it was clear Social Credit had been swamped, electing only two M.L.A.s to the Liberals' thirty-six and the C.C.F.'s ten. Less than a week later Ernest Lapointe, the federal justice minister, announced that Aberhart's 1938 debt legislation was being disallowed. (Earlier, King had tried to pull some Social Credit teeth by passing an amendment to the Bank of Canada Act making all directors of the bank government nominees, thus ensuring at least nominal public control of this central monetary-policy institution.) The federal government had the secure backing of the financial establishment and its journalistic supporters. The Montreal *Gazette* huffed:

[The Aberhart government] has now run amok through a field of radical legislation that is without precedent in any country, civilized or savage. It has legalized theft. Having attempted to exploit the banks, to muzzle the press and to tie the hands of the courts

. . . it has proceeded to the enactment of laws which are equally if not more vicious.*

Aberhart's drive to implement Social Credit reforms at the provincial level had been finally and decisively beaten down. "No power known to man can force on seven hundred and fifty thousand people laws which they have made up their minds they will not endure," Aberhart wrote to King; but Aberhart knew that, short of insurrection or a nationwide Socred drive to take federal power, the battle was over.

And so, from mid-1938 on, the Aberhart government was left only one choice: to use such powers as a province has at its command to increase purchasing power and control debt, and to maintain a vigilant and unbending posture against the money power. As ritual gestures, the government refused to co-operate with the Rowell-Sirois Commission on Federal-Provincial Relations, and underwrote a generous publication program by the Social Credit Board, which propagandized across the land. And in the realm of provincial power, Aberhart sponsored what he called "the Interim Program".

The Interim Program had two objectives: to create a quasi-provincial bank, the Treasury Branches, to give Albertans a limited measure of control over the issuance of credit; and to encourage industrial growth and keep money in Alberta with a "buy Alberta" campaign.

On August 29, three years after the landslide 1935 mandate, cabinet authorized the creation of a widespread system of branches of the provincial Treasury "to receive deposits from the public and to enter into contracts with depositors governing the manner of repayment." For rural areas especially, the Treasury Branches were a quasi-bank (although the government was very careful never to call the system that) in which savings could be deposited and from which loans could be secured. The Treasury Branches were in competition with the banks, and provided a service in many small centres where the banks would not locate. By the end of 1939, there were 315 branches, sub-branches and rural agencies of the Treasury Branches.

The effect of the branches was not to cut deeply into the Alberta operations of the chartered banks – the branches were too conservatively administered, and had too few reserves, for that – but to provide a standard against which the chartered banks' performance could be measured; and in that sense, the branches were an effective prod to better banking practices in Alberta.

The "buy Alberta" campaign was conventional mercantilist eco-

* May 12, 1938.

114

nomics and had nothing to do with Social Credit theory. The last gasp of real Social Credit practice was the issuance by the Treasury Branches of what were called "non-negotiable transfer vouchers". The government was very careful not to call these "money", "credit" or even "social credit". They were called "instruments" – but they were really a form of Social Credit dividend on a very small scale. Anyone doing business with the Treasury Branch received a three per cent bonus if they purchased at least one-third of their goods from "buy Alberta" firms. The three per cent bonus came in the form of transfer vouchers, which could be used as cash with other merchants prepared to accept them (prepared, in other words, to do business at the Treasury Branches and deposit the vouchers in *their* account, thence to be paid to *other* merchants who would do business at the Treasury Branch . . . etc.). It was possible to have the Vouchers redeemed in legal tender, with special permission – but obviously the government hoped that enough people would have enough faith in the system not to do this, or its benefits disappeared. It was only a form of extra credit and purchasing power if the people *believed* it was.

The system of vouchers did not work well. Wholesalers boycotted it (as they had earlier boycotted scrip), the vouchers were useless for doing business outside the province and once the war was on, the system collided with federal rationing policy, which was aimed at reducing consumption, not stimulating it. The system was finally abandoned in April 1945.

By late 1939 it was clear an election could not be far off. Aberhart's term of office had nearly run out, and predictions of the election date were being made daily. The Independents were now organized as a relatively united group and were nominating candidates in various ridings.

In the two years since their by-election victory in Lethbridge, the Independent Party* had made political strides. With the considerable financial and organizational backing of the provincial Liberals, they managed to field a strong slate of candidates including James Walker, a redoubtable U.F.A. Farmer from the south and Andy Davison, the mayor of Calgary and an old Aberhart critic. Their appeal to the people was an anti-Aberhart one, pure and simple. They recalled Aberhart's slips and delays of the past five years, dug up all the painful remainders of the government's embarrassments, and coined a slogan: "Never mind the Buggy – Save the Horse."

Aberhart fought back hard. In one radio speech he rumbled:

* The party had various titles – Independent Party, Independent Citizens Association of Alberta, Unity Party.

The Independents, or whatever they now call themselves, are simply a union of the old line parties. Those running as 'independents' are not honest independents at all, but simply representatives of the Liberals and Conservatives with no constructive proposals to put forward . . . their favorite political trick is to promise to restore the credit of the Province. What credit? The credit of Alberta was ruined long before Social Credit came into office. Farm credit was nonexistent before 1935 . . . you farmers, you men and women engaged in private enterprise, you know that you now enjoy more credit than ever before because since 1935 the banks have had to loosen up and provide a little cash!

And in one of his most famous speeches, Aberhart struck the old chord:

The voters know who it is who has been fighting for their God-given rights during the past five years. So let them roll out their barrels of money, these big shots and their deluded henchmen. I say let them begin at once their double-dealing, gossip-mongering whispering campaigns . . . the mothers know who has brought comfort to saddened hearts!

But Social Credit was in serious difficulty. The government's 1935 House strength had been badly whittled down by defections and floor-crossings. Its 1940 House representation had dwindled to forty-seven from fifty-six in 1935. Economic recovery had been tortuous: tax collections and spending were up, unemployment had dropped one-third from 1935 levels. On the other hand, 1938 was a bad crop year and world grain prices were poor; farm income in 1939 had fallen to 1935 levels. And the best Social Credit had been able to do had been to prevent large-scale foreclosures and beat back the financiers for awhile; that, and provide people with their most desperately desired commodity – hope.

The election results were a major setback for the Socreds. A larger turnout of voters than 1935 returned the government with only a plurality – the Socred popular vote dropped from fifty-four per cent to forty-three per cent. Here were the returns:

1935						1940*					
S.C.	LIB.	CONS.	U.F.A.	IND.	LAB.	S.C.	LIB.	CONS.	U.F.A.	IND.	LAB.
56	5	2	—	—	—	36	1	—	—	19	1

* The reduction in the total number of seats from sixty-three in 1935 to fifty-seven in 1940 was because of a general redistribution in 1939.

In ten seats, Social Credit won with majorities of less than 200 votes. The government lost Mrs. Edith Gostick, Mrs. Edith Rogers and Solon Low – two party luminaries and a cabinet minister. And while Aberhart easily won a Calgary seat, he ran a narrow second to an independent in the city-wide standings – his old critic, Mayor Davison.

There was one bright light: Manning, the youngest cabinet minister, somehow managed to hold himself clear of the backlash. He ran in Edmonton (like Calgary, a multi-member constituency) and topped the polls easily, winning over his nearest competitor, Independent J. Percy Page, by more than 4,000 votes.

With the war, Social Credit entered an interregnum. Like all parties and provincial governments, Social Credit spent the early 1940s in the economic buoyancy and political hiatus of the war effort. While continuing to snipe at Ottawa's submission to the financial interests, Aberhart willingly agreed to suspend any attempt to implement Social Credit doctrines; indeed, the need for added purchasing power had diminished considerably in Alberta. The provincial economy entered an upswing; unemployment dropped dramatically, thousands of farm people came to the cities to seek work and a better life. There were good crops and grain prices more than doubled between 1940 and 1945. After 1941 farm income began to once again attain the exhilarating levels of the late 1920s and personal income doubled between 1940 and 1945.

The gloom of the Depression began to lift.

Aberhart pledged Alberta to a full defence of the war effort, urging only that money be conscripted as well as manpower. He spoke out against war bonds because he felt they unnecessarily put the country further into the debt of the banks. He was harshly criticized for this by the Eastern press; some journalists, carried away by the same hysterical super-patriotism that produced the campaign to intern Japanese-Canadians and confiscate their property, hinted that Aberhart was a secret Nazi sympathizer.*

It was a dispiriting time for Aberhart. Government had lost much of its relish for him and the never-ending barrage of press criticism had taken its toll. But the greatest blow to his pride was yet to come.

In 1941 leading officials of the University of Alberta announced that in recognition of Aberhart's services to education in Alberta – and they had been many – the institution was going to confer upon

---

* C.S. Burchill, "Taming the Trojan Horse", *National Home Monthly,* May 17, 1941.

him an honorary doctorate of laws and invite him to address convocation.

For the record, Aberhart had been an old friend of education, whatever his run-ins may have been with some schools of educational philosophy. He had fought to retain educational spending even at the peak of Depression retrenchment pressures. As Minister of Education he had launched a streamlining plan for rural school districts. And he had given years of his life to helping thousands of students across southern Alberta. The University's award was clearly merited. Aberhart began to feel younger than his sixty-two years.

But when the recommendation went before a committee of the University's Board of Governors for formal approval, it was rejected without warning. An unofficial statement from Aberhart's university critics said, "Premier Aberhart's record was not one that could be approved by an institute of learning." It was a petty, vindictive act, and Aberhart was thunderstruck.

The president of the University, W.A.R. Kerr, resigned in protest. Aberhart, summoning up great poise, simply declined an invitation to address the convocation. He had been at work on his convocation speech when the word came through.

In the 1943 session Aberhart's health began to deteriorate. His strength ebbed away, and he remarked to Alf Hooke in the corridor one day that he couldn't understand how a man could feel so weak and still remain alive. When the session ended he went to the coast with his wife for his customary holiday, uncommunicative as ever. When he arrived at Vancouver, he needed assistance to walk down the train platform. He went for an immediate examination and tests, and was told he had serious cirrhosis of the liver. He tried to pass it off to his family as a minor thing but was soon back in hospital, where he stayed.

Optimistic doctors' notices were issued, but he began to fail. On June 23, without any dramatic last words, he died. He was buried in Vancouver after his wife told the press she wanted it that way. "We were too unhappy in Alberta," she said.

With him, they buried an era. Aberhart did not conceive the idea of Social Credit but he transformed it from a concept into a fighting movement. For the best part of a decade he dominated Alberta politics. He had no significant rivals. A man with great talents and weaknesses, he fairly crackled with personal magnetism. His leaving took something vital out of Canada's public life.

The cabinet went to Vancouver for the funeral and then returned to Edmonton to convene a special caucus to choose an heir. There

118

could be little doubt as to his identity. There was only one man who had had Aberhart's absolute confidence and always stood at his side: Manning. The only other contender, Solon Low, was a man of considerable ability but lacked Manning's obvious pedigree. On June 3 a short meeting was held behind closed doors and in less than an hour an unrecorded vote elected Ernest Manning the new premier of Alberta. He was thirty-four years of age.

CHAPTER SEVEN

The New Leader

To the extent that 'Social Credit has failed in Alberta', i.e., has not been tried, the root cause has always been evident – a persistent determination not to recognize that when Mr. Aberhart won his first electoral victory, all he did was to recruit an army for a war. That war has not been fought; and Mr. Manning declares in the plainest terms that he will not lead that army into a fight. Perhaps reasonably, he prefers to ride at its head in ceremonial parades.

– Major C.H. Douglas, 1948

Ernest Manning had inherited a government, but it was a government that had been badly rocked at the polls by a dissatisfied electorate, a government that had lost some of its sense of direction and purpose.

In his first four years of office the thin, quiet young premier was able to restore the government's standing, purge the party's internal dissenters, silence the party's internal ideological clangour* and decimate the opposition in a fateful election.

In all of this he was to prepare the way – perhaps unwittingly – for the major turning point in Alberta's social and economic history: the discovery of oil at Leduc in 1947. Between 1943 and 1947, he built the foundation of what was to become the Manning Era.

Manning took office quietly; there were no obvious or immediate important changes in policy or personnel. The government's continued loyalty to its traditional objectives was quickly affirmed and any doubts that Aberhart's passing may have occasioned among the party faithful were put to rest.

Change was not dramatic, but it soon became obvious in small ways that change was taking place, that Manning was very clearly his own man, and a quite different sort of leader from Aberhart – less flamboyant, less emotional, less charismatic; more cautious, more rational, more calculating; cooler.

---

* In the late 1960s Manning and Harry Strom were to discover that the clangour had only been temporarily suppressed and driven underground. The whole debate was to erupt again in 1969, with embarrassing results for the leadership.

From the beginning of the war on, Social Credit's stance had become more pragmatic; how much of this owed itself to force of circumstances and how much to the inevitable cooling of ideological fires, no one can say. Whatever, in 1942 the government had expanded its system of free cancer clinics and provincial health units and Manning, as Minister of Trade and Industry, had defended the government's Insurance Branch (which provided both fire and life insurance) on the ground that "we can save the people of the province money by providing protection at cost and at the same time keep the money at home." At the 1943 session the Minister of Health, Dr. Cross, endorsed the principle of national health insurance (even though Aberhart was known to be vehemently opposed to the Beveridge Plan). Said Cross: "Approximately 50 per cent of our people cannot afford to pay for necessary hospitalization and medical attention and we don't want them, in the new order [after the war] to suffer unnecessary pain or be filling premature graves because of their inability to pay."

On February 1, 1943, the Judicial Committee of the Privy Council in London – Alberta's court of last resort on constitutional disputes – laid to rest the last major offensive of Social Credit, the Debt Adjustment Act. The act grew out of the Western agrarian radical tradition; Alberta's appeal was supported by the governments of Saskatchewan, Manitoba and New Brunswick. The death notice of the Debt Adjustment Act came at a time when it was becoming increasingly clear that Social Credit was becoming a pragmatic government. And on becoming premier, Manning did nothing to change this trend.

When the 1944 session opened under his premiership, he showed this clearly, introducing free maternity hospitalization, increased school support grants, a Power Commission to oversee faster rural electrification and stricter regulation of natural gas producers at Turner Valley.

One year after becoming premier Manning called an election without warning (the government's term still had a year to run). That election, on August 8, 1944, was to mark the great watershed of the Social Credit movement.

Manning's strategy was to knock out the opposition by exploiting the growing strength of the C.C.F. At the time the socialists were riding very high; in 1943 the Gallup Poll had shocked many Canadians by disclosing that the C.C.F. was the most popular party in the country with twenty-nine per cent of popular support, versus twenty-eight per cent each for the Liberals and Tories. In 1943 the C.C.F. won power next door in Saskatchewan, and came out of nowhere to win thirty-four seats and become the official opposition in Ontario.

Although the C.C.F. was undoubtedly riding a crest of wartime popularity, it probably was not yet a major factor in Alberta; but Manning was able to shrewdly exploit popular *consciousness* of the C.C.F's growing power and turn it into a weapon against the Independents. The Independents were beginning to falter, and Manning sensed this.

The party "with no pride of ancestry and no hope of posterity", as the Liberal *Edmonton Bulletin* once called them, was increasingly divided. The coalition had been an uneasy one from the beginning because neither the Liberals nor the Tories really trusted each other in it, and a truly "independent" consciousness had failed to develop. Moreover, the Independents had only the vaguest of positive ideals; the only major thing on which the two constituent parties agreed was that Aberhart had to go. Unfortunately for them, he was now gone.

In another sense, the very success of the Independents in the 1940 election also contributed to their undoing. In the darkest days of the 1930s, when Social Credit seemed so invincible, a united front of the "outs" made good sense. But the Independants had won nineteen seats and a large chunk of the popular vote in 1940, almost beating the Socreds. The closer the Liberals got to power, the less inclined they were to carry the impotent Conservatives with them. In 1942 two Liberals who had been elected as Independents bolted the coalition and announced that they would sit as just plain Liberals. Manning decided to strike.

In 1940 the Socreds had fought the campaign on essentially unreconstructed lines. Social Credit presented itself as a party of radical monetary and debt reform, and the opposition focussed on Social Credit's radical aspirations and practical failures. The opposition charged Aberhart with leading the province down a path of political frustration and economic paralysis. The result was the near-collapse of Social Credit power.

In 1944 it was quite different. For the first time, Manning presented Social Credit as a solid, sensible free enterprise party threatened from the left by the C.C.F.

A defence of the party's positive and progressive accomplishment and reminders about the threat posed to freedom and free enterprise by the C.C.F., were made the two central issues of the campaign. The C.C.F. stood for "bureaucracy and regimentation", Manning said, at the same time as he defended the government's social and economic achievements – highways, land for returning veterans, free T.B., cancer, and polio care, increased pensions, maternity hospitalization, tax cancellations and "more than 2 million dollars in reduced insurance premiums."

Led by an Edmonton printer, Elmer Roper, the C.C.F. promised a "co-operative" system that would build housing with provincial loans "at cost", provide rural electrification, increase pensions and provide rural nursing services and free medical services and hospitalization. C.C.F. attacks blasted Social Credit for "going conservative" and charged that Social Credit had forgotten the little man and was too concerned about maintaining the goodwill of the power and oil companies. "These are the big shots", said Roper.

Manning's deliberate polarization of the campaign worked, drawing many businessmen to Social Credit support for the first time. Even many Independents deserted their sinking coalition and climbed aboard Social Credit. Most of the daily newspapers, which in 1940 had supported the Independents, swung their fire to the C.C.F. Some even supported the government. Said *The Edmonton Journal,* on July 8th, 1944:

> Readers of the Journal do not need to be reminded of all the criticism it has had to offer of the present Alberta administration. It still stands by this. But ordinary fairness demands recognition that under Premier Manning, the government's record has been such as to warrant much greater confidence in it than during the early stages of its career.

Manning's strategy worked. The Independents were ruined as a viable force, and the C.C.F. was beaten back. Popular confidence surged back into Social Credit and the "Manning Era" began. Social Credit's popular vote jumped from forty-three per cent in 1940 to fifty-two per cent and the party took fifty-one of the fifty-seven seats in the House, leaving the C.C.F. two, the Independents three, and the Armed Forces representative one.

The results showed that the C.C.F's growing strength – around which Manning built his campaign – was no chimera: the C.C.F. boosted its popular vote from 34,316 in 1940 to 70,307, and ran second in thirty-one ridings (although a close second in only four).

To mark their death as a viable force, the Independents dropped to second-last place in the popular vote (ahead of the Communists, with 12,000) to win 47,239 votes – as against 130,603 four years earlier. The Independent coalition fell apart in all but name* and the Liberals hoisted their old banner again. They were to find it tough

* It was formally dissolved in 1948.

sledding, though: when J. Harper Prowse became Liberal leader in 1947 he found many traditionally Liberal fund sources had dried up. "We've got a business oriented government now," they told him. "Why rock the boat and let in the C.C.F?"

Manning's debut as Socred leader had been, to put it mildly, impressive. It caused many raised eyebrows in the province, even within the Social Credit ranks. The young premier was only thirty-six, and quite untested. When he had embarked on his first campaign tour, up through northern Alberta, nervous party officials tried to persuade him to take some grizzled veterans with him. But Manning had kept calm, as always, and cool; and again, as in 1940, he led the polls in the multi-member Edmonton riding, beating Elmer Roper 14,271 to 5,253.

A few days after the election, League secretary Orvis Kennedy joined Manning at Manning's farm north of the city; they worked together on the barn awhile, then ate their lunches on the roof and went over the composition of the new cabinet. Kennedy favoured Solon Low for Minister of Education, to fill Aberhart's spot, but Manning instead picked Earl Ansley, the teacher and veteran Socred from Leduc. Manning had first met Ansley at a Socred meeting in Red Deer in 1933; Ansley was a stubborn believer in Douglas's theories, a fact that was to cause Manning trouble soon. He had also played a role in the insurgency. But he was a hard worker and Manning hoped he would outgrow his past. Manning felt the same about Alf Hooke, whom he appointed as Provincial Secretary. Hooke, as an insurgent, had damned Aberhart's "Hitler" tactics; Manning told Kennedy he was willing to give him a chance because "he was the only man who came back to Aberhart after the insurgency was over and apologized, and said he didn't mean any personal harm."

Gradually, Manning began to impose his personal stamp on the government.

In 1940 the province had applied to Ottawa for a charter to operate a provincial bank, and had been turned down. On becoming premier, Manning tried once more in 1944 and Alberta was again rebuffed. All that was left in the field of credit-formation was the so-called "interim program" of measures through the Treasury Branches and the Marketing Board, the system created in 1938 to try to generate new purchasing power by constitutional means.

Manning continued support for the ordinary loaning program of the Treasury Branches and the aid-to-industry program of the Marketing Board (set up to enable small manufacturers to benefit from the board's ability to get cheap bulk prices for large stocks of raw materials, and to finance inventory). But in 1945 the government discontinued the "consumers bonus'" offered through the Treasury Branches as a form of constitutionally acceptable debt-free consumer credit. Under Manning the loaning program of the Treasury Branches was very cautiously expanded; there was a great fear that a test case in the courts might show the branches to be a *de facto* bank, hence unconstitutional. Elaborate procedural and terminological safeguards were created to avoid this possibility, as well as the always-feared possibility that a depositors' panic might weaken the Treasury itself (for all deposits were government-guaranteed). The deposit-to-loans ratio of the branches was kept very high, much higher than the chartered banks.

The Treasury Branches provided a useful service, to outlying and rural points especially, and were a beneficial prod to the chartered banks in many locales; but they never threatened to become a replacement for the chartered banking system.

The last remaining item of "old business" on Manning's agenda as premier was a settlement with the bondholders.

As the war's end drew near Manning realized that continued postponement of this unpleasant negotiation was no longer possible or even desirable. The provincial government's refusal to play the debt game by the bondholders' rules in the 1930s was needed in its time, but times had changed. As long as it continued, Alberta would be regarded as a poor place to invest money; the development of the whole province would suffer. Until 1945 there was an Ottawa-imposed freeze on credit that made it possible to avoid facing this. Now the freeze was coming to an end.

By 1945 Alberta owed $34,000,000 in defaulted principal and about $25,000,000 in unpaid interest. Ottawa began putting on pressure to reach a settlement based on the province's recognition of responsibility for the whole amount; in return for this, Ottawa promised financial aid to help meet the bills.

The young premier refused to recognize the full debt and said Alberta would advance her own, final, counter-proposal instead.

Manning had never liked the idea of defaulting on the debt but the desperate condition of the people and the bullheaded intransigence of the bondholders had driven the government to desperate measures. All through the late 1930s and early 1940s committees of bondholders had made refunding proposals to the government, and the government had made counter-proposals; it had come to nothing. And so, in 1945, Manning announced his government's final offer, which he threatened to put into legislation and end the matter once and for all. The proposal offered holders of old securities a new thirty-year bond at 3½ per cent interest plus a cash bonus for co-operating. Ottawa intervened, declaring this proposal too miserly, but Manning's ultimatum brought the bondholders to the conference table and a final settlement was worked out. The settlement was more generous to the bondholders than Alberta's proposal and Manning refused to agree to it until Ottawa agreed to compensate the provincial government for the difference. The final solution was a complete refunding of the old debt at an average coupon rate of 3.4 per cent interest (the lowest of any Canadian province), with the whole thing to be paid out by 1980. And so Alberta re-entered the North American investment community. Determined never again to let Alberta be caught in a morass of unpayable debts, Manning settled on a pay-as-you-go financial policy for the government, and stuck to it.

In 1946 Manning launched what was to be the government's last attempt to implement Social Credit; and the way he went about it showed how much his new spirit of pragmatism had come to dominate the government.

The occasion was the passage of the Alberta Bill of Rights Act, which once again attempted to implement Social Credit, only this time by constitutional means. The act argued that inasmuch as the B.N.A. Act gave the provinces' control over "property and civil rights" it must also have given the provinces the necessary authority to do what was necessary in order to enable every citizen to *enjoy* his property and civil rights.

Created partly in response to resolutions passed by the Social Credit League convention that year, the act was divided into two parts – the first guaranteed certain rights to every Albertan (free education, medical benefits and a guaranteed income of $600 per year for those over nineteen, plus the traditional "rights" guaranteed in constitutions), and a second part which created a Board of Credit Commissioners to license the chartered banks and set up a "consolidated credit adjustment fund" for the issuance to citizens of "credit deposits" (the Social Credit dividend) through the banks.

Clause 28 of the act specified that it would not be proclaimed until "after the question of the validity . . . has been referred to the Supreme Court of Alberta . . . and it is certified upon any such reference that this Act is valid." In 1946 the Alberta Supreme Court duly ruled that the first part of the act was constitutional but the second was not.

The death of the Alberta Bill of Rights brought to a head a simmering dispute between the "pragmatists" and "militants" of the party and ultimately led to the last chapter in the de-radicalization of Social Credit.

When the Bill of Rights was introduced in the House, the militants said that Clause 28 was an act of defeatism, not a piece of tactical realism. The militants began to voice their criticisms of Manning and his leadership more and more openly. And before long the last remnant of Social Credit in its more radical days, the Social Credit Board, came charging into the picture.

The board, we will recall, was created in the early years of the administration to work out a plan for implementing dividends and the Just Price.

In its early months it did a good deal of work in this area, but with the bludgeoning of the Social Credit legislation by the courts and the federal government in 1938 and 1939, the Social Credit Board was left with less and less to do. The outbreak of the war put the movement into a patriotically self-imposed suspended animation and the Social Credit Board turned away from policy-design (there was no policy to design) and became a government-financed propaganda agency. Its members travelled around the province giving lectures on Social Credit theory and the board became a clearing-house for official doctrinal literature. In 1939 alone it sent 272,900 pieces of literature around the country.

As the war wore on, the board became more and more isolated from the vital centre of power. The members of the board had developed a reasonably friendly relationship with Aberhart (when he could see them); when Aberhart left the scene, the members of the board (by their own testimony) found Manning much cooler. They continued to be cut off from the important decision-making in the government.

And so the board turned to the cultivation of greener ideological pastures. Partly in an attempt to explain why it had failed to produce a workable plan for reform, partly because it had too much time on its hands, the board began to delve into some of the more bizarre world-plot theories Major Douglas had hatched in the old country.

Like the board itself, Douglas had been forgotten. The English Social Crediters had gone through a series of amoeba-like splits and had turned into a narrowing circle of embittered little cliques. As Douglas began to rationalize why this had taken place he came to believe there was a malignant world conspiracy against his theories. This "conspiracy" came to embrace more and more participants until finally it included international banking interests, communists, socialists, freemasons, Pan-Germans, Pan-Americans . . . and the Jews. The more Douglas thought about it the more he came to see behind his troubles the hand of Jewish bankers and Zionist politicians. In 1939, just before the opening of the war, Douglas wrote a letter to Adolf Hitler in which he accused the "Jewish financial system" of causing misunderstanding between the democratic powers and the totalitarian group. He said:

> . . . The Jew is a menace to be dealt with as firmly or even as harshly, if necessary, as we deal with would-be immigrants with a well established record of terrorism and arson. . . . Jewry as a whole has become a permanent 'chosen' superior, dominant and ruling class . . . over the whole world . . . the Jew . . . is the parasite upon, and the corruption of every civilization in which he has obtained power.*

As the years went on, Douglas's anti-Semitism became even more open and pronounced. In 1942 he wrote:

> I believe that I am stating an ascertained and incontestable fact when I say that Germany, Great Britain and the United States, beyond any other great powers, have been at all significant times dictated to in matters of policy by Jews, and predominately by German Jews.**

In 1943 the Social Credit Board began to pick up the thread of Douglas's world-plot theories and weave them into its annual reports. In association with board adviser and former Douglas confidante L. Denis Byrne, the board reached these conclusions in its 1943 report which made reference to a "fund of evidence" pointing to "a plot, world-wide in scope, deliberately engineered by a small number of ruthless international financiers to accomplish their objectives." A listing of such financiers showed that many had Jewish names.

By 1945 the stance of the board was a subject of growing discussion in the province, particularly in Jewish and liberal circles who were understandably alarmed by it.

Manning's introduction of the Bill of Rights brought internal criticism from Denis Byrne, who by this time had been appointed Deputy Minister of the new Department of Economic Affairs. Byrne submitted several confidential reports to his superiors in which he strongly criticized the new direction of the government, and the Bill of Rights in particular. Byrne's reports hardly made him any friends in cabinet, although internal advice of this kind was one of the things he had been hired to give. An article Byrne wrote and published, attacking Zionism as a political movement, drew the criticism of the

* *The New Zealand standard*, November, 1941; reprinted in *The Peoples' Weekly* (Edmonton), February 10, 1945.

** *The Peoples' Weekly*, January 12, 1946.

Jewish community, which protested to Manning through Solon Low.

By 1947 it was obvious that the Douglasite militants in the cabinet and the Social Credit Board were becoming a political liability to Social Credit, as well as a challenge to Manning's new direction in leadership. It was clear the militants would have to be removed. When the time came, Manning went about the job with surgical skill.

The occasion was the publication of the board's 1947 Report. The report began with a repetition of the world-plot thesis and then went on to question the validity of the secret ballot. It proposed a signed, open ballot in which the individual voter would be liable to taxation only for those government programs he specifically endorsed on election day. It also called into question the desirability of political parties, arguing instead for non-partisan "leagues of electors" or voters' unions, carefully controlled from the bottom up and oriented to pressuring government for specific results.

The custom of the day was that the board chairman, A.V. Bourcier, M.L.A., always submitted a preliminary draft of the board's report to Manning for comments and suggestions. One night in March 1947, Manning rose in caucus to say that the board report had been tabled without his perusal or approval, and that its contents were unacceptable.

Manning then introduced a resolution reaffirming the party's loyalty to essential Social Credit doctrines but repudiating

> any statements or publications which are incompatible with the established British ideals of democratic freedom or which endorse, excuse or incite anti-Semitism or racial or religious intolerance in any form.

The resolution was passed. In November Manning announced that at the end of that fiscal year the board was to be dissolved. He had already cut the ground from underneath the board by his resolutions and by transferring its economic promotion of Alberta functions to the Department of Economic Affairs. Its educational and publishing functions were to be transferred to the Social Credit League, he said, denouncing the "little faction of Douglasites who think they have some special monopoly on the principles of Social Credit."

By the end of the year Manning asked for and received the resignation of John Patrick Gillese, the idealistic young editor of *The Canadian Social Crediter*, who had made the mistake of following his own ideological beliefs a little too avidly and giving full space to the Douglasites to state their case.

Bourcier, one of the original M.L.A.s from 1935, was deprived of his membership in the Social Credit League. And then, in January, L. Denis Byrne was asked for his resignation. Byrne's Minister, Alf

Hooke, was out of the country at the time and the request for Byrne's resignation was communicated to Byrne by Nathan Tanner, one of Manning's trusted lieutenants. Byrne quietly complied. That left the one militant in cabinet, the quiet, brooding Earl Ansley.

When the matter of Byrne came before cabinet, Ansley supported Byrne. Later, Manning called Ansley into his office and suggested that in light of the need for cabinet unanimity, perhaps Ansley should resign. Ansley stolidly replied that he couldn't see why this disagreement should be reason for his resignation. "All right," said Manning dryly, "I'm asking you for your resignation. Now you've *got* a reason."

For a time the Douglasites fought back with the few weapons they had left. They organized the Douglas Social Credit Council and printed documents accusing Manning of selling out the true faith. Their campaign came to nothing; the government was now firmly in the hands of Manning and men loyal to him, and the Douglasites never had been any good at power-politics. The time for them to have made their stand and gathered allies around them was when they were still in the government, with all the resources of government. Out of government they were helpless. One by one they drifted away to their old jobs as teachers, civil servants, insurance agents.

Manning had dispelled any possible doubt over who was in control of Social Credit. The last of the theorists were gone from the seats of power. The new tone of the government was centrist, pragmatic, careful – a reconciliation of traditional Socred theory with political and economic reality. The basic tone of the Manning Era had been set: balanced budgets, cautious reforms (in 1947 medical and hospital care was made free for recipients of old age, mothers' and blind pensions), and opposition to socialism.

What the Douglasites had underlined was a basic sociological fact which could only be ignored for a time, but which would have to be some day faced: namely, that the unique thing that gave Social Credit its basic *raison d'etre*, its ideology, was withering away and no new ideology or explicit set of purposes had been defined to replace it.

The onset of widespread prosperity provided an opportunity to forget this and to forge a new objective for the party: the re-election of Ernest Manning. After 1948 that became the real function of the party in the minds of most Albertans and, indeed, of many party members.

Only one thing was now needed to signal the death of the old order in Alberta and usher in the Manning Era, and it happened just before 4:00 p.m. on a cold February 13, 1947, near a small town called Leduc: a solid stream of thick black crude oil shot to the surface of an oil well named Imperial Leduc No. 1 and was ignited with a roar.

A small crowd of roughnecks, officials and newsman looked on while a huge black ring of smoke slowly rose into the sky. More than 5,000 feet below the ground, in a rock formation that had once been a coral reef in a shallow inland sea, a huge pool of oil had been discovered.

CHAPTER EIGHT

How Manning Used Power

Nothing in Social Credit's past equipped it for the onslaught of prosperity brought on by oil. The movement had been created to fight the economic stagnation and mass poverty of the Depression; after 1948 the province entered a sustained boom unlike any it had ever experienced. Defeating generalized poverty and managing prosperity are two quite different modes of politics and few Socreds were prepared for the dizzying spin of events that accompanied Alberta's entry into the glossy world of fast-talking industrial promoters and smoothly manicured corporation presidents.

Manning's great accomplishment between 1948 and 1968 was to manage the government efficiently, honestly, and even with vision, as it was swept forward on the crest of this huge economic wave. Manning was a builder, and he built well: the tremendous income the government received from oil exploration and production was plowed back into first-rate schools, universities, hospitals, roads and social services. Yet in the process of managing these resources and winning seven straight elections, Manning unwittingly laid the basis for a fast-paced secular society increasingly foreign to his own values – a society that changed much faster than his own political party's ability to respond to change. In short, the very social changes that Manning helped to bring about eventually produced the kind of restless and rootless urban society to which Social Credit could not appeal.

Manning always believed that among Canadian political parties and governments, his was unique in one important respect.

The old-line parties, in Manning's view, were corrupt me-too groups interested only in getting power and keeping it; they lacked long-range objectives and a social conscience, both of which he liked to describe as Principle. The N.D.P. stood for Principle, but in Social Credit eyes it was Bad Principle, or Unsound Principle. Only Social Credit stood for Sound Principle, which was taken to mean an unshakeable opposition to high spending, bureaucracy and the Welfare State.

The rhetoric and the reality, of course, were two different things, just as they are in all political systems. His rhetoric notwithstanding, Manning went along with the general trend to big government; in fact, he owed an important part of his success as a politician to the fact that he knew when to yield to it, when to resist it, and when to seem to resist it. The electorate came to realize in time that with Manning they could have the best of both Principle *and* compromise. There was an almost delicious enjoyment about having a premier who could communicate the message that the government rested on certain basic, unchangeable policies – and who could then go on to give the people what they wanted.

1. *Spending and Big Government.*

"I hope you have not been leading a double life, pretending to be wicked and really being good all the time. That would be hypocrisy."

Oscar Wilde, *The Importance of Being Earnest*

A study of the Manning record – the budgets, the legislation, the government's priorities – shows that on many important issues, contrary to its usual rhetoric, the Social Credit government was a middle-of-the-road regime with a slight reformist tinge.

Between 1946, the last year before oil, and 1967, a generation later, Social Credit's spending increased three and a half times as fast as the population. During the 1950s, Alberta was the highest per capita spender of all the provincial governments.

According to Dr. Eric Hanson, a leading authority on government finance, by 1964 Alberta led the nation in per capita spending for education, was second only to Ontario in per capita spending for government generally, and was well above the national average for per capita spending on welfare, health, sanitation, agriculture, forestry, recreation and culture.

This was one reason a long succession of C.C.F. and N.D.P. politicians grew grey waiting for the fall of Social Credit: the bulk of Social Credit's high spending went into an elaborate structure of "people programs" in education, health, welfare. An example in the 1950s was the government's construction of a chain of superb "Senior Citizens' Lodges" in towns and cities across the province. More than fifty were built in small towns alone. At a time when Michael Harrington's best-seller, *The Other America*, was angrily condemning widespread neglect of the aged, Social Credit was providing pleasant, clean, attractive accommodation for more than 5,000 pensioners – a system of care for the elderly second to none in the continent.

The vast windfall of oil revenue was put into a superb network of paved highways, an Education Foundations Program that reduced inequality of educational opportunity across the province between rich areas and poor, hospital and medical insurance, the country's most generous students' financial assistance program, two superb cultural centres. The Opposition, the N.D.P. in particular, would have loved to have been able to portray Manning as a second Cal Coolidge; but the evidence just wasn't there. In 1966 Alberta not only outspent British Columbia, an equally prosperous province, it spent far more money on social programs than its "sister" Socred government.

Unfortunately, as Jefferson once noted, a government can do nothing for the people without doing something to the people. One price of Manning's programs was the development of Big Government.

In 1960 the Alberta section of the Canadian Bar Association conducted a study of the plethora of regulatory boards and tribunals in the Alberta government. It first went to an official to obtain a list; the official blushed and admitted he didn't even know how many boards and tribunals there were altogether. The Bar Association then compiled their own list and found 123, versus eighty-six for the much larger and more industrialized province of Ontario. They discovered that boards and regulatory agencies presided over the censorship of films, the production and distribution of oil and gas, the certification of labour unions and arbitration of industrial disputes, the right of entry onto private land for oil exploration, the rights of Hutterite colonies, the sale of securities, the zoning, redevelopment and tax assessment of land, the pricing of milk and food, the awarding of assistance to the blind, disabled, elderly, widows and mothers, the pricing of natural gas and electricity, the provision of farm relief, the fixing of working conditions and terms of apprenticeship, the sale of liquor, the compensation of injured workmen and the sterilization of mental defectives – among other things.*

* Of course many of these boards and agencies had nothing to do with the Welfare State; many of them were historical relics from pre-Social Credit days and several were a manifestation of the puritan tradition of regulating "immoral" conduct. The Liquor Control Board owed little to the Fabian Society and a good deal to Aimee Semple McPherson.

The Bar Association found that, like all governments, Social Credit had turned to the administrative agency or tribunal as a handy way out of the problem of day-to-day regulation of an increasingly complex society; boards and tribunals were basically an American innovation aimed at more rapid, expert and flexible regulation than could be provided by the courts or the civil service. Boards had become a fourth arm of government, distinct from the legislature, the executive and the courts; unfortunately, in some cases, they had become almost a law unto themselves. The result was that by 1966 Alberta was one of the most-regulated provinces in Canada; and the boards that provided the regulation had broad powers to define their jurisdiction, set up their own procedures, and remain immune to review or appeal in the courts.

In April 1966, a Special Committee made up of three private citizens and three M.L.A.s (two of them Socred backbenchers) was set up to study the powers and abuses of administrative boards and tribunals and recommend necessary reforms. Under the direction of Carlton Clement, Q.C., later appointed to the Alberta Supreme Court, the committee conducted its study and tabled its report. It recommended three reforms: broader rights of appeal from the boards to the courts, universal administrative guidelines for the boards (to assure basic standards of fair play, evidence, written decisions, etc.) and an ombudsman or Commissioner of the Legislature.

For a man of his libertarian principles, Manning was surprisingly slow to react to the problem the administrative tribunals presented. On a number of occasions he had down played the idea of an ombudsman as an unnecessary and incompatible graft of a Swedish institution onto the British parliamentary tradition; but at the 1967 session he announced that a search for an ombudsman was underway, and Alberta was eventually the first province to appoint one – George McClellan, former Commissioner of the R.C.M.P. Manning did nothing on the other recommendations of the Clement Committee, unfortunately.

2. "Free Enterprise."

Manning's relationship with business was always thought to be a close one, and often it was. Manning met the issue of nationalization of private power companies squarely in 1963 in a provincial general election; he led the fight against the implementation of the compulsory federal medicare scheme of Alan MacEachen; and under his leadership Alberta was generally thought to be an excellent place in which to do business, a province in which a businessman would receive from government sympathetic understanding, not hostility and suspicion.

At the same time, let us look at the reality as well as the rhetoric. Manning was a shrewd man who seldom let his ideology get in the way of his good judgment. While proclaiming itself a "free enterprise" government, Social Credit continued to operate a government-owned quasi-bank in competition with the chartered banks, a huge government-owned telephones system, and a government liquor marketing and control system that would have made Adam Smith turn over in his grave.

The Alberta Liquor Control Board was the most interesting anomaly. As inheritor of the old "temperance" tradition – which was as strong in the U.F.A. as in Social Credit in its earlier days – the A.L.C.B. was a government monopoly with virtually absolute power to market alcoholic beverages and control their consumption. An immensely lucrative government monopoly over the sale of alcohol (which made a net profit of $32,000,000 in 1966), the board was also a draconic regulatory agency with unlimited power to set prices, determine brands and cancel or suspend the licences and permits upon which thousands of Alberta businessmen depended for their livelihood. The Alberta Liquor Control Act empowered policemen to stop and search cars and belongings without a warrant; the act prohibited any court from reviewing or hearing an appeal from any decision of the A.L.C.B. The act openly revoked any right of Albertans to purchase or consume liquor, and then authorized the board to loan citizens back this right in small bits, at its discretion, as a privilege revocable at any time. One consequence of this was that a businessman holding a liquor license had no right to a hearing before the board, no right to present his own evidence, examine or refute board evidence (usually confidential inspectors' reports), no right to receive a written reason for a board decision and no right to appeal any board decision to anyone other than the cabinet itself.

It was puzzling that Manning could reconcile such a top-heavy system with his beliefs about free enterprise and his hostility to bureaucracy. To be sure, hotelmen scarcely led Manning's list of favourite people; and Manning had before him the precedent of Nevada, which legalized gambling (an enterprise similar to the sale of alcohol in its inclination to corrupt) only within the context of strict state regulation and a doctrine which held that the gambling licensee has absolutely no rights – only limited, revocable privileges.

Too, it must be said that this top-heavy regulatory system did prevent many of the abuses of the more loosely-regulated liquor trade south of the border, and delivered a fairly high standard of customer service. The only problem was that it constituted a bad legislative precedent, and it did lead to legislative absurdities (until 1967 it was illegal to make wine in one's basement or serve drinks after 11:30 p.m. on New Year's Eve) and administrative arrogance. The conduct of Liquor Board inspectors was sometimes arbitrary and unfair; one Edmonton businessman told of an incident where a lounge owner received a call from the board stating that an inspector had seen six women sitting at the same table in her beer parlour – an open invitation to immorality which he wanted stopped. One inspector didn't like the design of the bar stools in the new lounge of the Edmonton International Airport and refused to issue a licence for the lounge until they were replaced with some he did like. The chief inspector of the board refused to give newspaper photographers permission to photograph "name" entertainers in Edmonton bars unless the newspaper promised not to mention the name of the bar in which the entertainer was appearing.

In short, while Manning was friendly to free enterprise, strict free enterprise was only the formal code of Social Credit; its operational code was "good government", a broader and more flexible concept with a host of openings for state action. In general terms, Manning was friendly to business. On specific issues, when other things were at stake, Manning was capable of strong opposition to business, big business included. He was not blind to its abuses.

During the Manning years, especially after the birth of the N.D.P.,labour leaders often publicly lashed the government for "anti-labour" policies; but privately, the same leaders would admit that while there were many changes they desired in specific laws and regulations, on the whole the process of arbiting labour disputes was fairly and impartially administered.

In 1964 Canadian Pacific was attempting to close a giant, complex deal for the redevelopment of C.P. lands in downtown Calgary. The city needed the land and hoped to see commercial investment in it; the railway needed new land for its tracks and yards, if it was to move. A deal was worked out after long months of negotiation involving a complex transfer of lands between the two parties, tax exemption on the C.P.R.'s new land, and a seeming commitment by the company to invest a minimum of $10,000,000 in redeveloping its old property. The deal was seen to be critical to the future of downtown Calgary and the city fathers were on the verge of consenting to it when hearings on the matter were called at the legislature.

Manning studied the deal, decided it was neither fair nor equitable, and said so – promptly locking horns with the C.P.R.'s hard-nosed vice-president, Ian Sinclair. Sinclair growled that if there were any provincial wavering, the deal was off; then he referred to Manning as "my good man", which simply wasn't done. Manning stood his ground. During ensuing testimony, Calgary's city solicitor testified that the city had been bulldozed and that the deal gave the C.P.R. generous concessions yet committed it to little; under Manning's questioning, Calgary Mayor Grant MacEwan admitted the deal was "ambiguous and fuzzy".

The deal collapsed, and the C.P.R. went off muttering. That night Manning attended a board meeting at Edmonton Fundamental Baptist Church to decide whether the new lawn should be seeded in blue grass or red fescue.

The ambiguity in the relationship between Social Credit and business can be symbolized in two cases.

Manning's government was slow to deal with the need for interest-disclosure legislation for the consumer credit industry. Although the government passed the Credit and Loan Agreements Act in 1963, authorizing regulations to compel disclosure of interest rates in simple terms understandable to the borrower, it was not until just before the provincial election in 1967 that the government was "able" to find a formula that was "workable" – notwithstanding the fact that the British Board of Trade had one as early as 1965.

On the other hand, the Social Credit government was generally regarded by the nation's lawyers, landlords and creditors as far too friendly to the little man when it came to giving permission to foreclose a debt or evict a "deadbeat". The old Depression heritage of concern for the debtor was still alive in Social Credit; Manning's government pushed through innovative legislation to protect those deeply in personal debt and help them to rebuild their lives. The first of these acts was the Debt Adjustment Act, struck down by the courts in 1943. In 1958 Manning personally pushed through the House an Orderly Payments of Debts Act which set up machinery to protect those in financial trouble and help them to repay their debts in a fair way; this, too, was struck down by the courts as being in conflict with federal jurisdiction over bankruptcy.

Alberta continued to protect debtors through this period with the Debtors Assistance Board, which attempted to humanely arbitrate conflicts between debtors and creditors. Finally, in 1966, Philip Gibeau, chairman of the board, was sent to testify before the Commons Standing Committee on Banking and Commerce, and the federal government agreed to Gibeau's plea to pass legislation similar to Alberta's disallowed acts, legislation that would enable each province to "opt in". The Commons passed the legislation in 1966 and in 1967 Alberta became the first province to opt in, with a (constitutional, this time) Orderly Payment of Debts Act.

3. *Foreign Capital and the Oil Companies.*

One of the recurring central questions in Canada's history has been our relationship with foreign capital. How to develop, plan and control our own economy? How to find capital and technology? For Alberta (and the West in general) these questions had particular impact because, so often in past, central Canada had demonstrated often that she was incapable of responding to Alberta's economic needs. The people wanted development. Where were they to turn for help in making it happen?

After Leduc, they turned to the oil industry, and the oil industry was strongly influenced, in some cases controlled, by Americans. Today it is fashionable to believe that Canada can increasingly get along without foreign investment. But in 1947, at the birth of Leduc, what were the practical options open to Manning? There were really only two. One – bring in the Americans, under ground rules laid down to protect Alberta interests, and police them carefully, seeking at the same time to maximize public revenues from their operations. Two – go the Saskatchewan C.C.F. route and develop our own oil industry, using either a government-owned oil company or co-operatives. But how possible was the Saskatchewan option? Manning found it repugnant on ideological grounds, and there is reason to believe a majority of Albertans at that time would have agreed with him. And leaving aside the ideological question, there were more practical obstacles. Oil exploration was a notoriously risky and complicated business, a business in which virtually all the expertise resided in the private sector. How to find the oil without the private sector? And once it were found, how to produce, refine and market it in a world in which the large oil companies controlled access to so many markets? There was, finally, an overwhelming economic problem. Alberta oil, compared with oil availabile elsewhere in the world, in places like Venezeula and the Middle East, was very expensive oil to produce. Alberta's oil pools were small, by world standards, and they were located, often, in trackless and hostile terrain. This raised exploration and transportation costs dramatically. How possible would it have been to have marketed this expensive oil, especially in the face of a hostile oil industry?

The risks of going it alone were intimidating. Before Imperial Oil struck oil at Leduc, it had drilled 133 consecutive dry holes. Another oil company had spent $400,000 building its own road to get a drilling site, and $1,600,000 drilling the well – and it had been dry. A politician asks himself: what if the government goes into the oil business and then – like the Saskatchewan C.C.F. when it went into the shoe business, the box business and other businesses – starts losing money, the people's tax money?

And finally, Manning had to ask himself how selective the young province could afford to be about foreign capital. If you penalize one group of foreign investors, may you not find it difficult to attract other groups of foreign investors? Throw out one group, it makes the others nervous too. How attractive a place would Alberta seem to other investors if the government set about making things difficult for oil investors?

It is very easy, looking back from today, to exaggerate the amount of freedom Manning had to make the decision. In fact, his practical options were limited. And Manning was an eminently practical man. The final, and perhaps most important argument in favour of encouraging foreign investors and rejecting economic nationalism was an eminently practical one. Abstract economic sovereignty is important; but so are the schools, hospitals, libraries and social services that can be paid for from the returns on economic development. After so many years of hard work and suffering, didn't people have a right to a claim on that? It was not, after all, that Alberta was being asked to leave a blissful state of nature in which she was economically free and independent, and exchange it for bondage; Alberta had spent her whole life as a province in the clutch of outside investors. The real question in 1947 and later was whether to exchange Bay Street and British investors for investors from Wall Street and Houston. The answer seemed to be, why not? Next-door Saskatchewan had stuck up for her economic sovereignty, after all, and where had that gotten her? Her major export was people.

And so it was decided that Alberta would throw her doors wide open to all investors, and they came in a rush.

Today, Manning's stand must be judged in light of two questions: did Albertans gain a fair economic return from the foreign development of oil? And did the government do everthing possible to develop a technological and industrial base to enable Canadians to compete with, and participate at the highest levels in, these foreign companies?

Consider the first question:

Social Credit controlled oil development in this way. Since 1929, the provincial government owned the mineral rights under more than eighty-five per cent of the province's land. From the outset, then, the control over access to the oil and the conditions of its production was entirely in government hands and was a privilege, not a right. The drilling of a sample oil well went like this:

Company A thought there was oil beneath a given piece of land. It went to the Oil and Gas Conservation Board and put down a deposit; it was given an "exploration reservation" that entitled it to survey and test-drill to see if oil was present under the parcel. The deposit ensured that the exploration would be carried out. A road was needed into the site: the company had to build it and pay for it.

Company A found some oil. It was allowed to take a lease on the drilling rights on one-half of the exploration reservation. The other half went back to the province and was called a Crown Reservation. The right to produce from this went before the public auction. The highest bid ever received for a small parcel of land was $3,300,000 for a quarter-section of land south-west of Edmonton in 1953.

So far, the province reaped two kinds of revenue: deposits and bids for drilling rights. Once production began, the government collected a third form of revenue: production royalties. These were payable in cash or kind and were based on a sliding scale ranging from five to 16½ per cent of the value of production, depending on the total amount produced. The sliding scale was devised to encourage companies to keep small wells producing as long as possible, to get the maximum amount of oil out of the ground; higher royalties on the smaller wells would have led to many of them being closed down.

Revenue from oil bids went into the province's current revenue fund on the theory that it did not represent the depletion of the resource; money from royalties, which did represent depletion of a non-renewable resource, went into social capital (schools, roads, research, etc.) to replace the oil.

Did Albertans gain a fair return on the oil from this system? There are varying opinions on that, but certainly few Albertans felt cheated. Between 1950 and 1968 the system poured $2,350,000,000 into provincial coffers. The natural resource revenue (mainly oil and gas) in 1966 was $257,000,000. This not only had the effect of reducing taxes (Alberta was the only province in Canada without a sales tax) and funding a broad range of social expenditures, it also represented only the leading edge of oil prosperity. The oil companies built thousands of miles of road at no cost to the taxpayer; they purchased billions of dollars worth of supplies and services in the Alberta economy. They provided jobs for thousands of young Alberta school and university graduates. A whole range of new businesses and industries came into being to service the oil industry. From a predominately agricultural province, Alberta became a province in which, by 1961, nearly half the work force was employed in industries involved in or related to oil.*

* Eric J. Hanson, "Regional Employment and Income Effects of the Petroleum Industry in Alberta", a paper delivered to The American Institute of Mining, Metallurgical and Petroleum Engineers, New York, March 1966.

By 1961 the oil companies had spent $1,600,000 more in Western Canada than they took in – chiefly on exploration to obtain reserves for future production. While Saskatchewan's population stagnated some years and declined others, between 1946 and 1964 Alberta was the fastest-growing province in Canada, and per capita income more than doubled. In 1966 one out of every three dollars spent by the Alberta government didn't have to be collected from taxes; it came from oil companies.

The "golden years" of the Manning Era were a financial bonanza. Apart from its telephone system, the province did not have to borrow money from the end of the war until late in the 1960s. After 1966 expenditures on social programs began to rapidly catch up with this affluence; but by 1966 there was an accumulated government surplus (almost all of it loaned out to the municipalities for roads and schools) of $620,000,000. In the eight fiscal years between 1956 and 1964 Social Credit Treasurers *underestimated* government revenue seven times. In each of the seven years, deficits were predicted, but surpluses resulted; in each case, "unexpected" oil revenues did the trick. It was a land of milk and money.

But did Albertans get an opportunity to develop their technological and industrial base? Did Manning do enough to enable Canadians to compete with and participate in the oil industry?

The answer to that is more cloudy.

On two occasions Manning persuaded companies to offer large equity holdings to Albertans in exchange for permission for new developments.

The first was the bonanza of shares in the Alberta Gas Trunk Line Ltd., when the government made it the condition of permitting the building of the line that Albertans be allowed to purchase up to twenty-five shares each at $4.25 apiece. Thousands did (often making deals to purchase the shares of others, as well) and made very large profits (up to 400 per cent and more) as the stock took off; hundreds of young Albertans went to university on their parents' profits from Alberta Gas Trunk. The second involved a public offering of $12,-500,000 worth of convertible debentures in Great Canadian Oil Sands as part of the price for permission to develop the Athabasca oil sands. The G.C.O.S. debentures did less well.

Manning's only venture into large-scale economic nationalism was the Alberta Investment Fund, a page out of the book of the Canada Development Corporation, created in 1966. An offering of $10,-000,000 in investment certificates in denominations of $100 was put on the market to create a government loan fund for new Alberta industries. The certificates guaranteed a minimum return of 3½ per cent. The fund was half-heartedly and ambiguously promoted and advertised and the response to it was dismal: only $2,054,600 worth of certificates were sold, and the fund was shelved.

Manning's administration *did* underwrite the creation of an impressive system for *researching* new technology (the universities and the Alberta Research Council) and for *teaching* it (the universities plus two impressive technical institutes). With the exception of Great Canadian Oil Sands Ltd., however, Manning did not require the international oil companies to hire Albertans, fill a quota of top management positions with Albertans, or use made-in-Alberta equipment or know-how. Nor did he make any special arrangements to help Alberta or Canadian companies get into the oil industry on a competitive basis. To be sure, neither did any other government in Canada.

4. *"People Power."*

Manning was always a much more thoughtful and introspective politician than most of his contemporaries, and in the mid-1960s this introspection led him to conclude that Social Credit needed a new philosophical emphasis on people, a return to its roots as a humanist reform party.

A crucial actor in this process of renewal was Manning's son, Preston. During his time as a student of physics and economics at the University of Alberta, Preston accepted his father's conservative orientation but added to it an emphasis on the need for reform – a conservatism capable of serving and meeting social needs as well as industrial ones. "Free Enterprise" had always been, for Ernest Manning, a convenient label for an assortment of individualistic values; it did not preclude reform, and Manning was always somewhat nervous about the association between "conservatism" and "vested interests".

While at university, Preston became friends with Erick Schmidt, a bland young graduate student in sociology who had once studied theology. Along with Owen Anderson, a political science student who headed the campus Socreds, and Jim Ergil, a Turkish industrial engineer from the nearby Alberta Research Council, Schmidt was a decisive influence on Preston, and Preston was a powerful influence on his father. (Schmidt's background as a one-time candidate for the Baptist ministry, and his discretion, made him particularly acceptable to both Preston and his father.) Together, this group turned its attention to the question of reclaiming the Social Credit tradition of humanism.

The first public sign of the new look in Social Credit was the creation of the country's first full-fledged Department of Youth in

143

1966. Manning's surprise appointment as Minister of Youth (another M.L.A., Ray Speaker, had been touted for the position) was Robert Clark, a young teacher and amateur baseball player from Didsbury. At first the department was nothing more than a regrouping of civil service agencies from other departments, held together by its Deputy Minister, C.L. Usher, and the ingratiating grin and gee-whiz manner of its young minister. Only with the creation of the Alberta Service Corps, a volunteer social-action group for university students, oriented to serving the poor and disadvantaged, did the Youth Department come alive.

To head up the Service Corps, Schmidt persuaded the government to bring in Don Hamilton, an ambitious and hard-driving young United Church minister who had formerly managed the Edmonton Huskies football team. Under Hamilton's leadership, the Service Corps soon became an idealistic going concern.*

The other thrust of reform in Social Credit was far more serious, but much less public. It concerned the quiet development of nothing less than a social revolution among Alberta's native peoples.

In the early 1960s, in the midst of their vicarious involvement in the emotional struggle for civil rights in the United States, Canadians began to remember, with some guilt, that they too, had a racial problem. The Canadian Indian began to prick the conscience of Canadian whites.

The response of the federal government to the Indian's plight was very slow and uncomprehending; in fact, in the view of many Indian leaders, it was the bureaucracy and paternalism of the Department of Indian and Northern Affairs that was responsible for much of the Indian's plight.

It stands to Ernest Manning's credit that he was the first white political leader in the country to respond to the need to develop truly innovative programs to break the Indian's "poverty cycle".

Manning found two men to man the campaign. The first was Fred Colborne, Manning's Minister of Public Works, a burly, moustached veteran politican with the mien of a riverboat gambler but the social conscience of a one-time Roman Catholic who had read all of the modern Papal Encyclicals and taken them seriously. The second was Jim Whitford, a short, peppery "professional shit-disturber" (to use

---

* Collisions between the Service Corps and the settled gentility of the government were not long coming. The corps had to be dissuaded from publishing two recruiting posters – one with a giant humourous caricature of a stern Manning, his finger pointing, captioned "Uncle Ernie Wants YOU", the other portraying a student riding on a donkey, and captioned, "Why not get off your ass and help?"

his words at the time) who was appointed to become head of the government's Community Development Branch.

All through the early and mid-1960s, out in the bushlands and seldom in the headlines, Whitford and his men went into Indian and Métis communities to live and work with and develop the potential of the native leadership. The operative purpose of the Community Development Branch was to break down the traditional system for "handling" the Indian – to make the Indian aware of how the "system" worked and how he could use his resources to make it work for *him*.

What Whitford perceived was that, in the eyes of the white society, the native had become a problem to be manipulated. To the federal civil servant, he was the rather childlike ward to be led for his own good; to the local businessman, he was a sullen second-class customer, often to be duped with sharp retailing practices. To the missionary of whatever faith, he was the primitive to be brought under the protection and guidance of the mother church. Converted, but not consulted. By 1960, Alberta's once-proud natives were demoralized, lacking in confidence, under-employed, in poor health.*

Right from the outset, and somewhat deliberately, Whitford and his men were a thorn in the side of a good part of the Alberta establishment. They antagonized Indian Affairs officials, churchmen, white merchants, provincial civil servants, and often the Indians themselves. They were cast in the role of "change agents", and they threw themselves against barriers of ignorance, apathy and bureaucratic inertia with great dedication. Their objective was nothing less than the destruction of the legal and administrative relationships and racial attitudes perpetuating native dependency – the liberation of both white *and* native.

Whitford's chief field operative was a tough, charming ex-Indian Affairs officials, B.V. (Ben) Baich. Looking like a tanned Yul Brynner, the balding Baich provided field back-up to Whitford's resident officers, who were themselves a highly spontaneous lot. (One of them, Murray Smith, provoked an uproar in the civil service by gathering up a group of local Indian leaders – all without proper authorization – and flying them to an N.A.A.C.P. Convention in Milwaukee.)

---

* One of Whitford's top aides, who once worked as an Indian Agent for the federal government in northern Manitoba, described the dramatic change in his charges even between 1945 and 1960; in 1945 they were self-sufficient trappers, and were confident, even arrogant, towards whites; by 1960 they were, in his words, "sick men" who shuffled into the room, looked at the floor when spoken to, and "drank to forget".

Beginning in 1966, the Community Development program began to break into the headlines as its activities resulted in growing native action. In remote Fort Chipewyan, on the shores of Lake Athabasca, the local community development officer encouraged the natives to begin asking questions about the way in which they were treated by the local Hudson's Bay Company store, the only one in the community. The natives eventually accused the local H.B.C. factor of opening their mail to cash welfare cheques for back bills. When an Indian beat up the factor and threw him out of his own store, the Indian was arrested and charged; the government supplied a lawyer to defend him. And, in July 1966, a group of several hundred unemployed indians from Wabasca, a bush settlement 280 miles north of Edmonton, marched on the legislature and demanded an opportunity to develop their own modern sawmill. Out of their meeting with Manning emerged an agreement in which the government bankrolled and equipped a logging co-op for the Indians, gave them first shot at a generous logging contract with Federated Co-Ops, and guaranteed the natives fair wages and equitable treatment.

Some of Manning's cabinet ministers, upset by the march, muttered that it had been organized by the Company of Young Canadians. Actually, the catalyst had been Ben Baich.

The word eventually got out about the Community Development Branch, and one of Manning's ministers, Henry Ruste, came to him and asked that Ben Baich be fired. Manning told Ruste he should complain to Whitford.

The Wabasca experiment, years later, was not a financial success by the standards of industrial society; but there is no question it was, an unprecedented social experiment.

In March 1967, not long before he called his last election, Manning formalized his campaign to renew Social Credit by tabling in the legislature a White Paper on Human Resource Development. This paper, which was largely written by Preston and Erick Schmidt, expressed a new government commitment to rationalized, comprehensive "people services" for the development of "free and creative individuals". "The Government believes that the time has come for the people of Alberta, through their representatives, to declare explicitly their intention to make human resources development a supreme provincial concern. The time has come for an explicit commitment of private and public energies toward facilitating, to the greatest extent possible, the free and creative development of every human being in the Province of Alberta." As the White Paper put it in its "interpretive statement":

Concern for human values and human needs is the dominant factor underlying the Government's determination to do everything in its power to enhance the role of free and creative individuals, in and through the maximum development of the province's total human and physical resources.

As the "charter document" for a new era in public life, the White Paper was composed in an unfortunate wooden prose and the very poor choice of the term "*human* resources" was repugnant to some. Nevertheless, the White Paper was noted for the important statement that it was, and optimism was voiced about its announcement of the creation of a Human Resources Research Council to sponsor more and better research into social problems and to feed this research into a more sophisticated government decision-making.

To highlight the new thrust, Manning tabled in the legislature at the same time seven comprehensive reports on poverty in selected Alberta communities – an Indian Reserve, a Métis community, a depressed mining area (the Drumheller Valley) a marginal farming locale, a homesteading area in the Peace River country, and poverty pockets in Edmonton and Calgary. This was a sample of putting the social sciences to work for decision-making; the reports had been researched the previous summer by sociologists and graduate students at the University of Alberta and the Unversity of Calgary. In fact, the ink was still wet on them when they were handed to Manning for tabling.

As the last years of the Manning Era came into view, Manning was groping for a new direction, a new ideology that would express more adequately his objectives. For him, "free enterprise" was no longer, by itself, enough. Human Resources Development was to become the new ideology of Social Credit its new reason for being.

Could it succeed, this eleventh-hour attempt to shake up an aging party and government and infuse them with new purpose and commitment? The ironic answer was that the very conditions that enabled Manning to impose the Human Resources Program on an often apathetic cabinet and caucus were the very conditions that had drained the life out of Manning's own political party. Because Manning had such personal standing, he was able to carry the judgement of his colleagues in power. But partly because of his personal standing, his very domination of the time, much of the life had gone out of the Social Credit party and, indeed, the leadership elite of the government. This meant that the party could not effectively interpret or sell the Human Resources Program to the electorate; it also meant there was an excellent chance once he retired, that Manning would be replaced by a man with no real commitment to the Human Resources program. If that happened, the drive to renew Social Credit would falter.

CHAPTER NINE

How Manning Kept Power

In 1948 a most unusual thing happened in Alberta: the multi-party political system fell into a twenty-year coma. A unique form of government by one party and one man came into being to take its place.

During that twenty-year period, Ernest Manning stood over the public life of Alberta like a colossus. That anyone else could or should be premier – or that any other party could or should gain power – was, for many voters, unthinkable.

Public interest in politics itself slumbered. Even the Social Credit League of Alberta grew drowsy.

Yet, while this was happening, the Social Credit government remained quite responsive to change and the formal institutions of the democractic system remained healthy. The interests and demands of a wide range of groups in Alberta were canvassed and responded to by Manning's government. The press remained free – in fact, explicitly anti-Social Credit publications came into being for the sole purpose of defeating the government. The courts remained independent, speech and religion remained unfettered, elections were held regularly and honestly, and there continued to be an opposition in the legislature, albeit a tiny one.

Nor did there develop the widespread government graft, corruption and patronage that came to be associated with long-time one party rule in other provinces such as Newfoundland and Quebec. And, in spite of all this (or perhaps because of it), Ernest Manning was able to win seven straight provincial elections.

What happened? What was Manning's secret? And what were the

consequences of Ernest Manning's era for the province and party he represented?

1. *The Political Context.*

Alberta as an agrarian society had a long tradition of one-party dominance. The Liberals ruled the province from its inception in 1905 until 1921 and the United Farmers ruled it from 1921 until the advent of Social Credit. Part of this dominance could be explained by the homogeneous nature of Alberta's farm economy: there was really only one class of people, farmers.*

The discovery of oil and Alberta's industrial takeoff ushered in a host of social changes that broke this homogeneity in the 1950s and 1960s.

The discovery of oil broke the Depression psychology and created in its place an almost euphoric optimism. In the first years after 1947, many could not bring themselves to believe the implications of oil's discovery; eventually it sank in. More than 200,000 immigrants came into the province; personal income rose by more than four per cent a year.

The influx of immigrants and the merciless economic rationalization of farming, which squeezed more and more small farmers off the land, combined to produce a tremendous flood of people into the cities. Edmonton and Calgary took off. In 1946 sixty-two per cent of Albertans lived on farms or in tiny hamlets; by 1961 sixty-seven per cent of Albertans lived in urban centres, mainly Edmonton, Calgary, Lethbridge, Medicine Hat and Red Deer.

With urbanization and a tremendous expansion in the province's educational system, came rapid changes in attitudes and values. People were becoming "citified" and secularized. The arrival of widespread prosperity brought with it greater mobility and a tremendous increase in cultural activities.

Higher education raised levels of critical awareness. Prosperity increased the propensity to consume, and this in turn drew Albertans more deeply into the great commercial and advertising net of the North American economy. Organized religion and tradional small-town values began to wane. Alberta's stereotyped reputation for powerful religiosity became more and more unreal as the genteel,

---

* Of course there were many other causes as well – two of the most important being the influence of strong leaders (Henry Wise Wood, Brownlee, Aberhart) and the prairies' traditional dislike of "party politics" (i.e., dislike of any political organization calling itself a party, as opposed to a League, a Movement or an Association).

middle-of-the-road churches marked time and fewer people came to take organized religion as a really serious matter.*

In short, the economic and social revolution brought on by oil changed the face of Alberta dramatically and complicated Manning's political plans greatly.

The greatest problem Manning faced as a politician was that he symbolized a set of values – and a personal style – that was increasingly out of step with the Alberta of the 1950s and especially the 1960s. By 1961 there were 280,000 voters in Alberta who were too young to have experienced the Depression. By 1961 the province was in an era in which money and credit were easy to get and debt bore no stigma – but Ernest Manning and his colleagues were still preaching that consumption should be restrained, that debt meant slavery. In 1961 Manning was still preaching that the traditional values were best, that the family was the foundation of society; but the traditional values were fast disappearing and the family was under attack from many quarters. In 1961 Manning was still a supporter of the "old morality" in sexual and personal relationships. But in the cities, and even many of the small towns and rural areas (far more than a lot of older people knew or cared to admit), morality was rapidly changing: sexual freedom was growing, drinking was common, the drug revolution was just around the corner. In 1970 the Alberta Department of Education commissioned an experimental film on drug abuse for use in the drug education program in the public schools; when the film producer travelled around the province doing his research, he found that the place in which drugs were most freely available to all comers was the small town of Ponoka, a town in a sleepy, conservative rural area, with 4,000 souls.

How could Social Credit come to grips with this kind of social and cultural change? How could Social Crediters escape becoming "yesterday's men"?

2. Manning's Powerful Charisma

Social Credit's greatest strength as it faced this problem was the personality and image of its leader. Although Manning's paternalis-

---

* Alberta was portrayed for many years as "the buckle on the Bible belt", but the image had little reality. Even by the broadest definition of the term, "fundamentalists" made up barely ten per cent of those Albertans who even claimed a formal religious affiliation in the 1960s. It was sometimes argued that Manning's power rested on a fundamentalist support. But if this were true, fundamentalists should have been either numerous or influential, or both. And generally they were neither.

tic leadership style offended some, his tremendous moral stature, modesty, and obvious great ability combined with his privatism to produce an unbeatable mystique.

The foundation of this mystique was his weekly religious radio broadcast, carried coast to coast. Never a flamboyant speaker, but rather a somewhat serious, almost scholarly preacher, Manning impressed many listeners (including occasional listeners, who did not share his fundamentalist views) as a man of great sobriety and purpose – an impression which, in the midst of the materialism of the 1950s and social and intellectual turmoil of the 1960s, many Albertan's found appealling.

Manning had clung to a reasonably fixed set of religious values for all of his adult life; he inherited Aberhart's weekly radio program, which began in 1927, and continued it through until the present. Politics was his life's work; but in many ways religion was his life's love. Manning always maintained that what he originally wanted to do in life was to become a full time lay worker for the Prophetic Bible Institute; that was what he was doing when Aberhart received his "call" to politics, and no doubt he might still be doing it if Aberhart had not.

Like most of Canada's more than 1,000,000 evangelicals, Manning stubbornly held that the "mainstream" Christian churches had gotten off the rails, that what Canada and the world needed was a return to the fundamentals of Christianity, particularly a return to reliance on literally-interpreted scripture and an intense personal conversion experience. For such Christians, there was no pain in forsaking the "things of this world"; the "true Christian" had an "inner joy". He was "spiritually regenerated". The aim of the church was not collective action to improve the lot of man but the preaching of the Gospel to lead men to "accept Jesus Christ as their personal saviour"; such men will manifest their salvation in a concern for others.

Now in the "feud-amentalist" tradition, Manning's own church, the Edmonton Fundamental Baptist Church, was a tightly-controlled, somewhat exclusivistic congregation.* But it was in his capacity as head of the Back to the Bible Hour that Manning came each Sunday to most Canadians.

Manning's coherent, tightly reasoned sermons (he was never, to use his critics' favourite phrase, a "Bible-pounder") were easy to

* From its constitution: "At every meeting to extend the right hand of fellowship, the Covenant of the Church must be read and agreed to by all Members present. Should any Member refuse to agree to the Covenant, his membership is automatically suspended until he has made a satisfactory explanation to the Official Board."

follow and often related to current events. With an annual budget of $130,000 and a staff led by Social Credit League Secretary Orvis Kennedy's son Ed Kennedy, the coast-to-coast broadcasts help establish Manning as a lay religious leader of some importance. (It was Manning who persuaded six Canadian leaders – John Roberts, Ross Thatcher, W.A.C. Bennett, Duff Roblin, Joey Smallwood and Lester Pearson to sign a letter inviting Billy Graham to conduct his first Crusade in Canada.)

To be sure, Manning's religious activities frequently raised the hackles of his government's critics. Yet no one really dared openly accuse Manning of promoting his religious views for political purposes; Manning was too obviously sincere. This left the critics in the difficult position of being able to argue only that, in some sense, a political leader should keep his views to himself. It was not a powerful argument, partly because Manning demonstrated on several occasions that he would not allow his personal religious views to influence important policy questions – the matter of liquor for example. Alberta's liquor laws, once primitive (although no more so than in many other provinces not run by fundamentalists), were rapidly updated after the late 1950s and, by the late 1950's were probably about on a par with most in Canada.

Manning referred to this problem obliquely in a Back to the Bible Hour broadcast February 5th, 1966, which was devoted to the theme, "in any unregenerate society, the will of the people is bound to come into conflict with the will of God."

Referring to the Israelites in *I Samuel,* who in spite of God's will expressed through the prophets, wanted a king, Manning noted that God instructed Samuel to "protest solemnly unto them and show them the manner of the King that shall reign over them", which Samuel did. The people, however, were unmoved, and Samuel reported this to God, who replied: "Hearken unto their voice and make them a King." The lesson drawn from this by Manning was that when the will of the people conflicts with the will of God – as it often will in a society of the "unsaved" – the people must be allowed to have their way, for only by having their way, and suffering the consequences, will they come to see the error of their prideful stubbornness.

This emphasis in Manning's life was criticized by some,* but generally speaking it contributed to his image as an honest, sincere, upright man, a leader who could be trusted almost absolutely.

Manning's aura was also strengthened by his air of mystery: he

* When he was a cartoonist at *The Edmonton Journal,* John Yardley Jones never tired of drawing Manning Lamps bearing signs saying, "let there be light",

was an intensely private man. For a time, the Mannings lived in the city, near the University of Alberta; eventually they moved to a farm north-east of the city, on the bank of the North Saskatchewan River, and there they lived a quiet, tightly-knit life. Manning kept a herd of dairy cattle and a hired man to run the place; whenever he could, Manning liked to put on his coveralls and work on the machinery himself. Manning's wife Muriel, a tall, handsome, strong-minded woman provided both domestic strength and musical leadership for the Back to the Bible Hour (she was a talented pianist). The fourth member of the Manning family, their first son Keith, was brain-damaged at birth in 1940. He was educated in special schools before coming back to live with the family in his late teens. The main responsibility for carrying on the family name fell on Keith's younger brother Preston, born in 1942, and he carried it well. He won a Governor-General's medal for scholarship in grade nine, finished grade twelve with a ninety-three per cent average, was off-ered three separate university scholarships and then graduated from the University of Alberta in physics and economics in 1964, later joining Manning's business consulting firm, set up after his retirement.

During his premiership, Manning's private world was seldom vi-olated; the Mannings had a very small circle of close friends, and apart from these they seldom entertained. Cabinet wives were invited out once a year for tea; there were no social functions sponsored by the Mannings other than that. Manning rose every day at 7:00 a.m., drove his own car to work (he disliked using the chauffer), generally returned after 6:00 p.m. for dinner; at home he worked on upcoming speeches and Bible broadcasts, spending ten to twenty hours a week on that alone. In winter, there were frequently speeches to give or trips to make. In summer, when there was time, there was work around the farm. His eating and reading tastes were simple – al-though he was raised on the prairies, he liked to read about sailing. The Mannings took winter vacations, usually in Arizona, where they later purchased a home.

Manning wall-plaques saying "Thou shalt not" and cases of beer labelled "Ginger ale . . . of course." (For many years, brewers were not permitted to advertise their beer, instead they advertised "ginger ale"). Two popular Man-ning jokes of the time: St. Peter searching through new arrivals for a psychia-trist, then asking him, "come in and help us out. We're having a little trouble with the Supreme Being; he thinks he's Manning." Another, Manning looking for a burial plot. He finds a nice one but protests its high cost. The owner says, "but Sir, it has a lovely view looking west to the mountains, north to the forests, south and east to the prairies." Manning replies, "you don't seem to under-stand. I'll only be needing it for three days."

The sole exception to this pattern of intense privacy and formality was that all during his premiership, Manning had a publicly-listed telephone number. This subjected him to the usual variety of drunks, pranksters and cranks, but he always insisted that it also provided a "court of last resort" for people in trouble or having difficulty with the government. Often Manning or his wife were able to help out people with genuine problems. Sometimes it had comic consequences, like the time a woman called in what seemed like great distress and said that the welfare cheque hadn't come through and she had nothing to feed the children. Muriel roused the Deputy Minister of Public Welfare from his dinner table and put him on the trail of a grocer to round up a hamper for the woman. When Muriel called the lady back to tell her the hamper would be on its way later that evening she was told indignantly, "that isn't soon enough. I have to go curling, you know."

The public effect of this intensely busy and somewhat remote life-style was to lend an air of mystery to the Manning family. Everyone knew that "Mr. Manning" (as he was almost universally known; probably no more than a half dozen people ever called him "Ernest") was premier and that he was "there" somehow, but his public appearances were sufficiently rare that he was never overexposed. Manning did not invite familiarity.

At the same time, when he did speak on public questions (or even during his infrequent interviews) he conveyed a tremendous sense of assurance about his own views. Somehow he managed to avoid sounding pompous or arrogant; his tone and phrasing were those of a man who had obviously thought long and hard about the matter, had studied all possible evidence, and who had arrived at demonstrably sound conclusions. After a while, many Albertans came to regard his statements as obvious simple fact, quite unlike the claims of the "politicians".

As Manning won election after election, opposition political leaders had to face the herculean task of persuading themselves that he could ever be beaten. Few of them had enough fortitude to try and prove him wrong. A long succession of Liberal leaders (J. Harper Prowse, Dave Hunter, Adrian Berry, Mike Maccagno) and Conservative leaders (J. Percy Page, Cam Kirby, Milt Harradance, Ernest Watkins) came and went through the revolving doors of the opposition offices in the Legislature and made little lasting impact. Their despair was still being felt as late as 1967, as witness this article in March of that year by Ernest Watkins:

The election, whenever it comes, will superficially be very like the last. Each of the three opposition-party leaders will open his campaign with the plea that what the province needs is a stronger opposition. And the contest will close with an exhortation from the premier to vote for his team, backed by a fairly blunt warning that any riding that cuts itself off from direct contact with the government . . . will be very foolish indeed. . . . Ernest Manning as an individual, and the Social Credit party as an organization, are formidable opponents in any election campaign. But the opposition in Alberta is further handicapped by the fact that over the last five years there has been no broad public issue, still less any wide discontent here.*

3. *Manning's Management of Issues.*

One of Manning's consummate skills was the management of change; he knew when to stand firm and when to bend before an irresistible wind. In this sense he was an effective practitioner of the politics of consensus.

He knew when to accomodate change. In the mid-1950s he publicly predicted that cocktail lounges would never be permitted in Alberta: shortly thereafter, he introduced legislation to set up local plebescites to permit them. In late 1962 he saw that some form of government action on medical insurance was inevitable and began negotiations with the medical profession and the private insurance industry to hammer out a scheme.

He was sensitive enough to criticism to register it internally and coolly study its popularity. His relaxation of the censorship system and Sunday blue-laws came on the heels of concerted media campaigns.

He shopped around for good ideas wherever they could be found. There seems little question his excellent programs for the elderly were owed in part to constant agitation on behalf of the elderly by the C.C.F. through the 1940s and 1950s.

He had a good sense of timing, carefully rationing out new policies and programs for maximum impact. He introduced cash payments to all citizens ("oil dividends" as they were popularly called) the year before the 1955 election, a "five year plan" of community facilities and old-age homes before the 1959 election. In the 1963 election the Liberals tried to make public power an issue by promising to nationalize Calgary Power Ltd. if elected; the day before the election, Manning capped long months of quiet negotiations with the doctors and insurance companies by announcing that a subsidized medicare scheme would be implemented in Alberta. The effect of this move

* Alberta: Electing the Elect", *Saturday Night,* March 1967.

was devastating: public power lost whatever hold it may have had on the public mind, and the government was resoundingly re-elected.*

Finally, Manning was very good at squeezing every last drop of advantage out of his government's major accomplishments. The announcement of the design, building and extension of the Alberta Resources Railway was stretched over several years.

Against all of this, of course, it must be remembered that the public sector in Alberta was enormously wealthy; the tremendous yearly income from oil made it possible to provide a high level of services and public facilities without high taxation. Manning was able to build a Jubilee Auditorium for cultural events in each of Edmonton and Calgary in 1955 entirely out of current revenue! Affluence was a constant cushion for the government. What Manning did was manage this affluence very effectively.

4. Manning's Organizational Weapon: The Social Credit League.

One major basis of Manning's strength was that he kept virtually everybody happy some of the time. In doing this he had the backing of the Alberta Social Credit League, which served to channel popular "feedback" to Manning, and to deliver the good news on the hustings.**

Through most of the Manning Era, the Social Credit League was a pillar of government strength. And the strength of the League was the strength of practical men working hard at routine tasks.

The central source of the League's strength in this period was its executive director, Orvis Kennedy.

Kennedy was living in Oyen, a farm community near Calgary, when he first heard Aberhart over the radio in the autumn of 1924. Few people in the district had radios at the time; the practice was to have a radio owner play his set over the local party telephone line and people along the line would listen in by placing cardboard "horns" over the receivers.

---

* "State medicine" was a Social Credit plank in the 1935 election. According to a Social Credit M.L.A. at the time, W.R. King, Aberhart was prevented from implementing it only by its cost and financial conditions at the time. *The History of Alberta, Political and Financial, 1905-1938*, (n.d.), p. 17.

** Manning also relied for information on a private network of confidantes, a daily clipping service, and occasional public-opinion polls by a U.S. polling organization.

Kennedy was a jovial hardware man and in 1926 he came to Edmonton to work in a large hardware firm. In 1928 he began a drama club in the Masonic Temple and became active in the United Church Young Peoples movement, where he met W.A.C. Bennett, another hardware man, who preceded him as president of the Young Peoples group at Central United Church. Kennedy met Aberhart during a visit to Edmonton in 1934, just as the Social Credit crusade was getting into high gear. Kennedy offered his help and subsequently joined the first Edmonton Area Social Credit Council.

Although he sat for a time as an M.P. in Ottawa, Kennedy spent most of his life as a highly proficient political technocrat. His great flair was for the backbreaking hard work, long hours and infinite attention to detail that kept the League a smoothly-running political apparatus.

Tight and tidy organization was Aberhart's trademark, and he left it on the League; for the Manning Era, Orvis continued this tradition and ran the day-to-day affairs of the League with virtual autonomy. For most of the Manning Era, the League had between 12,000 and 15,000 paid-up regular members between elections (the number increased at election time, as in all parties, from the selling of memberships that accompanied the nominating process). Most members were "regular" members paying two dollars a year in dues plus one dollar a year for each member of their family up to a maximum of five dollars; a smaller number were "sustaining" members at ten dollars a year.

Regular membership was open to Alberta residents who were either Canadian citizens or British subjects and who subscribed to the twelve purposes of the League which ranged from "the study of Social Credit principles" and the liberation of Canada "from the yoke of the present financial system" to the abolition of poverty and the fostering of "the universally recognized principles of Christianity in human relationships".

At the local level the League was built of a series of hierarchies beginning with the "group", a local association of ten or more League members with their own executive. Groups formed into Constituency Associations, which held an annual convention each year before the provincial convention; the association was composed of delegates from each poll in the riding plus the constituency executive and representatives from the Women's Auxiliary and local Young Peoples' Branches. Each constituency executive also appointed voluntary, unpaid organizers called "key men".

Over all there was a provincial Board of Directors consisting of twelve members elected annually. Late in the Manning Era the board consisted of Manning as provincial leader, Orvis as president, three vice-presidents (J. Arthur Davies, Ian Smith and Francis Porter), five district representatives, Earl Smith of Bow Island, Dr. Ross Lawson of Calgary, George Sterling of Benalto, Ron Clark of Edmonton and Ralph Jasperson (North Rural); there was also a Young Peoples representative, Richard DeWitt of Calgary, and a Women's Auxiliary representative, Mrs. Ruth Landeryou of Lethbridge (wife of a Socred M.L.A.).

Although in theory there was provision for deep involvement of the League in election planning (a "strategy committee" made up of Manning, Orvis, and "two or three others"), there is no evidence it was actually operative.

In social composition and organizational structure, the League had far more in common with the C.C.F. and N.D.P. than either the Liberals or the Conservatives. As opposed to both old-line parties, Social Credit had an articulated structure with grass-rooted local units, an ideology to which at least lip-service was paid, and an ongoing series of activities to strengthen the involvement and loyalty of party members.

The League was, through the 1950s and yearly 1960s, a splendid instrument for getting out and delivering the vote. As a system for articulating the needs of the whole population, however, it was running into trouble.

When the militant Social Credit phase of the government dwindled, the League began to devote more attention to the need to improve day-to-day policy in Alberta. At its conventions, in addition to expressions of purely local grievances and ritual declarations of loyalty, the League passed a wide variety of resolutions which provide an interesting profile of its residual populism.

At the 1952 convention there were resolutions advocating higher pensions. controls on high drug prices, lower pension ages, higher family allowances and pensions, a better deal for farmers dealing with oil companies. In 1955 there was a resolution (which was withdrawn) asking the government to enter the auto insurance field, and the convention saw passage of resolutions advocating free drugs for pensioners and the return of twenty dollar "transfer vouchers" for the needy.

Running through many of the Social Credit conventions of the 1950s and early 1960s there was an undercurrent of agrarian radicalism and populism. Sometimes it was suppressed; sometimes not. (A 1955 resolution deplored "an increasing trend in provincial and constituency conventions towards having all convention matters prearranged and regulated from the official level without sufficient expression of opinion from the delegate level." It lost.)

At the 1960 convention, resolutions were brought in (they never reached the discussion floor) asking for a greater provincial role in public housing, for investigation of companies "taking advantage of their shareholders", for a straight-majority vote on fluoridation and for an investigation of the rate structure of Calgary Power Ltd. "with the viewpoint of obtaining a better rate for consumers of electricity in this province."

As a powerful democratic force, however, the League was weakening. For one thing, its advancing age and failure to recruit young blood put it more and more out of touch with a younger population. For another, it was not encouraged to put real, effective pressure on the leadership. Early in its history, government leaders took a leaf from the book of the United Farmers and began appearing at League conventions to "reply" to League resolutions; often their replies indicated only that the League's ideas were impractical or unrepresentative. Several times, Manning told League conventions that the League was only one voice to which the government had to listen. The result was that the 1965 League convention looked like a reunion for survivors of Vimy Ridge (newspaper photographers had a field day).

And so, in 1966, the League began a quiet campaign behind the scenes to try and retire some of its older faces in favour of new blood. And inevitably, one of the victims was Floyd Baker.

Now, Floyd Baker was one of the reasons why Social Credit held power so long in the first place. He typified the kind of hard-working, loyal, devoted if rather unimaginative men on whom the movement depended.

Baker was elected in the original 1935 landslide and retired from the Legislature in 1967, at the age of seventy-two. He was never defeated.

He personified Mr. Small Town Canadian – a non-smoking, teetotaling United Churchman of the old school, a retailer and contractor, a man accustomed to stocking store shelves, weighing nails and shaping metal with his hands.

Floyd's talents did not lay in the direction of eloquence or political theory; they lay in the direction of hard work for his constituents. Here is what he once said:

I take care of my people. I look after 'em. I'm out in the district (Clover Bar, northeast of Edmonton) going to funerals, helping out. If they need me, I'm there. If there's money being collected, I chip in. I've contributed to five district churches. Last year, I organized a work gang to dig a ditch to drain a slough. I arranged to have the government send in men to trap and move some beavers who had dammed up a creek. If a church or community hall needs some eavestropping or a furnace, I put it in for 'em. No charge. I take care of my people.

At his retirement Baker was bald and occasionally absent-minded, but he radiated nervous energy. "If you ever stop moving you're finished," he said. His memory for names and events was as sharp as ever; a colleague recalled that Baker was once helping him in the Socred party newspaper office in 1946 when a stranger came up to Baker and said, "you probably don't remember me . . . " Baker paused just a minute and said, "now just a minute neighbour, let me see . . . it was in 1934 and we were campaigning up at Bonnyville. Our car got stuck up to the axles and we stopped at your farm." He remembered the man's name perfectly.

The campaign to modernize the League was not entirely successful in the Manning Era. In the nominations for the 1967 election the head office of the League launched a determined drive to nominate new candidates and in several ridings there were vicious battles between Orvis Kennedy and his men and local M.L.As who fought for their lives. In one riding, Bow Valley-Empress, the head office pushed Perry Olson, brother of Bud Olson, but he was defeated by a grass-roots candidate, rancher Fred Mandeville. The modernization was frustrated not only by the reluctance of party warhorses to retire, but also by the party's image for fustiness and religiosity. The result was that, in the last years of the Manning Era, the League had become, to far too great an extent, a cheering squad for the government.

One consequence was that, by the mid-1960s, Manning had grown frustrated by the lack of new ideas and personalities coming out of the League and had reached into new realms for people and ideas. In addition to picking up suggestions from senior civil servants, Manning frequently stepped outside of the civil service and political circles altogether. He reached into the University of Alberta for young Erick Schmidt, and Schmidt and Preston Manning maintained a more intimate association with Manning in the planning of new directions than most of Manning's own cabinet ministers. Yet not until after Manning's retirement did Schmidt even take out a membership card in the League. Manning's other innovation in his search for ideas and people was a modification of the u.s. Presidential Study Commission. In 1963 Manning appointed the Committee on Revenues and Expenditures, a joint study group composed of

M.L.A.'s from both sides of the House, representatives of Chambers of Commerce, labour, School Boards and Hospital Boards and civil servants. Its report on the spending policies of various government departments and the inadequacies of various programs, was carefully read throughout the province, and some of it was acted on.

The one thing that Manning did *not* do to buttress his power in Alberta was to resort to broad-guage gerrymandering.

Gerrymandering and over-representation of rural voters have been commonly used to sustain aging governments in Canada and the United States for as long as memories go back. The consequence has generally been corruption, local government inefficiency, and political cynicism on a wide scale.

But even prior to the 1970 redistribution, which brought Alberta constituencies into a fair approximation of the urban-rural distribution of population, Manning's power did not depend significantly on the urban-rural imbalance that did exist. Edmonton and Calgary had more than fifty per cent of the province's population but only thirty per cent of the seats in the legislature. Some rural areas were greatly over-represented, especially in the extreme north-west and south-east. At the same time, Social Credit generally won about fifty per cent of the vote in Edmonton and Calgary (versus 58.9 per cent in rural areas in 1963). A study by a young University of Alberta political scientist found:

> A general redistribution would not enhance the positions of the Opposition parties in the urban centres presently. Granted that the position of the Liberal Party was improved [in an imaginary re-drawing of constituencies to abide by absolute representation by population] in a few Edmonton ridings and the same would probably happen in Calgary for both the Liberals and Conservatives, a definite change in the voting behavior of the electorate would be necessary to elect candidates from these parties.*

What *did* happen as the result of the urban-rural imbalance is that Social Credit drifted out of touch with the society that had spawned it. Because too many Social Crediters, in the party and, often, on the backbenches of the government, had their minds and thoughts "back home", the government began to lose touch with many of the things that were happening in a rapidly urbanizing province. One example was the housing crisis faced by young families: although cabinet minister Fred Colborne was eventually able to swing the government toward change, there was a painful lag in the government's response

* Orest M. Kruhlak, *The Politics of Redistribution: Alberta,* March 24, 1966.

to the unique needs of young families in city apartments, faced with meagre prospects of ever being able to afford their own home.

5. *Scandal-Avoidance.*

A major factor in Manning's success through this whole period was that his government was never tarnished with a significant scandal. In 1955 two Social Credit M.L.A.'s, Jack Landeryou and Roy Lee, were found to have purchased a building which was rented to the provincial government. Both men resigned from the House but were subsequently re-elected by their constituents. Despite the tremendous temptations that must have been presented to various ministers in the heyday of the oil boom, not a single major scandal or story of wrongdoing was unearthed. In 1967 and 1968 a fledgling N.D.P. member of the legislature, Garth Turcott, levelled charges that two Manning cabinet ministers, E.W. Hinman and Alf Hooke, had wrongly used their influence and knowledge for personal gain. A judicial inquiry was held into the charges and the two ministers were exonerated, although chided for lack of discretion in some of their business dealings.

What this meant, through the 1950s and most of the 1960s, was that the Opposition parties were generally deprived of any raw material with which to fashion a weapon against the government. Manning accommodated the government to changing times and conditions, responded to a wide variety of social needs, and ran a "clean ship".

6. *The Winds of Change.*

It would have been extraordinary if this success story had gone on forever, and so, like all success stories, it began to come apart. The homogeneity of the province was starting to disappear. A whole generation of newcomers – young people and immigrants – presented Social Credit with an increasingly impassive and unresponsive audience. These strange faces were not angry with Social Credit, simply somewhat bored by it. Many of them resented Manning's strong, almost aristocratic leadership and the Social Credit movement's old-fashioned style. They felt no sense of identification with the government.

The climax of this process was the 1967 general election. Social Credit opened the election with a new slogan, "horizons unlimited," and a new accomplishment, the Alberta Resources Railway.

But it became obvious the old magic was not working as it once had. Building from almost nothing, the young leader of the Progressive Conservatives, Peter Lougheed of Calgary, managed to field a slate of impressive new candidates, and to launch attacks on Social Credit as a "tired" party that was smug and complacent. The highlight of the campaign came when Manning accepted a challenge to appear at a public forum in Edmonton's Macdougall United Church along with the other party leaders. The young Tory leader cut an impressive image at the forum, which was televised. He did not defeat Manning, but he gave a good account of himself; the newsworthiness of the event lay in the fact, not that he had won, but that he had survived.

On election day, June 6, the Tories almost doubled their popular vote, from fourteen percent in 1963 to twenty-seven per cent, thus becoming the leading opposition party and a serious challenger to a government that had not had a serious challenger for years. The Tories elected a corporal's guard of six M.L.A.S.

The long coma of the multi-party system was drawing to a close. Alberta politics was beginning to look different. Not long afterward, Manning decided that it was soon time to retire. All that remained was the last, desperate battle to save Social Credit from its enemies – and from itself.

Part Three
Fall

CHAPTER TEN

Succession

In the 1940s Manning had to labour long to establish his supremacy. By the 1950s and 1960s it had become a tradition. Many Albertans could not conceive of anyone else being premier. In February 1967, a prominent Alberta political scientist (and Liberal) said to his friends: "This government will stay in power for the next ten to twenty years."

A consummate realist, Manning knew better. With each election, the voices that spoke wistfully of change were speaking a little louder. The 1967 campaign had been a distinct warning· for a significant part of the public, Lougheed was becoming a credible alternative. Lougheed had served notice that he would head up a probing, active and imaginative opposition, something Social Credit had not faced since the halcyon days of J. Harper Prowse in the mid-fifties.

Political realignment had never gotten off the ground. At the beginning, the campaign had attracted some media attention but it had never reached critical mass; in the end it was viewed by senior and influential Conservatives at the national level as an interesting curiosity. Manning wanted to make the party system more ideologically rational, but few others seemed interested; there were, perhaps, too many "socialists" among the Liberals and Conservatives, and too many "opportunists" among the New Democrats.

Finally, Manning's restless intellect had grown weary with twenty-five years of government routine. It is possible to become bored with being even a premier. The vital excitement which Manning felt in politics as a young man (especially in the days when Social Credit had seen itself more as moral crusade than an incumbent government) had been replaced with the monotony of endless rubber chicken banquets, federal-provincial fiscal conferences, cabinet sessions and sittings of the legislature on frosty February nights.

It was time for new leadership. It was time to step down.

He left behind, by any fair measure, an unequalled record in Canadian politics. He had spent virtually his entire adult life in public office. He had presided over the creation of an excellent network of physical and social services for the people. As a government leader he stood alone; it was a common gibe to say that God had put the oil and gas in the ground, not Social Credit, yet it was true that his government had spent the oil and gas revenues in a way that had brought great benefits to the people. Not only had it been well spent – little if any had found its way into the wrong pockets. The great explosion of wealth brought on by Leduc had presented enormous opportunities for graft and corruption, and yet, despite this, Manning had run a clean ship, free of scandals. Can one imagine what the oil and gas might well have led to, had they been discovered in Newfoundland or Quebec? He had been, in the words of the Bible, a good Steward of all that God had provided.

His legacy as a politician was more ambiguous. As a politician, Manning resembled no one more than Williams Ewart Gladstone, the stern and upright defender of British Liberalism in the nineteenth century. Like Gladstone, Manning was a politician profoundly concerned – some would say obsessed – with questions of morality in politics, or, as Manning usually put it, Fundamental Principle. Both men were profoundly religious: Manning devoted his spare time to the Back to the Bible Hour, Gladstone to walking the streets of London slums trying to convert streetwalkers. (He helped to found the Church Penitentiary Association for the Reclamation of Fallen Women.) One student of Gladstone wrote:

> For Gladstone, every important political issue was a contest between good and evil; and if he could not discover good on one side and evil on the other, he failed to discover importance and was not interested. Sometimes his hearers could not fail to find it thrillingly appropriate. At other times the note seemed forced, and the speaker pharisaical; he might even seem insincere, but those who knew him, even though they might have been political opponents, knew that this was no case on insincerity. To Disraeli on the other hand, even when he was most convinced of the importance of the task he was undertaking, his opponents appeared as no more than perverse and wrong headed. Political questions were to him, as he often said, matters of opinion and not of right and wrong. . . .

Disraeli was inclined to err on the Machiavellian side, Gladstone on the other; for it is an error to discover moral issues where none are in fact at stake, though a lesser error than to be blind to them when moral issues really arise.*

Both Gladstone and Manning were held in awe by the public of their time (though Gladstone's adulation was punctuated by periods of intense unpopularity on account of his foreign policies). Both stood apart from their colleagues and had no cronies.

The effect of Manning's long dominion over the government and the party had not been salutary however. He had never cultivated a successor, and there was no one obvious candidate when he retired. There were philosophical cracks within the government, which his immense influence and prestige had been able to paper-over; but with his departure they were certain to open again. He had driven the human resources development program through with his sheer prestige, but several important cabinet figures remained unconvinced of its wisdom, if not actively opposed to it. He did not enjoy the cut and thrust of political debate, and he did not encourage the refinement of this trait in his followers; but the province was entering a more political era. There was going to be a need for fresh, even idiosyncratic, thinking if Social Credit were to let in some fresh air. But he had never actively encouraged this. There was deadwood in the government, which he had allowed to accumulate. Beneath the shiny record of achievement the party was showing its age. Could it respond to the need for rapid change?

The regime which he was about to hand over, in short, was superficially solid but there were some real questions about its ability to adapt to the new politics of the 1960s.

There was a very long time in Alberta when people appreciated the strong personal leadership that Manning offered. By the mid-1960s, however, even though he still aroused great respect, more and more political independents were asking whether the time had not come for a more consultative and participatory style of government. It was the era of participatory democracy, supposedly (Trudeau was to endorse it); and from the cities, from the young, from the business groups, from the universities and their environs, came a growing hunger for a new role in provincial affairs.

The urban middle class had been slow to accept Social Credit in the 1930s, but in those days the urban middle class was small; by the mid-1960s it had been swelled enormously by industrialization and

* D.C. Somervell, *Disraeli & Gladstone* (Garden City: Garden City Publishing Co., 1928), pp. 65-6.

the migration to the cities brought on by farm consolidation and the steady squeeze on uneconomic small towns; and now it was beginning to demand political change.

It isn't clear when Manning decided to retire because the decision was a well kept secret for some time. During the session in the winter of 1968, however, Manning spoke about his retirement to four trusted colleagues – Anders Aalborg, Russ Patrick and Harry Strom, all in the cabinet, and Randy McKinnon, who had been appointed head of the Alberta Advisory Council after his defeat in 1967. When Manning suggested they should begin thinking about the succession, they turned to Aalborg. But Aalborg, who later told friends he wanted the job badly, was not free to take up the option. Several years earlier he had suffered the harrowing experience of a serious heart attack; he feared a recurrence. They turned, at one point, to Strom – but he laughed as he shook his head.

A few weeks later, Preston Manning began to discuss the problem quietly with some of his friends. The group included Erick Schmidt, the sociology graduate student who had worked with Preston on *The White Paper* and *Political Realignment;* Owen Anderson, a graduate student in political science who knew Preston from when they were both members of the Young Socreds at the University of Alberta; and Erick's friend Don Hamilton, a businessman whom Erick had recruited as first director of the Alberta Service Corps.

Schmidt, Anderson and Hamilton felt that the slender younger Manning should contest the leadership, and there was a good deal of weight to this view. The party was going to need a strong and imaginative leader, and Preston, his wordly inexperience notwithstanding, had many of the right attributes. Fair and slight, like his father, on the platform he was transformed into an even better speaker than his father – he had the Manning voice and technique of marshalling his arguments, but more forcefulness. More important, he was young (twenty-three at the time) and a prolific generator of ideas. A brilliant student in high school, he was slightly less conservative than his father ideologically, and brought to his study of politics a real gift for synthesizing ideas and searching out new interfaces between intellectual disciplines. In addition to a conventional honors degree in economics, he had had exposure to more exotic training: he had studied the better part of a year at the giant aerospace engineering firm of TRW Ltd. in Redondo Beach, California, producing a thick study on the applicability of general systems theory to socio-economic development models, and he had a host of ideas on how modern systems analysis and management theory could be applied to overhaul politics and government.

170

The group went to see the premier with their proposition. He heard them out quietly and said there were indeed several good reasons why Preston should run, but there were more good reasons why he should not. The dynasty issue would be raised. Preston was very young and inexperienced in practical politics; he would have difficulty controlling a cabinet of much older and more experienced men. It would be whispered that he was not fully his own man. No, the idea was "unsound".

Preston's friends were disappointed, but pressed on: who, then, did Manning think was qualified to lead the government? It was during this discussion that the name of Harry Strom was put forward. Manning said that he had known Harry for some time and that he had much to offer. He was experienced in the legislature; he had no enemies; he had dealt fairly and creditably with the cities as Minister of Municipal Affairs and with the farmers as Minister of Agriculture; he was a supporter of the human resources development program. He would give Harry his private endorsation, he said, but he would not do so publicly nor would he play any role in the campaign.

Schmidt and Preston knew Harry slightly from working in and around the government; Owen Anderson knew him a little (Owen was born and raised in Medicine Hat, just down the road from Harry's farm at Burdet); Don Hamilton did not know him. In point of fact, Harry Edwin Strom was not generally well known in most of Alberta, certainly not in the cities. During the 1950s and 1960s when picking a possible successor to Manning was a favourite parlour game in Alberta, his name had never been mentioned; instead, the favourite choices of onlookers had always been Russ Patrick, Gordon Taylor, sometimes Aalborg or Reierson. But Strom? A dark horse at best.

The basic facts on Harry were mildly interesting: fifty-two years of age; tall (6′ 3″) and rangy; born and raised on a family farm at Burdet (one of eleven children) but spent part of his childhood in Calgary with a brief stop at the old Calgary Institute of Technology (where he studied automotives); six children; good family man; member of the Evangelical Free Church, but not pushy about it; quiet, friendly, honest, homespun. In his early years he had held a Social Credit party card off and on from 1935, but had never been active in the party through the Depression or the war, even to the extent of attending a convention or working in an election; in 1952 he was narrowly defeated in his first try for a nomination in the riding of Cypress. Active in local affairs as a school board member, councillor, and participant on local committees on rural electrification, telephones and cattle, he gained the nomination for the 1955 election and was elected to the House. He received his first cabinet appointment, under Manning, in 1962.

In practical political terms, he had been around Social Credit long enough to be acceptable to the old-timers without having been around long enough to be thought of as an old-timer himself. He was a compromise candidate, the kind of man likely to be acceptable to many factions.

For Preston Manning's group of young reformers the question was: was Harry with them in terms of commitment to thoroughgoing root-and-branch reform of the government and the party? To find out, they met with him a number of evenings in the basement rumpus room of his house and probed his conception of government, his objectives and values; and they told him what they had in mind. He seemed to them a genuinely likeable, open man, receptive to suggestions and not opposed to change.

He was an excellent listener, a man with whom they felt they could work in harness. On the other hand, he was not anxious to contest the leadership. He said it would be very hard to fill Manning's shoes. He said, with obvious sincerity, that he was not politically ambitious, and that he feared the strains on his family.

The young turks weighed Harry against the alternatives, and he came up strong. Anders Aalborg (even if he could be persuaded to run despite his heart): sober, careful, respected across the province by the older generation but would have difficulty appealing to youth or city-dwellers. Rather unimaginative. Gordon Taylor: well known and respected everywhere in Alberta as a superbly dedicated and honest Minister of Highways, but lacking experience in other portfolios. A reformer by bent, yes, and a forceful personality, but a notorious loner. Would he work in a group setting and be receptive to proposals for change from others? Doubtful. Ray Reierson, Minister of Education, also Telephones: energetic, respectable performance in several portfolios, unquestionably intelligent, but volatile, strong-headed and hot-tempered. Able, but difficult to work with. And so they went, down the list, until they concluded that Manning was right: Strom was the best of the available alternatives. He was a poor speaker, not highly analytical – but he could lead a team.

Strom was the safe choice, Preston the bold but risky choice; Preston and his friends chose to support Strom. With some persuasion, Harry agreed to run. And so a member of the group quietly rented a suite of rooms on the sixteenth floor of Edmonton's Holiday Inn and the Strom Team Headquarters, as it was called, was filled with wall-size organization charts, stacks of leaflets, clicking Gestetners, ringing telephones and harried secretaries.

None of Harry's "brain trust" had ever organized a leadership contest before, but then again neither had any of their potential opponents; in fact, in its whole history, Social Credit had never before had a leadership convention per se. They were gifted amateurs, drawing from what they knew of the party, from John F. Kennedy's convention campaign of 1959-60, from the political science texts.

An elaborate organization chart was drafted as follows:

Candidate – H. Strom & Committee

Campaign Director: Bob Clark

Assoc. Director	General Manager	Associate Director
(Norm Crystal)	(Don Hamilton)	(Ron Southern)

Policy	Communications publications	Special groups	Organization	Planning Scheduling	Special Events
(Schmidt)	(Anderson)				

speech – Media – Photographer

brochures
biography
literature

Many of the boxes were left blank, unassigned; they were to be filled in later. What the brain trust lacked in experience, it made up for in sweat: they frequently worked long into the night, long before the candidacies had been declared. Bob Clark, Manning's Minister of Youth, acted as liaison with the Manning cabinet, cultivating the support of party and government elders, backbench M.L.A.s and local party officials. Don Hamilton ran the office full time pulling together the efforts of the volunteers and office staff in conformity with a critical path developed by Preston. Erick Schmidt wrote some of Harry's campaign literature and supervised production of the posters; Owen Anderson wrote Harry's major policy speeches and position papers. A bright, self-effacing Edmonton chartered accountant and land developer, Gordon Rasmussen, was recruited to raise money for the campaign.

The general consensus in the Strom organization was that the serious challenge would come from Gordon Taylor and Ray Reierson, Taylor especially, Aalborg having declared himself out of the running. Aalborg was cultivated; he indicated he would come out in support of Strom. Taylor and Reierson, no matter how many other candidates might enter the race, were certain to be the class of the opposition.

It was decided, from the outset, to be open about the objectives of the Strom Team: Strom would be portrayed (and indeed his young aides saw him in this way, and he did not object) as a man who would responsibly modernize the party and get the government back in touch with alienated voters in the cities, in the middle class, and among youth. But it was to be a soft sell: most convention delegates were likely to be middle-aged and elderly people who had supported "Mr. Manning" for many years; they would have to be brought along gently. Thus, the key-note brochure of the campaign, which was sent to all members of the party, began in its answer to the title question, "Why Strom?" on a reassuring note:

> The Honorable Harry Strom is unquestionably loyal to the principles and traditions of the Social Credit movement. He was one of the few cabinet ministers to campaign actively for the few Social Credit candidates in the last federal election. Harry Strom has firmly stated his convictions that the principles upon which our movement was founded must be preserved and communicated to others.

Only after this was the note of change introduced:

> At the same time Mr. Strom realizes that to preserve principles, they must be continually reinterpreted to meet new conditions, and communicated to new people (not simply repeated over and over again to those who already accept them). All members of the Strom Team are Social Crediters and every piece of literature and advertising used by the Strom Team has been prepared by persons who hold a Social Credit membership. [This may have been, in addition to a reassurance of safety, a sly dig at Reierson, whose campaign was directed by a professional advertising agency.] In addition to young men and women, the Strom Team also includes many well-known party veterans.

To symbolize this dual concern with reform plus tradition a slogan was formulated: "A new era on a strong foundation." This tied in nicely with Manning's statement in the White Paper that the building of the basic economic structure in Alberta was now completed, and it was time to turn to the building of a new social structure.

The "team" nature of the Strom candidacy was a strong element:

> If elected leader and Premier, he will make specific efforts to build a team of Cabinet Ministers, MLA's, party members, special consultants and advisors whose collective efforts will continue to give Albertans the kind of leadership they have grown to expect from a Social Credit administration. . . . Harry Strom doesn't talk too much, or try to do everything himself. He prefers to listen carefully, raise pertinent questions, and then make sound decisions . . . he is not afraid to delegate responsibility.

On his religious beliefs:

> Harry Strom is an active Christian layman who believes that Christian principles are relevant and applicable to politics and public affairs. He has held executive and teaching positions within the Evangelical Free Church and has long participated in the work of other Christian organizations and service groups. His personal faith will not be expressed in terms of inflexible positions on such matters as Sunday movies, Sunday hunting or liquor regulations (he believes that these matters must be decided by plebiscites in accordance with the will of the majority). Rather, his faith is exhibited in the honesty and integrity he brings to public office, the genuine concern and compassion he shows toward all people and the stability he maintains in times of stress. . . .

Only on the last page did the pamphlet speak specifically of reform:

> The new leader and Premier must not only be firmly committed to the party's principles and traditions, he must also be open minded and forward looking to insure that the party and the government remain up-to-date and in tune with the aspirations of the people. Harry Strom possesses both of these characteristics. He is completely open to new ideas and suggestions. He is not afraid to make changes . . . this is what makes his candidacy so attractive to young people . . . he does not propose to lead a government simply designed to preserve the status quo. . . .

On September 27th Manning officially ended weeks of public speculation about his retirement by announcing it to caucus and then to the media. On October 8 Ray Reierson announced his candidacy, and the next day – he had not wanted to be first candidate officially into the race – Harry jumped on a Twin Beechcraft with his advisers and for two days hopped from north to south, announcing his candidacy in Lethbridge, Medicine Hat, Calgary, Red Deer, and Grande

Prairie. In each centre he struck a note of moderate reform saying that his "ultimate objective" was "the social development of Alberta". He defined this as "the creation of conditions, and the reform of existing institutions with the objective of building a province where all our citizens may develop socially, economically and politically and do so to their fullest extent . . . so that we may become a truly free and creative people." He signified his intention to spell out his policies and objectives more fully as the campaign progressed.

On October 11th Edgar Gerhart, then a promising backbencher, joined the race. Son of an able, tough Municipal Affairs minister under Manning in the 1940s and 1950s, Gerhart was one of the only two lawyers sitting on the government side, and articulate and pragmatic politician whose reputation for tough realism was belied somewhat by his portly appearance. Gerhart always spoke his mind: he could be expected to add a note of frankness to the campaign.

The same day, Gerhart was joined by an unexpected candidate, Dr. Walter Buck. In his mid-thirties, Buck was the youngest candidate, and a complete unknown; a dentist and businessman in nearby Fort Saskatchewan, he had sat on the government backbenches since 1963 without making much of an impression. No one in the press gallery of the legislature could remember a single thing he had ever said. His press conference at the Chateau Lacombe therefore came as a surprise to the major candidates.

Finally, on October 12th, Gordon Taylor entered the contest, rounding out the slate.

From the beginning of the race it was Strom versus the Others. Strom had a solid organization, with different lieutenants assigned to speechwriting, research, finance, cultivation of the M.L.A.s, and cultivation of the convention delegates. Gordon Taylor had little organization. Ray Reierson relied upon the efforts of an advertising firm. Gerhart admitted that his organization was "mostly heart" and no one could figure who was backing Walter Buck.

The same pattern prevailed in policy. The Strom campaign produced a steady stream of policy proposals, position papers and backgrounding documents; the other candidates made statements on policy sporadically if at all. Gordon Taylor opened his campaign with a blast at able-bodied "welfare bums" who exploit the government and take bread out of the mouths of the truly needy; these "malingerers" should be thrown off the welfare rolls, he insisted. Strom came back with a thoughtful analysis of how many malingerers there really were, based on the figures of the Department of Public Welfare.

Quoting chapter and verse, Harry said that only 10.9 per cent of those receiving welfare in Alberta were even potentially employable (the rest were mothers with dependent children, the aged, and the physically or mentally handicapped). To turf out the unemployed employables would not only fail to make them regular members of the labour force (most had severe attitudinal or training problems that stood in the way of steady work, it would also unjustly punish their families. A better course, he argued, would be to identify these people and then give them a personalized program of training and counselling to fit them for work – with a follow-up relationship between government and co-operating employers, to assure integration into the world of work. This was a humane and progressive proposal, which preceded by some time the Nixon Administration's much-heralded "family assistance" program developed by Daniel Moynihan.

The young advisers to Strom felt deeply about this issue: for years, the favourite sport of the right wing in Social Credit had been taking cheap shots at people on welfare. To this wing of the party, Strom had thrown down the gauntlet. In the minds of the Strom group, no better issue could be found on which to separate the traditionalists from the reformers in Social Credit.

The policy input of the Reierson, Gerhart and Buck campaigns was negligible. Reierson talked about the need to scrutinize government spending more closely and maximize educational opportunity; Gerhart's only platform was that Social Credit had to become more open to change, and "get expenditures under control".

And so the campaign wound on through October and November. For the candidates themselves, it was a part-time campaign: Strom, Taylor, Reierson and Gerhart had cabinet portfolios to take care of. Their workers could work full time; the candidates themselves could travel and speak only sporadically. Around the province, the Social Credit party organization sponsored a series of local meetings to enable convention delegates and just plain party members to meet the contenders. For those who hoped to see, at these meetings, evidence that the succession contest was drawing new people into the party, the evidence was disappointing.

At a meeting in Calgary, at the Palliser Hotel, the room was full of elders. Two bald men in their sixties or seventies stood against the wall sipping the grapefruit punch and discussing long-distance running at the University of Manitoba in 1924. At a later meeting in the Calgary Public Library, two modish young people, a married couple, stood out in a room of older people like communists at a prayer meeting.

As Minister of Highways, Gordon Taylor was able to get around the province a good deal on ribbon-cuttings and bridge-openings. Brisk, erect, quick-tongued and never a man to forget the underdog, Taylor got his share of publicity. At a bridge opening at Ponoka, he spoke at a municipal luncheon and was presented with the inevitable white stetson. He joked about his bachelorhood: "I've been looking for the right girl for years now but I've never found her. Maybe it was because I didn't have the right hat. You may have changed my life."

As the campaign moved through October the interesting question for the Strom group was the growing speculation surrounding a possible Alf Hooke candidacy. In many ways the most interesting alternative to Strom, Hooke was the oldest (sixty-three) of the possible candidates and, apart from Manning, the only survivor from 1935. A white-haired bantam rooster of a man, Hooke cut a brave but desperate figure. Over the years, like many of the Douglasites, he had drifted steadily to the right. He still believed, deeply believed, in monetary reform, but monetary reform had died as an issue in Social Credit. He was left with a deep-seated and doctrinaire "free enterprise" position. His preoccupation was fighting the growth of "the welfare state". He was not just opposed to the growth of government spending and taxation – that would have been explicable enough; he was even opposed to the human resources development program, which contained a strategy for reducing government inefficiency.

Hooke was a professional politician, and a good one. He knew and understood the people of his beloved riding of Rocky Mountain House (where he had been a school principal for many years). But he was a man whom history had begun to pass by.

He wasn't quite sure why he opposed Harry Strom (although Strom's association with Hooke's old enemy, Erick Schmidt, had something to do with it), but he felt that somehow Strom represented a decisive break with the party's past. And so rumours began to drift out of Rocky Mountain House that the old warrior was getting ready to fight a last stand against any dilution of pure Social Credit by the Strom organization. He was getting ready to become a candidate.

Would a Hooke candidacy injure Strom's chances? It seemed to Strom's advisors unlikely that Hooke could draw many votes, but there was a danger that the old stump orator (still the best Social Credit had) might try and alarm older people in the party with horror stories about Strom's dangerous advisers.

On October 29 the local constituencies began meeting to choose delegates to go to the convention, which would be held in Edmonton at the Jubilee Auditorium on December 4th and 5th. The tempo of the campaign began to heat up. In earnest, the candidates began to solicit firm commitments of support from the chosen delegates. Approaches were made to the sitting M.L.A.s to see whether they would attempt to deliver their delegates to a favourite candidate.

On November 8 Strom made a speech in Red Deer at which he unveiled the first of his policy initiatives. He spoke with concern about the deteriorating quality of life in North America's larger cities and the need to commence bold urban planning to prevent urban deterioration in Alberta. To accomplish this he proposed a major commission to study the future of Alberta cities and to develop guidelines for planning the parks, transportation system, recreation, pollution control, education and urban renewal that would be needed to develop healthy and stimulating cities in Alberta. The commission would include representatives from the city administrations and would aim at proposals with some chance of early implementation.

The Strom "idea campaign" had a good deal grass-roots thrust behind it. Strom had a number of citizens' committees around the province, working to develop imaginative policy proposals for consideration by the Strom campaign organization. One such group in Calgary, headed by young Socred lawyer Bill Downton, presented a report on November 5th with no fewer than fifty-three policy recommendations which had come out of meetings with over 300 people in the Calgary area. The recommendations included relaxation of blue laws, reapportionment of seats in the legislature to give the cities a larger voice, relaxation of government secrecy and party discipline in voting, a permanent premier's office in Calgary, cabinet meetings around the province, rotated sittings of the legislature in the various cities, greater use of plebescites on controversial issues, removal of education costs from the property tax, an ombudsman in each city to protect residents from abuse by city administrations, subsidized day care centres, training programs for deserted wives, mental health reform, automatic review of the tenure of deputy ministers each five years, no-fault auto insurance and the creation of an "iconoclast's club" of original, thick-skinned thinkers of all political persuasions to meet with the premier at regular intervals and subject government policy to criticism and suggestions.

Not all of these recommendations were accepted by Strom, yet by the eve of the convention Strom had made thirteen specific major policy proposals including, in addition to welfare reform and the urban life study,

- Reform of government budgeting through adoption of "programmed budgeting" techniques to bring greater efficiency and analysis to government spending and the creation of new programs;

- A stronger role for Alberta in national decision-making and a new voice for the West in national deliberations;

- A "Citizens Committee on the Constitution" to study B.N.A. Act reform and work to develop a broad provincial consensus on the best direction for constitutional change in Canada;

- A "Head Start" program in the schools for disadvantaged children;

- A full-scale study of how best to adapt the Alberta educational system at all levels to the social and economic needs of the people until the year 2000;

- A broader role for the backbencher, a government office in Calgary to make government more accessible to people in the south, and major reform of Indian education in northern Alberta.

Each of these policy positions was unveiled in turn as the campaign went on. There was a purpose in this: Strom wanted to pace himself, he wanted to maintain a steady momentum from the beginning of the campaign to the end, and he wanted to keep before the convention delegates his developing image as the middle of the road reformer who could keep the party united. A study carried out by Owen Anderson's fledgling public opinion survey group in the spring, on behalf of the executive of the party, had asked a representative random sample of 715 party members for their views on the party. One of the questions asked was open-ended: "Name one or two persons whom you think might become Premier should Mr. Manning retire?" In the response, 9.79% had named Taylor, 6.85% Strom, 5.31% Aalborg, 5.17% Preston Manning and 3.64% Reierson; 53% had no opinion.* It was obviously important to develop in the minds of potential delegates a much clearer perception of who Harry Strom was and what he stood for. It was obvious from the poll that *no* candidate commanded any decisive spontaneous upwelling of grass-roots support.

Between September and the convention the Strom campaign suc-

* Among the "others" which members suggested for leader, Peter Lougheed received 1.82% of the response, which was more than several Socred Cabinet Ministers, and more than twenty-two other Socred M.L.A.s also named. The absolute numbers are less impressive, of course; on a sample of 725 people, 1.82% is thirteen people.

ceeded in its main objective, which was to identify Strom as a reformer and a strong contender – if not the strongest contender. This was not to imply that his opponents were reactionaries. Gordon Taylor, a populist to his fingertips, was always respected as a man unafraid of strong new measures to equalize opportunities. Ray Reierson, a tall, slightly stooped figure with flowing hair and a rather evangelical speaking style, was not a man to play the free enterprise ritual either; when it was proposed, before the convention, that Alberta Government Telephones should be sold to private enterprise in order to satisfy the principle of free enterprise, Reierson jumped in angrily. A.G.T. was already owned by all the people and served all the people well, he said. How then would the people gain by the sale of such a valuable property?

By the eve of the convention, Strom had accumulated a formidable list of backers. Aalborg, the senior statesman, backed him. So did Youth Minister Bob Clark, young Minister without Portfolio Ray Speaker, Agriculture Minister Henry Ruste and Northern Affairs Minister Al Fimrite. Several backbench M.L.A.s had publicly given their support; several more had pledged to make their support public at the convention. Technically, the speeches, posters and literature of Strom campaign had been the most professional. The presence of Preston Manning in the Strom group had been duly noted by the party grapevine. On the basis of all this early evidence, Strom was the front-runner.

And yet, as the delegates began to arrive to register at the Jubilee Auditorium on Friday afternoon, December 4th, there was a growing electricity in the air. Outside, the weather was frosty and still; little snow had fallen and a giant red and white Ray Reierson billboard had been parked on the front lawn, right next to the main entrance. Inside, technicians strung cables across the plush carpets of the lobby and stationed television cameras at critical points. Representatives of the candidates buttonholed delegates, passing out buttons and hats and banners. On the stage of the auditorium itself, two giant portraits of Manning stared balefully down at the empty seats. A huge electronic tote-board, borrowed from the Edmonton racetrack, of all places, had been erected to tally the votes of the candidates.

The convention delegates, their faces a tableau of middle Alberta, wandered through these proceedings with a mixture of awe and excitement: this was their first leadership contest ever, their first exposure to the hoopla and rah-rah that had long characterized the other parties, but never, until now, Social Credit.

Incredibly, in the centre of the rotunda, a thumping hard-rock band was belting it out, led by a huge, twitching black female singer – all courtesy of Edgar Gerhart. This bizarre cultural confrontation gathered a crowd of incredulous Social Credit onlookers – small-town hardware merchants with steel-rimmed glasses, schoolmarms from Rocky Mountain House, wind-burned farmers from Mundare. In culture shock, they walked slowly around the bandstand, like a group of villagers inspecting a landed U.F.O. Inside the auditorium, barely heard over the electric guitars, a German oompah band was trying to get a snake-dance going.

Behind closed doors – in the basement of the auditorium, and across town, in the larger hotels – the first meetings between candidates and their workers, and candidates and candidates, began to discuss, in hushed tones, who might throw their support to whom. As these meetings took place, Party Secretary Orvis Kennedy had a meeting of another kind with officials of the Young Socreds. There had been a plan afoot to introduce at the separate Young Socreds' convention a resolution to advocate legalization of marijuana. Fearful that it might attract the "wrong kind of attention," Kennedy persuaded the Young Socreds to withdraw it. And so Day One, the day of registration, ended.

Day Two, voting day, began with more serious jousting among the candidates. The delegates were assigned to separate groups which met in different parts of the auditorium. Each candidate was to appear in turn before each group, outline his objectives and philosophy briefly and then answer questions. Harry Strom strode from group to group, a tall, smiling figure, seemingly relaxed and confident. Gordon Taylor's supporters began to pass out the yellow plastic hard-hats that were to become their trademark at the convention and greeted their candidate enthusiastically. Strom had said publicly that only eleven per cent of those on welfare were employable; taking up the issue afresh, Taylor told the various groups that even one employable person receiving welfare is one too many. Alfie Hooke had been nominated as a candidate at the last minute by Paul Jenson, pink-cheeked farmer and academic from Hooke's riding: "if you can't beat him, join him," concluded Jenson with a grin. Alfie went from group to group to drum up some enthusiasm for monetary reform. Taking his glasses off and putting them back on for oratorical emphasis, Hooke flailed the air and desperately tried to rekindle the old fires, the old Depression memories. But it wasn't working. Alfie was still a fine orator, but the delegates weren't listening. He might as well have been speaking to them from the inside of a soundproof plexiglass box.

When the meetings with the candidates finished, the delegates went to a large meeting room in the basement for their traditional "buzz group" to discuss organizational matters. In keeping with tradition, the meeting was closed to the press and other outsiders. That finished, the delegates drifted away to dinner, admonished to return at 6:30 p.m. to begin the balloting.

As the voting began, Manning sat impassively with his wife, in the front row, his face betraying not the slightest emotion. The ballots were passed out to the delegates spread across the main floor and the two balconies overlooking the large stage, where, under the tote board, a long line of Social Credit ladies, dressed in green Alberta Tartan plaid blazers, waited to count the votes. It took about an hour for the ballots to be distributed, marked, and passed back to the stage for tabulation. As each new sub-total appeared on the tote board, accompanied by a roar from the supporters of each candidate, it became apparent Strom was indeed the front runner, but that he would not generate enough votes to gain the necessary majority on the first ballot. The total:

Strom	814
Taylor	282
Reierson	255
Buck	184
Gerhart	137.

The only surprise was the runners-up: Buck's appeal to the noncommitted delegates had been underestimated by most insiders, and Gerhart's over-estimated. A shaken Gerhart stepped before the television cameras to say that he had been "shot between the eyes . . . but I'm going to take my medicine like a man." He would not throw his group's support to any other candidate, he said; but as the second ballot began he put on a Strom button. (The previous night he had met with Reierson, who was trying to organize a "stop Strom" campaign, but the meeting ended without commitments.)

The pressure swung to the unfamiliar newcomer, Buck: Strom was far ahead, but not too far to be caught if the right amalgam of votes could be mixed; crucial to the mixture would be the 184 votes Buck had collected on the first ballot. Would Buck drop out and throw his support to Taylor or Reierson? Buck stalked from the auditorium with his lieutenants, and huddled. Then he came back in and announced, "no commitments. I'm staying in." The odds against an effective coalition lengthened. Reierson leapt up, put on a Taylor hard hat, and strode onto the stage to go the microphone and announce his withdrawal and his support for Taylor. But Orvis

Kennedy, who was convention chairman, stepped between Reierson and the podium. Right before the 3,000-odd delegates, and the astonished television viewers, the two engaged in a muffled shouting match, Orvis contending that that the rules did not permit a candidate to throw his support to another. Finally, Kennedy relented and Reierson announced his decision, angrily shouting, "I never thought I would live to see the day when a Social Credit candidate would be denied the right to speak to his own supporters." And so, just after 8:00 p.m., the second ballot began.

As the constituency-by-constituency results flashed on the tote board, it became obvious that the stop-Strom movement had failed. In less than fifteen minutes from the end of the second ballot, Strom was building up a distant lead. The final numbers:

Strom	915
Taylor	606
Buck	147

Bedlam broke out and Strom was mobbed by his supporters. Gordon Taylor rushed to the stage to urge the delegates to make the vote unanimous. The delegates began to drift out of the auditorium, some to the Strom victory party in a suite at the MacDonald Hotel, others to gatherings where they could lick their wounds. Interviewed on television, N.D.P. leader Grant Notley told newspapermen the Strom victory would have "disastrous consequences" for the Conservatives by "modernizing" the Social Credit image and leaving the Conservatives with nothing but a "me too" position. After midnight, Harry Strom went to bed with a deep sense of aloneness and an almost crushing sense of the responsibility that awaited him. And Social Crediters headed home to their constituencies with the unfamiliar but exhilarating feeling that they had participated in the beginning of the rebirth of their movement.

CHAPTER ELEVEN
Reluctant Messiah

"The objectives of [President Eisenhower]? They are hard to name. What are the objectives of the housewife next door? To get on with her workaday chores, to continue to exercise a certain influence and control over the household, to like, and be liked, to contribute to the general tranquillity – and, always, to live yet another day."
> – William F. Buckley Jr., *Up From Liberalism*

"There is nothing more difficult to take in hand, more perilous to conduct, or more uncertain in its success, than to take the lead in the introduction of a new order of things."
> – Machiavelli

Nothing in Social Credit's past equipped it for the prosperity that accompanied the discovery of oil at leduc in 1947, yet Ernest Manning – in many ways an unlikely man for the task – had met that challenge and built a dynasty on his success.

Nothing in Social Credit's past equipped it, either, for the new political demands of the late 1960s. How does an old organization, deeply set in its ways, go about becoming young again? How does one reverse hardening of the arteries in an organization? In utter fairness to Harry Strom he had bitten off one of the most difficult assignments in politics.

As Harry Strom drove to the office his first day in power, he was inheriting a government that had built, and built well – an excellent system of social services unrivalled in the land, from schools, colleges, institutes of technology and three universities to voluntary medicare, the Treasury Branches, social assistance. Of the Alberta health care system, the Toronto *Globe and Mail* was to write:

> The Ontario health care system is excessively confused, uncoordinated, complicated and wasteful . . . for patients, doctors, paramedical workers and hospital workers . . . the Alberta system, by contrast, is businesslike, designed to provide the most service with the fewest civil servants . . . it is simple, and simply explained . . . it is uniform for the poor and the middle and the rich. The people like it: I have never observed a public program more wholeheartedly supported.*

* "The Alberta care plan: Lesson for Ontario", *Globe & Mail,* March 4, 1971.

Social Credit had built an excellent highways system, a strong welfare program, an excellent, expanding educational system. It had innovated many new social programs, including promising new approaches to opportunity for native people. And it had done all this while managing the public's money honestly and thriftily on the whole. In all governments, certain departments are prone to graft because they are dispensers of major contracts and other favours – departments like highways, and public works. But under Social Credit, even these two departments were unsullied by scandal.

So Harry Strom took over a strong, clean government. That was a definite plus for a new premier. And there were two more pluses as well.

To begin with, he was now premier, and the premier's office holds tremendous potential for defining new issues, appointing new personnel and creating new images of leadership. A new premier can bring a whole new cast and style to a government. Strom had no illusions about the difficulty of the task before him; at the same time, he was taking charge of an office which has implicit in it great potential for setting into motion major change and reform. Tradition holds that a new leader is given a period of grace in which to make his imprint on the administration. That precious time of grace was now open to him.

Finally, and this was important, Strom had the asset of his supporters – people in the party who were ready for change and expecting it, able backbench politicians ready for a challenge in cabinet, young advisers with a host of ideas and proposals, and a provincial media that was at least open to be persuaded that the government was being modernized.

These were the factors that favoured basic change and modernization in Social Credit. What about the factors that would make change more difficult?

First there was the condition of the Social Credit party. In the long years of the Manning Era it had become badly rusted. The government had come to treat it not as its major link with the people, and not as a serious contributor of new ideas for policy and practice, but as a kind of aging cheering-squad to be trotted out at election time. The government did not take the party very seriously; there was some doubt whether the party took itself seriously. Most important, perhaps, was the fact that the majority of party members lacked any reforming zeal. In 1935 the party had been a hotbed of hatred against injustice. Party members felt an almost religious determination to build a more just society. By the late 1960s, all that was left of this was the party's peculiarly religious style, which by this time had become a comforting ritual more than a driving force.

Second, there was the condition of the government itself. It had been a solid government, an honest government, at times an imaginative and highly progressive government. But it was also a government which, over thirty-four years of power, had developed its own ingrained habits, procedures and leading personalities – all of them resistant to basic change. Sprinkled throughout the civil service, and indeed among the elected members themselves, were many people who would regard Harry Strom as the new boy on the block who would have to bloody a few noses before he would be taken seriously.

And finally, as in all equations, there was a factor that could be labelled neither positive nor negative, but simply unknown: the leadership qualities of Harry Strom himself. Would Harry Strom be able to draw upon the qualities of vision and drive needed to bring about basic change? Would he be tough enough to knock heads together and put his personal stamp on the government?

Social Credit lasted thirty-six years. The last Social Credit administration, that of Harry Strom, lasted thirty-three months. The days of Harry Strom were days of paradox. In terms of legislation, it was a very successful administration with solid accomplishments to its credit. Building on what Manning had left behind, Strom's administration streamlined the civil service in several key areas, created an Ecology Corps to give unemployed students an income and a role to play in environmental protection, began an innovative pre-school program in disadvantaged areas of the largest cities, created Canada's first Department of the Environment and invested it with sweeping powers, mounted new initiatives against drug abuse, built a college system across the province, instituted a visionary educational planning program, created an important, new kind of university and improved communication between the civil service and the people. At the same time, the Strom administration was a *political* failure, in that it did not effectively communicate to the voters a feeling that there had been a real change of substance in the government since the departure of Manning. In terms of good legislation, good social policy, innovation in government programs, the Strom administration was productive and successful. But politically these things counted for little. They did not lead to new electoral alliances, new support for Social Credit among traditional critics or renewed support among traditionally sympathetic but independent voters.

This deep sense of paradox was shown at its most vivid in the contrast between what Harry Strom was really like as a man, and how he came to be perceived by the people.

As a private man, Harry was well known for his courtesy, gentleness, honesty and simple friendliness. He could put any visitor, no matter how humble, at ease. He was an eminently comfortable man to be with, a good listener (he had been the youngest of eleven children in a farm family; he had learned to listen). In terms of religious beliefs, he was almost as conservative as Manning, yet he never exuded the least sense of piety or rigidity; he could hold his religious views without making people feel ill at ease. He disliked stuffed shirts and enjoyed poking fun at them. A true Scandinavian, he had no sexual hangups and was an unassuming social democrat in his private life. His children went to an ordinary public school. He drove an ordinary car and lived in an ordinary suburban bungalow. His government chauffer was deeply frustrated: Harry liked to drive the government car himself, and enjoyed revving it up at red lights. He liked to sneak out of the house after dark and drive his son's Honda.

People who worked with him loved him, even when he drove them to distraction; yet seldom did his immensely likeable qualities come through to the average voter, who often perceived him (on the basis of his appearance on television) as dour and inarticulate.

In many ways Harry represented the things that were best about this old Alberta. Yet by the mid-1960s the old Alberta was passing: the small towns were dying and with them the certitudes of small-town life. Social Credit knew how to speak to the farmers and the people in the small towns. But how to reach the new Alberta, an Alberta of secular prosperity, big cities, a growing class of professionals and managers and intellectuals, a province increasingly dominated by young people who did not remember the Depression and newcomers who were not schooled in the ancient rituals of voting Social Credit because it was the only hope of good government? Alberta had become more like the rest of Canada, and was losing its regional distinctiveness. Social Credit would have to sell itself all over again to this new Alberta. If there were to be dramatic and attractive changes in Social Credit, Harry Strom would have to support them firmly. He would even have to *personify* them.

This, then, was the situation which Harry Strom inherited on a cold December day in 1969 as he took office. The moment he entered the legislative building he faced four major groups contending for his ear and for control of the new administration:

The Elders
The Elders were those men and women whose roots stretched back to the Depression, which was for Social Credit what the Long March

was for Mao Tse-tung. The Elders were not numerous when Strom took office, but they were to be found at all levels in the government and the party. One was Alf Hooke, the old populist orator, who had thrown so many roadblocks in the path of the human resources development program under Manning. Alf held the position of Minister of Lands and Forests. Another was Francis Porter, the grave, white-haired member of the party provincial executive from Drumheller. Similar men and women could be found in the party, especially at the local constituency level, and in the government backbenches. They were not numerous, but they were usually vocal. What they stood for, first and foremost, was ideological purity. They still believed deeply in monetary reform. They wanted the party to continue fighting that battle against all odds. They were deeply suspicious of "newcomers" to the party or the government and had their faces firmly turned toward the past.

It must now be said that Harry Strom handled Alf Hooke badly. Hooke had given most of his adult life to the movement; he deserved to be given an honorable sinecure. While Social Credit did not practise extensive patronage, and did not have available for this purpose a Canadian Senate, or the courts, something could have been found for Hooke had Strom been willing to look. But to Strom an arrangement of this kind smacked of a "deal"; and so instead of arranging a graceful exit for the old warrior, Strom called him in and asked for his resignation from cabinet.

Hooke needed to go – but not this way. The consequence was that Hooke became an enduring enemy not only of Strom and his young advisers, not only of reform within the party, but even of Ernest Manning. Manning and Hooke had both given their adult lives to the cause. Yet now Hooke had been banished from the cabinet, while Manning had been showered with honours, given company directorships and appointed to the Senate. Hooke was deeply wounded by Strom's act, and he struck back. For the next three years he peppered Strom with letters aimed at undermining Harry's fragile self-confidence: the letters,which came on the average of twice a week (and were often reinforced by similar letters from Hooke's supporters) intimated that the average voter was becoming alienated from the government by Harry's dependence on his "socialistic" young advisers and that Social Credit needed a return to solid principles. Strom never replied to these letters, but they kept coming right until the 1971 election.

Hooke's campaign took on strange forms. A young farmer and academic from Hooke's riding, Paul Jenson, had gone to the podium at the leadership convention to put Hooke's name forward; there had been a tacit understanding between the two that when Hooke retired, he would support Jenson as his successor. In 1971, after Hooke announced he would not seek re-election, Jenson ran for and won the nomination in Hooke's constituency. But instead of supporting him, Hooke undermined him; Hooke's supporters spread the word that Jenson (who had once run for the N.D.P. federally) was "unreliable" and "not to be trusted." Before the election was called, Jenson was forced to resign and a new candidate, who had Hooke's support, ran in his stead.

Strom evicted Hooke from the cabinet, but he did not follow this up against Hooke or the other Elders. Hooke remained an accredited member of the party* and so continued to work from the inside. Even with Hooke gone from cabinet, Strom was painfully aware of the continued presence and occasional influence of the Elders, but he was unwilling to take further action against them.

Strom felt a strong need to keep peace in the family. Having alienated them, he took no further action against them. They thus remained in the party and worked harder than ever to resist change.

The Courtiers

The Courtiers were those young advisers and executive assistants who came to be dubbed "the young Turks" or "the invisible government". The group included Strom's two executive assistants, Don Hamilton and Owen Anderson, Erick Schmidt (who had been an adviser to Manning), Preston Manning, Social Credit party president Bill Johnson (who was also president of the Social Conservative Society) and this writer.

It was generally believed that the Courtiers had great influence over Strom, and indeed it is true that on certain issues and at certain times, the Courtiers were able to win their way. The Courtiers bombarded the government with a host of policy proposals: the ones which gained acceptance were early childhood education, the educational planning commission, the Task Force on Urbanization and the Future, *Land for Living* (an Erick Schmidt idea, this four-colour government information magazine was published quarterly and sent to every home in the province). Constitutional research and the creation of an Intergovernmental Affairs office under the premier were the thrust of Owen Anderson; Alberta's new stance in federal-provincial affairs was the outcome of proposals brought by the writer and Owen Anderson.

The government had a number of executive assistants in addition

* Hooke's party membership was finally revoked after the 1971 election.

to these, although most of the rest acted in an administrative capacity.*

The influence of the Courtiers did not extend across the whole field of government. In a host of important areas – the general level of government spending, new taxation, housing, transportation policy, major urban policy initiatives, the selection of Social Credit candidates, the reform of the premier's office and shakup of cabinet, the timing and planning of the election – they had little or no influence. In these areas, the decisive inputs came from other sources.

Nevertheless, the Courtiers soon gained a reputation for power and influence they didn't really possess. They were bitterly hated and feared by the Elders, who resented their loss of influence and feared the consequences of admitting these dangerously unorthodox young men into the anterooms of power. The Elders were not timid about circulating rumors that certain cabinet ministers, even the premier himself, had fallen too much under the spell of "these people". The actual relationship between the Courtiers and the cabinet was much more complex than this. During most of the Strom period it was not easy to determine *where* power lay, exactly; it usually lay in a shifting and constantly changing coalition of cabinet ministers, executive assistants and sometimes party officials. And the makeup of this coalition shifted from issue to issue and problem to problem.

In fact, the premier and his cabinet ministers generally managed to manipulate their advisers at least as often as their advisers manipulated them.

The most important relationship, for the future of the government, was the one between Harry Strom and his two advisers, Don Hamilton and Owen Anderson. When appointed, both were in their late twenties.

They formed an interesting pair. Hamilton was the practical one, Anderson the supreme theorist. Hamilton had been a private businessman who had built a restauarant and a frozen pizza factory; Anderson was an ex-Mormon, a moody, introspective musician and graduate student in political science. Anderson fed Strom most of his policy proposals; Hamilton urged him to crack heads together.

At the outset, both saw Strom as an essentially decent and gentle man who was open to change; both of them felt, it seems, that they could persuade him to adopt their view of politics. As their relation-

---

* An exception to this rule was Don Potter, executive assistant to the Agriculture Minister, Henry Ruste. Potter was the source of many of the progressive measures brought in by Ruste, especially the Agriculture Department's new thrust in encouraging the marketing of Alberta produce and the increased processing of it within the province to create jobs.

ship wore on, however, it gradually became evident to them that Harry was, in his quiet way, determined not to be manipulated. His tactics were indirect, never frontal; instead of blocking their suggestions outright, he would stall them off or change the subject.

Immediately after he took office, Strom agreed to once-weekly planning meetings with "the boys" at Government House Library. These meetings would be to get away from the pressures of the office and set objectives, determine priorities, and make plans for the modernization of the government and the party.

By mid-1969 it became evident to Anderson and Hamilton that the meetings were not resulting in much action. Each week they brought up the same items – cabinet reorganization, reorganization of government departments, purchase of a government aircraft to reduce wasted travel time, introduction of Harry's campaign promises. To all of these Harry seemed agreeable enough, yet the discussions never seemed to result in action. Finally, just to test how serious Harry was, Hamilton copied the previous week's agenda, put a new date on it, and brought it to the meeting; and Harry didn't seem to notice. Hamilton did the same for the next three weekly meetings, again without eliciting any apparent recognition.

Ernest Manning was invited to a meeting; he told Harry that he must act boldly, to establish himself as the Leader, that the time was ripe for change. Harry became nervous, looked at his watch, said he had forgotten an important appointment, and left the meeting.

Several weeks later, Anderson and Hamilton stopped scheduling the meetings.

The Mandarins.
The word conjures up the image of the archtypal Ottawa Mandarin – cool, elegant, educated in the right schools, ironic, mid-Atlantic accent and all that. Social Credit's Mandarins were cut from a somewhat coarser cloth than this, although they lacked none of the Ottawa Mandarins' skill in the use of power.

As the Manning years wore on, the civil service got older, too: the departments of government developed their own traditions and their own senior civil servants to administer them. There were a number of weak ministers. Where this happened, where there was a vacuum of leadership, the civil servants increasingly took the initiative. Gradual but important changes took place. Several deputy ministers crossed that indistinct line that separates giving advice from running the ship.

In the Strom administration the consequences of this growth of civil service power were politically serious. When Strom took office, several departments of government were receiving their leadership not from elected officials but from long-time civil service czars who were generally very bright and able but who had been allowed to accumulate far too much influence over policy making. Alf Hooke had waged an ongoing battle with the senior officials of his department, the Department of Public Welfare; in the end, his officials won out.*

The Deputy Minister of Labour, Ken Pugh, a fatherly pipe-smoking figure, became the de facto power in the Department of Labour; Hubert Somerville, the tough and strong-headed (but effective) Deputy Minister of Mines and Minerals dominated this all-important department in charge of the province's oil industry.

One of the strongest Mandarins of all was Provincial Auditor Keith Huckvale. An employee of the legislature, and not an ordinary civil servant, Huckvale's formal duties were to audit the province's books and report once or twice a year to the M.L.A.'s. In fact, thanks to the province's "pre-audit" system which made it necessary for Huckvale to approve every expenditure *before* it was made, his powers were much broader than they seemed. Huckvale parlayed this, and an advantageous strategic position (the Deputy Provincial Treasurer, the Deputy from whom the vital financial planning and fiscal advice should have been coming, was hesitant) into an unwritten position as chief financial adviser to the province.

With not so much as a single economic planner on its staff,** the Treasury Department had become a limp, negative influence on government fiscal decision making and planning. Strom's Treasurer, Anders Aalborg, was an aging teacher and not an economist; he brought to his job a rigid fiscal orthodoxy that would have found him a place of honour at the head table of the Canadian Bankers Association.

The civil servants under Aalborg were no better: like Aalborg, their idea of an economist was a retired small town bank manager. Into this vacuum, Huckvale moved as a kind of *eminence gris* on whom Strom came to lean for fiscal and budget advice. Huckvale was

---

* The officials took a much more intelligent position on welfare than Alf Hooke did, to be sure. What I am concerned with here is not the rightness or wrongness of Hooke's position but the principle of democratic control of government policy by elected officials.

** The Treasury had a bright economist during this period, Al O'Brian, who was head of the fledgling Budget Bureau. But the Budget Bureau was thwarted administratively, and at one point O'Brian quit the government to take a position at the University of Alberta.

chartered accountant, not an economist; Strom seemed unable to perceive the difference. He began to take Huckvale with him to federal-provincial conferences and listen gravely to his advice. Whenever Huckvale thought the government was spending too much money, he would call a press conference and say so! Strom saw this as forthrightness, not impertinence. A civil servant had no business telling the public that the government "couldn't afford" medicare or was running up deficits that were too high or how sound the economy was. Huckvale was quite uninterested in the government's political survival, yet Strom treated him like a confidential adviser.

The more aggressive and self-confident senior civil servants came to realize that they could get away with taking chances, that Social Credit would not rein in its senior Mandarins. Indeed, in the three years of Strom's administration one was dismissed.* This was one example of Strom's failure to impose his personal stamp on the government.

When a Social Credit cabinet minister did not control his department, he would often indulge in a binge of nay-saying to convince himself that he was really boss; for a few weeks, everything the deputy would bring in would be vetoed. Ministers like Ambrose Holowach, the Minister of Culture, Youth and Recreation, were unable to see the vital difference between this and imposing positive leadership and direction on the department so that it became a working part of responsible government.

A classic case of the government's loss of control over the civil service was the Human Resources Research Council. Created by Manning on the suggestion of Erick Schmidt in 1967 as one of the keystones of the human resources development program, H.R.R.C. was a first in Canada. It was to be a social science research agency, independent from government in the day-to-day sense but intimately tied into the policy-making system. Manning's intention was that H.R.R.C. would assemble a staff of competent economists, sociologists, political scientists, anthropologists and other social science researchers (Schmidt was a graduate student in sociology when he proposed it) to do research designated by the government, on topics which had a direct bearing on future policy. This research would

* Just prior to the 1971 election, the clerk of the legislature, who headed up the civil service in the legislative building, issued an edict that no "political" speeches from the premier's office were to be xeroxed on the government's equipment! Rather than discipline him, Strom handled it cooly. He called in the clerk, Bill MacDonald, and with a straight face said, "Bill you know I rarely make any *political* speeches. If I'm going to be making one, I'll let you know in advance."

define options, explore costs and benefits, and go directly to the decision-makers.

In practice, under the auspices of its director, Lorne Downey, H.R.R.C. took off on its own directions and the government (even though it had cabinet ministers sitting on the H.R.R.C. board of directors and Downey reported directly to the Minister of Education) lost control to the academics. H.R.R.C. did less and less work on matters bearing on government decision-making and more and more esoteric work of little practical value to government. For this failure to harness social research to public purposes, the politicians must bear at least some responsibility.

The Barons
There was a fourth group of power-brokers whom Harry Strom had to contend with and this consisted of the stronger cabinet ministers, whom we shall call the Barons. These were men whose ability, long experience, personal forcefulness or a combination of all three, had built up a sphere of unchallenged influence in cabinet. These men – Gordon Taylor, Minister of Highways; Ray Reierson, Minister of Telephones; Edgar Gerhart, Attorney-General; Anders Aalborg, Treasurer; Jim Henderson, Minister of the Environment – were the "heavies" of cabinet. This does not mean that they necessarily exercised strong influence over Harry Strom or even their colleagues; often they had little influence outside of their own portfolios. But within their area of responsibility, cabinet generally deferred to their judgement.

For Social Credit this had its good side.

With little interference, Taylor was able to build an excellent provincial highways system. Under Reierson, Alberta Government Telephones delivered good telephone service to outlying areas and adopted the latest technological innovations in communications equipment. Under Henderson, the government was to move effectively into the protection of the environment. Henderson was the Department of the Environment's first minister: he put upon it the lasting imprint of his own firmness. This intervention took place at a critical time for Alberta: the province was able to prevent before it happened the despoilation of the air, water and soil that had accompanied industrialization so often elsewhere.

The younger Social Credit ministers like Bob Clark, Minister of Education, and Ray Speaker, Minister of Welfare (later the Department of Health and Social Development) while junior ministers, also functioned in the Baron tradition. Both men ushered in highly useful and promising departmental innovations – Clark, the college system, extensive curriculum reform, and budget controls that were effective without crippling the system; Speaker, amalgamation of the Department of Health and the Department of Welfare into a single department, Health and Social Development. Both were able to place their imprint on their respective portfolios. Both men were able to establish good working relationships with their deputies without surrendering to them; Clark was probably the more aggressive of the two in terms of overriding the civil servants or taking a stand with his collegues when he thought there was an important public issue at stake. Speaker let the very promising welfare-retraining program (which Harry Strom had promised and which had been inaugurated as a pilot project) die when cabinet mossbacks opposed it for being "too expensive".

Strom's failure to take charge of the Barons was not politically all that damaging as long as the Barons were basically progressive or even moderately creative politicians, as these men were. In the absence of strong guidelines from a premier, such men will act on their own initiative and the consequences of their acts will frequently be positive.

The problem for Social Credit was three-fold: (1) the Barons were more like a stable of thoroughbred racehorses than a team of draught-horses, and they did not always pull together to create a uniform image for the government; (2) sometimes the Barons carried their independence to excess, acting without consulting their colleagues and landing the government in hot water; and (3) not all of the cabinet members were Barons. Some were unimaginative drudges who had long outlived their political usefulness.

To begin with, the Barons did not attempt to undermine Harry Strom as the leader figure, but neither did they worry excessively about building him up. Major policy pronouncements often came from the ministers, rather than the premier. This reinforced the impression of a government without a strong leader.

Second, the Barons were strong-headed and sometimes landed the government in unnecessary hot water. Attorney-General Edgar Gerhart inflamed relations between the government and the Civil Service Association right on the eve of the 1971 election by threatening to evict striking jail guards from their government-supplied houses and calling a press conference to show Conservative party signs on the lawns of Civil Service Association executives as proof of an alliance between the two.* Gerhart liked to think of himself as a tough guy; his belligerence on this occasion exacerbated a poor situation. Ray

* There may have been, at least at the senior levels. Several days before the election, the C.S.A. published a newspaper advertisement which began, "Every dog has its day . . . for thousands of Alberta civil servants this day comes soon. . . . "

Reierson did the same as Telephones Minister, when Alberta Government Telephones got into a hair-pulling contest with the municipally-owned Edmonton Telephones system, again on the eve of the election.

This issue blew hot and cold for several months in 1971 and began to heat up again at the worst of all possible times, right before the election. The anti-Social Credit *Edmonton Journal* played it to the hilt, citing A.G.T.'s refusal to allow Edmonton Telephones to serve new suburbs in west Edmonton as decisive "evidence" of an anti-urban bias in Social Credit. The city administration fell on the issue like a starving man on a scrap of bread; flaming full-page newspaper advertisements excoriating this hateful act of discrimination toward Edmontonians appeared regularly in *The Journal.*

The government's failure to cool this issue before the election was not entirely the fault of Reierson – municipal politicians and senior civil servants, and *The Journal*, did not want it cooled – yet Reierson must bear responsibility for failing to use his influence with the board of directors of A.G.T. to defuse this confrontation. And Harry Strom must bear responsibility to failing to compel the stubborn, strong-headed Reierson to find a way out of this crisis.*

One of the most important Barons of all was Provincial Treasurer Anders Aalborg. Strom took office as the entire Canadian economy entered a downturn in 1969; the phenomenon of "stagflation" (inflation plus high unemployment) was beginning to take hold. No single provincial government could hope to solve this problem by itself; but it could take the boldest possible action within its sphere of legitimate powers to minimize the damage and impress the voters with its determination to do everything possible. But Aalborg was not a man for bold measures. On the contrary, he was as orthodox in fiscal matters as a small-town banker, and many good proposals came to an untimely end in cabinet on the rocks of Aalborg's obsession with a balanced budget.

Aalborg became Treasurer after E.W. (Ted) Hinman, a clever and philosophical politician from the Mormon heartland at Cardston, was asked to step down from the position by Manning. Hinman, like Aalborg, was an orthodox man in fiscal matters but there the resemblance ended: Hinman might have found room to manoeuvre within his orthodoxy. Aalborg's main contribution in cabinet was a knee-jerk opposition to anything labelled spending. He even managed to torpedo Strom's campaign promise to implement Programmed

* When the election came, Social Credit lost every single seat in Edmonton. The "A.G.T. issue" certainly played a strong role, though not the only role, in this rout.

Budgeting, an inexpensive concept that would not have stimulated the sluggish economy, but which might at least have built some bridges between Social Credit and a sceptical business community.

The final problem was that not all of Strom's cabinet ministers were Barons. Some, were men who had run out of drive and ideas.

It was fine to operate on the principle of letting each minister do his own thing when the minister had sound objectives in mind and the will and ability to realize them. It was a recipe for stagnation to extend to all Ministers this kind of *carte-blanche* when some were so demonstrably inept. The Barons were left alone to do good things; the drones were left alone to do nothing. The presence of these "non-Barons" was a double negative: not only did they contribute little, they became a passive and negative influence on the cabinet. With few ideas of their own, they could nevertheless be counted upon vehemently to oppose the ideas of others if the ideas pointed to any break with precedent or caution. They valued, above all, security and routine.

Half-way through the administration, Owen Anderson and Don Hamilton began to bring pressure on Strom to force all cabinet ministers to declare their intentions with respect to running again. Those who intended to retire, it was suggested, should be replaced; to leave them in cabinet would be to allow them to make decisions and influence policies for which they would not have to take responsibility at election time. A man should be in cabinet for other reasons than to acquire additional years of pensionable service. Strom was hesitant to being the matter up with his old colleagues. It was not until the last days of the administration that he brought pressure to bear on these men to declare their intentions; and even then he did not replace them on the cabinet.

In terms of cabinet, Strom had every opportunity to shape it according to his own design. It is not clear if he had a design; certainly he lacked the will to put one into effect. The day after the leadership convention he went to bed with the 'flu; visitors reported that he seemed overwhelmed with the magnitude of the job he had undertaken. At the first cabinet meeting over which he presided, he listened to all the ministers addressing him as "Mr. Premier" and then said wistfully, "can't it be just plain 'Harry' anymore?"

He was preoccupied with preserving the unity of cabinet, the government, the party. But he had a very defensive notion of unity. He thought it meant an obligation to old comrades, an obligation not to break with tradition or upset the Elders. For Strom, unity did not mean that the cabinet, government and party should support him in implementing new measures; unity was more an obligation he owed to others than something they owed to him. He could not see that a premier bears a different relationship to his cabinet than a rural school board chairman bears to his fellow trustees. One is *primus inter pares;* the other is one of the boys. Thus, the only dramatic change he made in cabinet was to fire Alf Hooke. No one else was replaced.

This failure did not go unnoticed. It was noticed by the Barons, noticed by the backbenchers, noticed, out in the public, by those who were toying with throwing their support (perhaps for the first time) to the "new" government. The latter, especially, saw Strom's failure to act as important evidence that the "rural mafia" was still in the saddle.

We have noted that Harry Strom had been given, as all new leaders are given, a period of grace in which to inaugurate his new order. This period passed without significant public change in the government's personnel or policies.

But there was another missed opportunity as well. For there was a crucial period in the life of the Strom administration when the government had its last chance to revivify itself with new blood and new public interest. This period, as nearly as these things can be measured, was probably the year 1969 – not too late in the administration to begin altering the Social Credit image before the election. At this critical period there were still many uncommitted voters who were watching the new premier with interest; there were still a significant number of ambitious, attractive new potential candidates waiting for even a hint of an invitation to run for Social Credit. These people were ready for basic change in Social Credit. All they needed was some evidence of change, some symbolic hint of different things to come from the Premier, some enticement and invitation to participate. The appointment of a few attractive new faces to cabinet would have constituted such a hint, such an enticement; or a ringing speech from the Premier calling for new policies and new men to administer them.

But the gesture was never given. Strom's advisers petitioned him to do something in this direction, no matter how small. Appoint Walter Buck to cabinet, they urged: the man is young, attractive, on his record a vote-getter. But Strom would have none of it. Walter Buck, he said, was too ambitious. When an attractive young Edmonton Alderman, Cec Purves, announced publicly his intention to seek a Social Credit nomination against Doctor J. Donovan Ross, he was rebuffed; at a public meeting at which Purves was present, Harry unaccountably blurted out to the audience, "I thought I should tell you I haven't promised Cec anything." (No one had suggested he had.)

199

And so the moment imperceptibly slipped by, never to return. And across the province new men interested in office began quietly to turn to Peter Lougheed's alternative.*

It was a day of youth in politics, but Social Credit was led by a man in his mid-fifties who had become a grandfather. It was a day in which Pierre Trudeau could go from being a law professor to a prime minister in only three years – but Social Credit wouldn't appoint an "untried" man to its cabinet.

By the end of the 1960s Social Credit still believed that it retained a mystical tie with ordinary people, with "the *real* Albertans". It saw itself as a little man's government, much as John Diefenbaker saw himself in a mystical relationship with "the ordinary Canadian". Yet this, too, was only part true, as Social Credit discovered one bleak day in the winter of 1970-71 when the National Farmers Union staged its march on the legislature.

The most powerful farm organization in Alberta at the time was the Farmers Union of Alberta (later re-named Unifarm) the lineal descendant of the old United Farmers of Alberta that governed the province from 1921 until 1935. But as agriculture had changed, so had the Farmers Union; by the late 1960s, it was a prosperous organization that had excellent ties with middle class and successful farmers but growing trouble communicating with the smaller and less successful farmers. Under the leadership of Roy Atkinson of Saskatchewan, a newer and much more militant farm organization, the National Farmers Union, was attempting to organize the smaller, more hard-pressed farmers, especially the farmers wiped out by drought in the Peace River country, into a militant political force that could catalyze basic change in Canadian agricultural policies.

These small farmers, caught in the squeeze between rapidly rising costs and slowly rising prices for their produce, were growing desperate. And those from the Peace country had a double problem: situated on the fringe of the sub-Arctic, the Peace country was notoriously prone to drought and early frost. Several years in a row there had been disastrous crop failures. And so they came, almost two thousand of them, on a bleak winter's day, and they gathered on the pavement by the front steps of the legislative building to meet their government and demand solutions. By late afternoon these husky, sullen men with jeans and wind-burned faces, and women with plain

* At least two ambitious and able men considered running for Social Credit, one of them going so far as to actively sound out Social Credit party officials on how to organize his nominating campaigns. Both were eventually turned off. Both ran as Tories, were elected in 1971, and immediately joined the Lougheed cabinet.

cotton dresses and a drawn look in their eyes were growing restless. They handed out free eggs to curious civil servants and eyeballed the building's jittery, white-faced security guards.

A bus drew up loaded with commercial security guards and dogs; an alert government aide, with pictures of Selma, Alabama, still fresh in his memory, intervened and told the driver to leave the area. The R.C.M.P. were hurriedly telephoned and told to send every plain-clothesman they could find, as fast as they could find them.

A little after 2:00 p.m. one of the N.F.U. organizers, a hugh farmer wearing a white ten-gallon hat and a fringed white buckskin jacket, physically lifted aside the terrified commissionaire at the front door, gently deposited him in the vestibule, and then the mob poured in through the door and into the main rotunda of the building. Crates of chickens were let loose to go squawking through the building. Chants of "we want Strom" echoed through the marble halls. Harry Strom was dumbfounded: what could he say to these people? This was the N.F.U. that had organized the tractor march on Ottawa and thrown eggs at the Prime Minister; the mood down in the rotunda recalled Petrograd on the eve of the Revolution. Harry was a farmer and knew farming, but what could he say to these people? They did not seem like the farmers he had known.

He came out, and spoke to them, agreeing to meet immediately with the N.F.U.'s representatives to see what could be worked out. The TV cameras which the N.F.U. had summonsed recorded the event for the news that night: the N.F.U. leaders were satisfied that they had made their point. The crowd finally went home, leaving a shaken cabinet.

In 1935 it had been people like this who had propelled Social Credit into office. Now here they were, marching on the legislature, unable to relate to Social Credit, or it to them.

Social Credit was a populist party still, but an aging populist party. Old age does odd things to populism, which has been described as a radical protest movement under middle-class leadership. As conditions improve and the leadership ages, populism tends to lose its radical fervour and, while still identifying with the ordinary people, comes to put greater stress on the ordinary people's conservative qualities. Times had been very good in Alberta. The tyranny of the banks was no longer a serious political issue. The monetary-reform wing of the party had dwindled. Social Credit was still a party with real roots in the people, but the question was, *which* people? Important and growing groups in Alberta – small farmers, on the Left; professionals, managers, intellectuals on the Middle and Right – were under-represented in Social Credit. But ties with the lower middle class, with people in the small towns and farming areas, were still strong. And so Social Credit more and more came to reflect their attitudes.

In the 1930s, Social Credit fought the banks and their allies; in the late 1960s it fought against higher salaries for civil servants. In 1970-71 Social Credit brought in its first billion-dollar provincial budget, and seemed awed by the monster it had created. Populist parties always have schizoid tendencies, strong internal tensions which are only controlled during economic or political crisis. But the crisis had passed, and the lower-middle class conservatism of Social Credit had become the dominant element in its personality.

Time and again, Social Credit had opportunities to re-establish contacts with its own historical roots.

In 1970 the party invited to its annual convention Louis Kelso, a U.S. attorney and economic theorist who was proponent of what he called the "second income plan". Adapted to Alberta conditions, the second income plan envisaged a system in which the government would make it possible, through financial incentives and deposit insurance, for the average citizen to assemble at little personal risk a portfolio of income-generating securities from which the citizen could draw a "second income".

Statutory changes would increase the amount of earnings returned to the investor as dividends; this, in turn, would make participating companies eligible for new financing under the plan. The second income of each citizen would become a significant income, a hedge against inflation and technological unemployment, perhaps, eventually, a guaranteed income sufficient to live on.

This was no pure Social Credit theory, by any means, but it was a theory compatible with much that Social Credit had said, and Alberta had at its hand, ready-made as it were, the financial system that would be needed to finance the stock purchases: the Treasury Branches. It also had the natural resource industries, a "natural" participant in such a scheme. Despite this fact, and despite the positive response which Kelso elicited at the convention, nothing was done to follow the idea up.

Strom was similarly tardy in seizing on the political potential of the "Alberta first" issue. At his first federal-provincial conference he did table a document, "A Case for the West", which spoke ringingly of past and present injustices toward the West in Confederation, and the need for new structures and policies to redress these grievances. But he was unable to follow this up with any consistency or forcefulness.

There is no doubt that the choice of Harry Strom was a fateful one for Social Credit; that much was obvious to government advisers early in the administration, and helped to account for much of the desperation they felt. Harry could hold the party together, but that was not enough. He was not a professional politician. He lacked the cynicism and callousness of many professional politicians, to his credit as a person, but he also lacked their will to win and their ability to transform day-to-day events into public issues. He once said that politics meant "healing the sick and comforting the afflicted", but he appeared to mean this in the sense that the phrase would be used by any good rural M.L.A. (and he had been a very good one): one should attend weddings and funerals, send congratulations on births and anniversaries, participate in barn-raisings and help constituents with pensions, passports and road culverts. It just wasn't in this decent, easy-going man to be a twenty-four-hour-a-day professional politician. He didn't ask to be made leader; when he said that certain things about politics seemed "un-Christian" to him, he meant it deeply. Often he would have no truck or trade with even the most elementary political manoeuvre. He thought that Social Credit was basically a matter of virtue and righteousness and he sought to adhere to these standards of conduct. He was, in some ways, the most tragic victim of Manning's doctrine that politics has no place in public life. This doctrine worked for Manning only because he did not practise it: in his own fashion he was a consummate politician. Harry Strom, however, naively tried to preach this doctrine *and* practise it, and the results were disastrous.

No accounting of the attempts to reform Social Credit would be complete without mention of the campaign to reform the Social Credit party itself.*

What image does the name of the Social Credit party conjure up? A little old lady in tennis shoes? A stern fundamentalist preacher, waving a Bible? A stout farmer with his wife and his pitchfork? The reality certainly had all of these elements, but much more. In fact, for most of its modern history Social Credit was a badly misunderstood party.

In late 1968 the party provincial executive commissioned Owen Anderson's public opinion pollsters to conduct an extensive study of the opinions and attitudes of the party's rank-and-file members. The results of this study, never made public, are an invaluable sourcebook of information on what Social Crediters were really like. To review the findings of this study today is to conclude that in certain

* Its formal title is the Alberta Social Credit *League.* It is, notwithstanding, a
  political party in every sense of the word and so I have taken the liberty of
  calling it a party.

respects, party members lived up to their stereotype, but that in other respects they were much a more diverse, interesting and unpredictable group than most gave them credit for.

Here were some of the respects in which the 715 party members interviewed in the study conformed to the Social Credit stereotype:

- 87% had lived in Alberta longer than twenty years;
- Almost 40% had been Party members longer than ten years;
- 51% went to church once a week or more often;
- 84% owned their own homes;
- 53% identified their ethnic origin as "Anglo-Saxon and Canadian";
- 24% were farmers.

On the other hand, they were far from comfortable economically: about sixty per cent had family incomes of less than $7,000 a year. Although Edmonton and Calgary contained fifty per cent of Alberta's population, only eighteen per cent of the party members came from the two cities. They were disproportionately small-town or rural, and less than well off.

Does this suggest a slightly redneck flavour? The additional evidence in the study said no. Thirty-six per cent favored legalized abortion; thirty-five per cent favoured government-financed day care centres (more than those who opposed them – thirty-two per cent); those favouring increased immigration to Canada from "a greater number of countries" was almost as great (thirty-eight per-cent) as opposed (forty-three per cent). Incredibly, forty-seven per cent said they approved, or strongly approved, C.B.C. news and public affairs coverage! Asked what should be done to increase public interest in government, they gave a fascinating range of replies:

"Have an N.D.P. member in power for four months." "It appears that once in office they are all the same and get into the same rut." "Eliminate the graft in the higher echelons." "Apply some shock treatments." "Get rid of some of the goody-goodies and get people who will work for the good of all. Too many 70 year-olds have too much to say now. They should retire." "I think Jesus will be coming to rule with a rod of iron any time now in the before (*sic*) 15 years more or less." "Pass some stupid legislation – but that is a silly question. As long as the government record is good why get [the people] interested?" "Form Social Credit League in Indian and Metis colonies and reserves. We should have more native people carrying membership cards." "Clean house." "As a workman I find it difficult to generate a discussion amoung workmen about politics. All they are interested in is money, beer, women. Seldom do I find a Social Credit supporter because of increasing hatred to Christianity." "Advertise like 'Brylcreme.' *It* came back!"

The survey showed that many rank and file Social Crediters saw nothing inconsistent about voting Socred provincially and Tory federally and that the inclination to vote Tory federally was *strongest with the young* – a disturbing piece of evidence. In a future provincial election how would younger voters generally feel about a Lougheed alternative, if young Social Crediters were this prepared to vote Tory federally?

Asked "what federal party could Social Credit work with?", sixty-five per cent said the Conservatives, only three per cent the Liberals. Thirty-six per cent agreed that Social Credit should get out of direct participation in federal elections and support another party. Boding ill for the later attempt to forge an alliance between Socreds and Liberals in the 1971 election was the discovery that the rank-and-file party members in the study had voted, in the last federal election, fifty-five per cent for Social Credit, twenty-one per cent for the Conservatives, and only 1.54 per cent for the Liberals.

The survey also showed that Ernest Manning's "political realignment" campaign had only succeeded in confusing and dividing the rank and file members of the party.

Manning had proposed the creation of a new philosophy, "social conservatism", which could be supported by both Social Crediters and Progressive Conservatives, but only thirty-seven per cent of party members said they liked the term; the rest said, "it is too close to the word socialism", "it would mean that we have quit federally", "prostitution", "I do not like any name that implies old line party", "it means a cautious Social Credit", and (my favourite), "I dislike anything with the word Social in it."

Political Realignment: What Really Happened
It may be well to digress here and recall briefly that the drive to reorganize Social Credit which began under Strom in March 1969, was not the first such attempt at reorganization; the first was Manning's campaign for "political realignment" which lasted approximately from 1965 until 1967.

No one is sure when the idea for realignment first occurred to Manning but a careful deduction from events would be sometime after the 1963 federal election, the year when Social Credit's strong showing in the federal election of the previous year began to unravel. In 1962, largely on the basis of Real Caouette's blitzkrieg through the Quebec countryside, Social Credit had taken twenty-nine House of Commons seats and had held the balance of power with the minority Diefenbaker government. In 1963, however, Diefenbaker fell, the Liberals took office, and the Socreds dropped to twenty-one seats. In both elections, the party elected only four M.P.s outside of Quebec, two in B.C. plus Robert Thompson and Bud Olson from Alberta. Ontario, as always, was still a blank (in Ontario the party had always been regarded as a curiosity), and the voting base in the West was clearly stagnant. It was obvious to Manning that many Social Credit voters in Alberta were still voting Tory federally.

In addition, a number of other things had happened behind the scenes which had reduced Manning's confidence that Social Credit would ever amount to anything federally.* First, there was the continuous bickering that had gone on between the provincial Socred organization and Manning's hand-picked federal Social Credit leader, Robert Thompson. Thompson was a chiropractor from Red Deer, a man with a sad, almost haunted look in his eyes; most of his adult life had been spent in Ethiopia as a missionary, Boy Scout representative and adviser to Haile Selassie. It was an exotic background, but one that ill equipped him, in Manning's eyes, for the rough-and-tumble of the House of Commons.

Indeed, Thompson had had great difficulty establishing his leadership. At the national leadership convention held in 1961, he had barely edged Caouette for the position; as a face-saving gesture Caouette (who commanded a formidable bloc of Quebec delegates) was made 'Deputy Leader'. But it was far from clear who was which; Caouette was by far the more forceful and audacious of the two. Manning distrusted Caouette, especially when Caouette demanded a party platform that would promise Quebec all customs and excise revenues collected in Quebec ports and a Quebec post office.

Nor did Manning think much of the way Thompson was running the national office. At one point Thompson ran up a budget deficit of $144,000; the money to pay the bills had to be raised by the Alberta organization. Thompson printed his own national party newspaper in Ottawa; Orvis Kennedy thought it devoted too much space to speeches made in the House of Commons and not enough to the accomplishments of Social Credit governments in Alberta and B.C.

Thompson was unhappy when , in the wake of the financial fiasco, Manning insisted on imposing Martin Kelln of Saskatoon as comptroller to control all major national office expenditures.

* I am indebted for many of these insights to Orvis Kennedy in a long interview held March 17, 1972.

Finally, and perhaps most important, Thompson didn't bother seeking the advice of Orvis Kennedy on national organizational matters. On one occasion, Thompson unwittingly allowed into the national party some cranks because he failed to first check out their names with Orvis; Orvis had a list of many of these "bad actors" from previous national organizing drives. One such official was thrown out of the party in Ontario when the *Toronto Star* called Orvis to tell him the man kept a swastika on his office wall.

In the face of all this, and Social Credit's long failure to expand its small foothold in the House of Commons in the 1940s and 1950s Manning reluctantly concluded that the experiment had failed; the "on to Ottawa" drive had petered out for good and it was time to study other options. He concluded that it was time to wind up the federal Social Credit party and use its limited resources to convert one of the "old line parties"into a vehicle more sympathetic to traditional Western Social Credit concerns.

Many Socreds had always supported the Tories federally, and a number of Tory business people had long expressed a private interest in Manning as possible leadership timber. Diefenbaker was not the kind of man Manning could support, but it was obvious Diefenbaker would be replaced as leader, and possibly soon. He selected the Tories as bride-to-be.

Manning's strategy was to ask the Tories to reform themselves, to become a more thoughtful party, a party of genuine commitment to "small-c conservative ideas", and not merely to electoral alliances. To become, in short, a true party of the Right. In return for this, the Tories would be offered the votes, funds and organizing resources that Social Credit could offer – and, if they were interested, Manning himself.

There were two big problems with this strategy. Unsophisticated ordinary rank-and-file Social Crediters would have difficulty understanding why they should now support the Conservatives when all their lives they had been taught to regard *both* of the "old-line parties" as sneaky, almost immoral. Also, it was a strategy which aimed at changing the whole orientation of a long-established *national* party – yet Manning's ability to deliver votes was entirely regional, perhaps provincial. Moreover, in light of the fact that Albertans had supported the Diefenbaker Conservatives massively ever since 1958, what more could the Tories hope to gain in Alberta from an alliance with Manning?

At the 1964 Social Credit convention in Red Deer a resolution appeared favouring the "philosophical realignment" of the Canadian political parties into one large "conservative" party and one large "socialist" one. This, too, was the kind of thing Manning had in mind: he wanted to offer the voter a clear-cut choice between two ideological alternatives. (He could understand, but never accept, that Canadian political parties are alliances of interest groups, not ideological movements with a philosophy.)

In the 1965 federal election, Preston Manning ran as a Social Credit candidate against a veteran Tory machine politician, Bill Skoreyko, in the heavily ethnic, working-class riding of Edmonton East. Ernest Manning endorsed his son in a lettter to voters: "Merely changing back and forth from one old-line party to the other, or from minority to majority government, will not significantly alter the situation . The real need is to elect new members dedicated to the restoration of responsible government at the national level."

Preston Manning worked hard, but went down to a heavy defeat, 13,596 to 6,762. If Ernest Manning had any doubts about the need for realignment, this sealed them. Why should a candidate like Preston be *fighting* the Tories? In a logical political system, a candidate like Preston would have been a Tory candidate. It was obvious that an effective national small-c conservative appeal could not be launched from a Social Credit platform. What was needed was a new political philosophy – which Manning called "social conservatism"– behind which both Social Crediters and many Progressive-Conservatives could rally.*

From the moment Manning began to talk about realignment publicly there was wide speculation as to his "real" motives. The beginning of a drive for the Tory leadership perhaps? That idea was probably not completely absent from Manning's mind, but it seems doubtful if it was a central motivation. Manning had been sounded out by Tories from Ontario on the leadership question. There were a number of financial backers of the Tories who would have supported a Manning campaign. Talks had been held about realignment with a number of influential Tories including Dalton Camp. But Manning was not much in love with politics, certainly not enough to be interested in actively seeking a new career challenge at his age. And he was a realist: what would his chances be of taking the Tory leadership in an open convention? No, it didn't add up.

None of the possibilities for co-operation discussed by Manning and shadowy figures in the Conservative Party ever amounted to

---

* Most rank and file Social Crediters did not find social conservatism all that appealing as a philosophy. In the 1968 membership survey, grass-roots Socreds were lukewarm about the very words; one respondent said, "there is such a group in Edmonton now and from what I understand they are not political and only the very upper class or monied or intellectuals belong."

much, save for one: for a time, there was a gentleman's agreement that if Social Credit would desist from running candidates in close federal ridings,the Tories would do the same in close provincial ridings. In both cases, the idea was to not split the free-enterprise vote and allow in the N.D.P. But this alliance was built on sand.

In 1967, under the new leadership of Peter Lougheed, the Tories ran a candidate in the always-tough Jasper-Edson riding, where the N.D.P. was strong. The vote split; the Socred only won by a hairs-breadth. When Peter Lougheed took an advance guard of Tories into the legislature as the official Opposition, the agreement was dead.

In 1967 Manning blew the trumpet charge of the realignment campaign with the publication of a book, *Political Realignment: A Challenge to Thoughtful Canadians.* In it he again set out his thesis that Social Credit had no federal future and that the federal Tories needed a dose of new thinking and new dedication to economic reform and individual freedom as envisaged by Social Credit. National reception of the book was generally lukewarm, and many commentators were mainly interested in whether it represented a personal drive for the Tory leadership. This distressed Manning, who had hoped that the book would stimulate some badly needed work on policy within the Conservative party. Preston and his friend Erick Schmidt attended the Conservative Thinkers Conference in Mont-morency, Quebec, to see how receptive the Conservatives were to Manning's thinking; but they returned home disappointed.

The federal Tory leadership convention of 1967 , which elected Robert Stanfield to replace John Diefenbaker, and Peter Lougheed's election to the legislature as Leader of the Opposition in the same year (thus ending what Lougheed described publicly as Manning's attempted "seduction" of the provincial Tory party) effectively brought to a close the realignment campaign. (A footnote to the closing was the by-election held in Strathcona East when Manning retired in 1969. The seat was contested by Social Crediter Bill John-son, a lawyer who was also president of the Social Conservative Society and a leading exponent of political realignment; Johnson was defeated by Tory candidate Bill Yurko, a virtually unknown engineer who pounded the sidewalks in the thirty-below-zero temperatures while the Social Credit party executive stayed home – they had their doubts about Social Conservatism. The verdict of the voters of Strathcona East echoed that of the nation's opinion-makers and the federal Tories: detached from Ernest Manning himself, Social Con-servatism had little sex appeal.)

In the final analysis political realignment was a strategy of conser-vation, not attack. Social Credit was slowly losing ground everywhere. Manning's intent was to make a virtue out of necessity:to cash in Social Credit's dwindling reserves while they were still significant, and use them to forge an alliance on the best possible terms with a stronger force, the Conservatives. He was bargaining from a position of weakness, but it was a gamble worth taking.

It was a clever and subtle strategy, but it had one destructive side effect, a side effect that completes the story of political realignment and returns us to the fate of Harry Strom's attempts to reform the Alberta Social Credit party after March 1969. The bad side effect of the political realignment campaign was that it implied, to both the general public in Alberta and to rank-and-file Social Crediters, that there were no really basic differences between the Socreds and the Tories. If that were true, they wondered, and if Manning had already admitted it was time to wind up the federal Social Credit party,then why bother keeping a *provincial* Social Credit party?

Good question! Canada is a federal nation; the affairs of Alberta and the nation are intertwined; if an idea is good enough for one it is good enough for the other. Why a rump Alberta Social Credit party indeed, especially with an alternative like Peter Lougheed (obviously a competent and trustworthy man) available? These were the kinds of thoughts that ran through many minds. And if Harry Strom could not calm these thoughts, Social Credit would find itself in a great deal of trouble.

This was the backdrop against which the campaign began to re-form the Alberta Social Credit party and get it in shape for the coming duel with Lougheed.

As soon as the leadership convention had ended and Strom took office, his aides began to pressure him to give top priority to a thoroughgoing reorganization of the party. Owen Anderson in particular had some bold changes in mind. What he proposed was a restructuring of the party to give it an independent economic base and a new expertise in the applications of computer technology and public opinion surveying to political organization and campaigning. In a paper entitled, "A Proposal for a New Form of Political Organization", he advocated that Social Credit free itself from dependence on traditional fund-raising by using its prestige to swing a sufficient mortgage to build a large office building; the profit on rents would be sufficient to provide several floors of free accomodation for the party in an attractive downtown urban setting, and the party would eventually acquire full ownership of a valuable asset. He also proposed that the party purchase permanent computer facilities in which every single piece of pertinent political data in the province – population movements, voting patterns, results of public opinion surveys, demographic data – could be stored, retrieved and analyzed for the formation of strategy. The objective would be to consciously shape a more representative and popular government according to the findings the computer analysis would suggest. Given a computer model of known voting trends and voter preferences, it would be possible to simulate in advance likely voter response to every conceivable policy option. Then it would be possible to adopt policies and tactics which would attract the kinds of new supporters in which the party was so deficient – young people, renters, urbanites, professionals, the intelligentsia.

Had this scheme been put into action, it is likely that Social Credit would have emerged with one of the most contemporary political organizations in the country. Alas, a more immune recipient for this graft of alien tissue could scarcely have been found. Strom and the Elders in the party were cautiously sceptical about the value of computers and public opinion surveys, and frightened by the implications of anything so unconventional as building a high-rise office building. What, the party assume a mortgage?

Strom went to an initial breakfast meeting at the Kingsway Motor Hotel in March 1969, to kick off discussions on party reform, and the meetings moved off in less adventuresome directions. The Anderson plan was considered far too visionary and ambitious. The drive to reorganize took the form of creation of eight "task forces" to zero in on selected areas. There were to be the following groups:

1. Steering Committee.
2. Planning and Programming Task Force.
3. Financial Task Force.
4. Membership Task Force.
5. Data Task Force.
6. Policy Review Task Force.
7. Communications Task Force.
8. League Task Force.

By about July it had become evident that many of these task forces were simply not going to get off the ground. There were too few qualified, enthusiastic people to man them properly. The whole effort had a limp quality about it; after the first meeting at the Kingsway, Harry Strom was seldom seen at meetings; certainly he did not throw his personal prestige behind the reorganization. Ray Speaker was chosen chairman of the all-important steering Committee, which was given overall responsibility and which reported directly to the premier, cabinet, party board of directors and caucus. It was the responsibility of the Steering Committee to oversee the work of the task forces. But of all the groups, only the Policy Review Task Force, the Membership Task Force, and the League Task Force, seemed to do any work – and their recommendations disappeared into the maw of the Steering Committee, never to be heard from again.

The big question was, how to reform the party when many people in the party didn't want it changed? The Elders were badly out of touch, but deeply in love with their rituals and traditions, which had become an end in themselves. This ingrained resistance could, perhaps, have been overcome had the premier personally thrown his weight behind the campaign. But once it got started, he left others – Bill Johnson, president of the League, Ray Speaker, Orvis Kennedy – to carry the ball. And they simply weren't enough.

What about the Young Socreds? Could they not have played a role? Unfortunately not. To the extent that there was a Young Social Credit organization though the 1950's and 1960s, it was consistently unable to attract the kind of people who could have played a role in modernizing the party or the government. Like the youth affiliates of most political parties, it was not taken seriously by the party leaders. Unlike the youth affiliates of most political parties, it did not even succeed in attracting the kind of ambitious, bright and aggressive young people who could later run for office themselves. At one point, in the early 1960s, the The Young Socreds at the University of Alberta came under the leadership of two clever young law students, Doug Sanders and Bill Downton, and for a time it seemed that the two might be able to turn the organization into a significant force. (At one point, they sponsored a debate on the resolution, "Resolved that Social Crediters are funny-money, backwoods Bible-pounders", with the losers to receive custard pies in the face. Downton and Sanders took the negative, attracted a large audience, but unfortunately lost the debate.) The Downton-Sanders period, however, was not representative of the movement. By the late 1960s the Young Socreds were a motley band which included children of government M.L.A.'s and older party supporters, graduates of Bible institutes and, just before the end, a successful candidate for Young Socred President who wore a Zorro hat and cape and adopted as his campaign theme song, "The Good, the Bad and the Ugly". (This prompted rude speculation as to which part of the title was named after him.)

And so the Young Socreds could not be expected to play a significant role in renewal.

As for the task forces, the Policy Task Force did months of work, met with many groups, and finally tabled fifty three policy recommendations. Of the fifty-three four were implemented (a citizens' environmental agency to conduct independent investigations of environmental problems; increased efforts to market Alberta agricultural produce abroad, especially in Japan; increased assistance to Alberta processors of Alberta agricultural produce; implementation of redistribution to reduce the rural-urban voting imbalance). Many of the rest were clever, and would have cost little or nothing to implement: automatic nonvoting seats in the legislature for the mayor of Edmonton and mayor of Calgary, to speak on behalf of urban concerns; earmarking of certain taxation revenues for the sole use of the cities, e.g., a special automobile licence tax; an unearned increment tax on urban property transactions; the limitation of tenure for deputy ministers to five years, renewable by contract; broader rights of appeal for individuals from civil service decisions.

The unhappy fate of these positive-but-cheap recommendations was an indication that those in control of the party were not really serious about renewal. These recommendations could have been brought to the floor of a party convention; if adopted, they could have become the basis of immediate government action. They would have been concrete evidence to doubting outsiders that the party was acquiring some new fire in its belly, that the party was the place to be if you wanted to have an input to the government. In light of the party's reputation for being a government cheering squad, this kind of evidence and reassurance was desperately needed. But it never came. Almost to the bitter end, Harry Strom and most of his cabinet regarded the party as an addendum to the government.

Some of the recommendations of the Policy Review Task Force were finally dusted off and incorporated in the party platform at the eleventh hour of the 1971 general election, when it was far too late.This deathbed conversion to reform produced the very opposite effect to what the cabinet intended. Confronted with a blizzard of new Social Credit promises – aid for massive new recreation complexes in Edmonton and Calgary, $1,000 cash grants for the purchase of first homes for young couples, and many others – sceptical voters asked why, if these ideas were sound, why they were not implemented earlier? As one writer of a letter to the editor of *The Edmonton Journal* put it, "for the past three years the Government has said there was no money for new programs, but now it is suddenly available."

The end result of the campaign to reform the party from within was cynicism and discouragement, not idealism and an influx of enthusiastic new recruits. A number of people were lured into the party by the promise of participation in this significant work of renewal. When they saw their hard renewal work go for aught, and their recommendations met with chilling silence, they went away again with deep doubts about the sincerity of those who had invited them. There is only one thing worse than to refuse to reform, and that is to promise to initiate reform and then not carry it through.

CHAPTER TWELVE

The Rise of Lougheed

"If we have to have an Opposition, it might as well be headed by Mike Maccagno."

— Ernest Manning

It would be totally wrong to think that there had never been an opposition to Social Credit. In 1940 the Liberals, Conservatives and remnants of U.F.A. banded together in the Independent Movement, and nearly defeated Aberhart. In 1944 the C.C.F.was riding the crest of a wave of popularity across the country, and Manning was only able to beat them off with a strenuous campaign. In 1955, J. Harper Prowse, a forceful and articulate Liberal lawyer took fifteen Liberals into the legislature to form an opposition that seemed on its way to major gains against Social Credit. For the entire Social Credit period, opposition to Social Credit was *de rigueur* on all university campuses and in many teaching circles; liberal clergymen disliked the party ; among the better people in the cities, the party was looked on with amusement. Social Credit was the political establishment, but it was never the social or economic establishment.

What kept Social Credit in power for so long, even when it was seriously threatened, was a widespread belief on that part of many political moderates and independents that Social Credit had delivered honest and efficient "good government"in the interests of all groups at least some of the time. For many years these people voted Social Credit (it was a standing joke in Alberta that no one would admit to voting Social Credit) and were untouched by persistent Leftist and academic criticism of Social Credit. They saw no responsible or moderate alternative to the government. Peter Lougheed's great initial accomplishment after the long interregnum of the Manning years, was to offer these moderate voters a respectable, non-Socialist alternative to "the governing party" as he called it. When

Social Credit's nemesis finally came, it came not in a frontal attack from the long-embattled fortresses of the Left, but in a smooth flanking movement from the Right.

Peter Lougheed ascended to the Conservative leadership in March 1965, with impeccable credentials. Scion of an old Alberta family, his grandfather had been leader of the Senate under Borden in the early part of the century and was a charter member of the Alberta frontier establishment. The young Lougheed was independently wealthy. He had the independence that wealth usually brings, but he also had ambition and drive – qualities that wealth often softens in those of the second and third generation. He was well educated (law, at the University of Alberta; commerce, at Harvard), experienced in business (Calgary's large construction and engineering firm, the Mannix group of companies) and had no political enemies. He had never run for provincial or federal office, yet he spoke with earnest authority about provincial problems. He was attractive, friendly and clean living.

Lougheed took over a party only one step from outright decrepitude. The Conservatives were without seats in the legislature. They had had a succession of lacklustre leaders in the 1940s and 1950s; in the 1960s they went to the opposite extreme and chose as their leader Milton Harradance, a flamboyant Calgary criminal lawyer who barnstormed the province in a converted P-51 Mustang fighter. Harradance had been succeeded by Ernest Watkins, an extremely literate and clever English lawyer from Calgary; but Watkins was far too much the intellectual for the role. In the 1963 election, Harradance went down the drain along with the rest of the Tory candidates, and later Watkins had quickly indicated his desire to retire from politics.

Lougheed's initial efforts were aimed at becoming better known across the province and attracting a core of ambitious, capable young politicians who could serve as the future elite of the party. He travelled across Canada, meeting with the reigning Conservative premiers, John Robarts, Duff Roblin and Robert Stanfield, to seek their counsel on policy and tactical questions. He was not afraid of hard work; even though he was not yet in the legislature, he worked almost full-time on the road, familiarizing himself with all parts of the province, building a grass-roots organization, becoming known at the local level and scouting for potential future candidates. He cultivated reporters, editorial writers and editors assiduously, taking them to lunch, soliciting their views. He never argued his own views too strongly but always left the impression of one serious, probing and concerned. When he was favourably commented upon by one writer or another in print, his organization would xerox the favourable reference and send it to other media writers; and so a kind of self-fulfilling prophecy of charisma was developed. At that point, he had little more to work with.

In his speeches and news releases he began to carve out a small but respectable niche in the political spectrum – critical of the government, but in a responsible way. His general themes in his first two years were that the government was "tired" and "complacent", that Alberta was too dependent on oil income, that Alberta needed much more secondary industry.

The 1966 Tory convention took as its theme "the future belongs to us" and Lougheed stressed, then and later, that he was building a future government, not an opposition. "We must continue with our program of convincing Albertans that we provide the most promising, the most enthusiastic, and the most responsible alternative to the present administration of the province," he said, enunciating "twelve guideposts" for party policy:

1. Public laws should be made in public.

2. Local government should predominate wherever practical.

3. The provincial government should give strong support to the need in Canada for an effective central government. Conservatives recognize the inherent dangers of eroding the federal government's powers.

4. Conservatives do not believe that the role of the provincial government is passive.

5. A provincial government should always have a long range plan for Alberta's future economic development.

6. Adequate warning of proposed new legislation should be given to those affected and a full opportunity should be granted to air their objections in a public forum.

7. Conservatives believe that provincial government should establish legislative priorities based on its financial resources, and publish these for public scrutiny. ("We believe in any establishment of priorities that stresses expenditure on all aspects of education, not just on the bricks and mortar of education, must be given the highest priority to equip younger Albertans to compete in the decade ahead.")

8. The greatest challenge to the province is to administer welfare in relation to need without detracting from human dignity.

9. The provincial government should always accept sound financial responsibility in its affairs and the affairs of municipal governments financially dependent on it.

10. The province should constantly struggle to organize and develop our natural resources by the private sector but in a way that provides "adequate returns to our own citizens".

11. The provincial government should not just preach free enterprise but also promote it by creating a "supportive atmosphere" [for business].

12. "Finally, we sincerely believe that God's endowment of this province with such abundant natural resources complemented by the skills and talents of our own people permit us to realistically set as our objective a society that is not inferior to any province or state in North America."

This was a very cleverly constructed personal platform for there was little or nothing in it which could not have been endorsed by most Social Crediters and political independents. It seems that an important part of Lougheed's strategy, almost from the moment he became leader, was to reassure the ordinarily pro-Social Credit voter that he had nothing to fear from the Tories, that a vote for Lougheed was a vote for a "safe" change. In a province with a history of infrequent changes in government, this was shrewd psychology. To those Social Crediters who now asked in irritation, "why change?", Lougheed supporters could retort, "why not?"

As the prospect of a 1967 general election drew closer, Lougheed began to develop in greater depth his critique of Social Credit.

Referring to the government as "a reactionary administration – reacting day to day", he attacked Manning's "myth of performance". (He never attacked the premier personally.) He made it clear that in place of a conservative administration which he branded as "old and tired", he was offering a shiny new one. Speaking before the MacDonald-Cartier Club in Edmonton in January 1967, he attacked the Socreds' management of the economy. Stabbing the air, Kennedy-style, he asserted:

We have been coasting on our petroleum revenues for the last decade – we have failed to use capital revenues from the petroleum industry – over one billion dollars – as an investment in the future by way of imaginative development, research and promotional programs . . . our attitude in Alberta seems to be – here we are – aren't we wonderful – come to us'. (Even Ontario with one-third of the manufacturing plants in Canada has more aggressive programs for building up its economy). . . . we have utilized this one billion dollars from the petroleum industry to establish a built-in level of provincial government spending – far larger than any other province on a per capita basis – $490 per person – double that of Ontario . . . we have been out-negotiated by the Federal Government and perhaps by other provinces . . . [and] finally the province has failed to provide the leadership for the municipalities – particularly the cities – to come up with plans and programs to keep the municipalities on a sound financial basis and doing so without unfairly penalizing the property taxpayer.

With a slight trimming and additions here and there, Lougheed was to repeat these points, and his "twelve guideposts", as his basic campaign themes right through to the 1971 election. He obviously decided on this "game plan" very early and stuck to it with remarkable tenacity.

When Manning called the 1967 election, Lougheed moved quickly. It was an election without major issues. The Socreds' chose the theme "Horizons Unlimited" and spoke proudly of their most recent accomplishment, the construction of the 300-mile long Alberta Resources Railway, built from Hinton to Grande Prairie to open up the rich resources of Alberta's north-western foothills.*

Lougheed ran a full slate of Conservative candidates, many of them attractive new faces. The stress in selection of candidates was youth, good looks, education and energy. Considering his later effective exploitation of television, it is interesting that Lougheed did not rely much on the medium in 1967. The stress in Conservative campaigning was the door-to-door blitz. In 1967 this was a bold and innovative tactic; many Socred candidates spent their campaigns sitting in their campaign trailers or working in their government offices. Lougheed himself worked very hard in his own riding, realizing the importance of establishing his grass-roots support and credibility; running against a lacklustre Socred backbencher, Donald Fleming, in Calgary West, he won easily.

The results of the Tory campaign were impressive. Lougheed's group elected a corporal's guard of six M.L.A.s (including the nucleus of Peter's advisory group – former Edmonton Eskimo quarterback Don Getty, who vanquished Socred cabinet minister Randy McKinnon in Strathcona West; Dr. Hugh Horner, a former Tory M.P., who won in rural Lac Ste. Anne, and Lou Hyndman, a young attorney from an old Conservative family – his grandfather had been Chief Justice of the Supreme Court of Canada – in Edmonton West).

* It became a financial white elephant, but not until several years later.

More important, he doubled the Conservative popular vote, from thirteen per cent in 1963 to twenty-six per cent. The Socred popular vote dropped from fifty-five per cent in 1963 to forty-five per cent in 1967, and the Liberals were already showing evidence of their steady decline toward oblivion: twenty per cent in 1963 to eleven per cent in 1967.

With his foothold in the legislature established, Lougheed began to use it for maximum political leverage. He refused to call his group the opposition; they were "the alternative government". To the irritation of the Socreds, the Tories began to act like a government, introducing their own legislation. They used the question period with deadly effectiveness; each day, the Tories in caucus would decide which Socred cabinet minister to zero in on; they would then each arise in turn to pepper that minister with questions, resolutions and veiled charges. When a minister showed the first sign of weakness, he was "called on" more and more often.

The more articulate and aggressive Socred ministers – Clark, House Leader Fred Colborne, Reierson, Jim Henderson, Gordon Taylor – were left alone. The weaker ministers – Holowach, Ross, Ruste, Wilson – were peppered mercilessly. Lougheed did not overexpose himself. Rather, like Manning, he held himself in reserve for the major speeches, the big debates. He never got involved in personal wrangles; he left that to his subordinates. Even within the confines of his small opposition, he played the role of premier.

From the 1969 session on, Lougheed had the benefit of a piece of unearned good fortune. The Alberta economy, in common with that of rest of Canada, was in a downturn. Unemployment was up. The government was internally divided on how it ought to respond to this; the Provincial Treasurer, Anders Aalborg, was opposed to any further spending or any further taxation. The result was a failure to move boldly against unemployment, a failure which the Tories scored.

Lougheed correctly understood that the legislature can be made into an effective pulpit with the whole province as a congregation. He knew that people would judge his potential as a premier from his behaviour as an opposition leader. He must be aggressive, incisive – but always statesmanlike and positive. This was the kind of note he struck in his first reply to Strom's first Speech from the Throne in 1969:

The Honorable Mr. Strom has assumed the responsibilities from Mr. Manning. We sincerely hope in the interests of all Albertans he will meet – as a legislator and not just as an administrator –

the challenges of modern, contemporary, changing Alberta. Unfortunately, we did not observe this and no indication exists of it in the Speech . . . it would seem appropriate, Mr. Speaker, for us at this time to look back over the past twelve months and see what has really been accomplished . . . we did very little in the field of mental health because we are still waiting for the Blair Report. We did nothing in penal reform because we waited for the McGrath Report. Yet the incidence of crime continues to increase in Alberta, a 23% increase . . . we are now changing the name of the Department of Welfare, but we are certainly not changing the trend [toward welfare] . . . our net farm income went down last year compared to 1967 . . . our rural population continues to decline . . . our property taxpayers took it in the neck . . . the cost of living continued to rise in this province, 3.8%, and the Government took no apparent action on a Royal Commission, the Batten Commission, that dealt with this . . . the cost of home acquisition continued to be beyond the reach of the average wage-earner . . . and the Dominion Bureau of Statistics stated the average weekly wage in 'good old Alberta' in October, 1968, is $109.34 and was still below the Canadian average . . . now let's look at what's omitted from the Speech to the Throne:

We were told last year [in the Socred leadership race] that there would be established an Alberta-wide commission on the constitution. No reference to that in the Speech from the Throne. Is it being abandoned? Why is it secret? And why are M.L.A.s excluded?

We were told last fall that there would be a major study on the aims and objectives of our educational system. No reference to that in the Speech . . . is it being abandoned? Perhaps it's secret too. Does it involve this expanded, dynamic new role for the M.L.A.s?

We were told last fall there would be a major study on the aims and future of the universities . . . a very timely thing. No reference to that in the Speech from the Throne . . . we were told last fall there would be an expansion of programmes called 'Head Start' programmes . . . we were told last year that there would be a broad, comprehensive study of the future of urban rights [sic] in the province. . . .

. . . this Speech is much more significant, much more significant, for what it omits than what it includes . . . it is a disappointing and depressing start for Social Credit after Mr. Manning.

From the 1969 session onward the nimble Tories chipped away

steadily, and effectively, at the self-confidence of the Socreds. They seemed to have a very shrewd perception of the Socreds' weaknesses and areas of self-doubt: knowing that some of the Socreds were already very defensive about the amount of influence possessed by some of their advisers, the Tories regularly needled the cabinet over who was "really" making the decisions and who "really" wrote this speech or that speech; in a Conservative government, Lougheed said, there would be no "hidden government" of paid advisers and executive assistants; the M.L.A.s would make all the decisions.

Lougheed's proposals were, on the face of them, eminently reasonable and statesmanlike: allow live television coverage of the legislature; permit free votes on more legislation; provide a vastly expanded and modernized role for the M.L.A.; open meetings of committees to the public; have an autumn session of the legislature each year to do housekeeping, thereby permitting the winter session to be shorter and more effective.

Time and again, Lougheed was able to score points because the government had grown sluggish in its ability to respond quickly to events. When a chemical plant closed without notice on the outskirts of Edmonton a Lougheed lieutenant was on his feet in the legislature the next day with an "alternative government" bill to make it compulsory for firms to give employees a minimum of one month's notice before closing a plant. Time and again, Lougheed was quick to seize on the political potential of government slips and delays; whenever the government would inaugurate a study aimed at reform, Lougheed could be counted on to gain mileage out of its composition, terms of reference, personnel, timing, or the implementation of its recommendations. In other jurisdictions in Canada, this would be routine politics; in non-political Alberta, it was bold manoeuvring.

This tactic made life much harder for those in Social Credit who were trying to reform the government from within; the Blair Report on mental health and the McGrath Report on penal reform were the products of this reform drive, and it was hoped they would be seen by the public as evidence of Strom government's new openness to change and reform; instead, Lougheed was able to convert them into "evidence" of the Strom government's complacency and slowness to change by demanding to know why their recommendations had not been implemented holus-bolus, and immediately. If the Socreds had been less responsible men, they would have simply implemented broad changes in these areas and not bothered with detailed studies first; they could then have impressed the voters much more with their reform spirit.

What began to happen, under the hammer-blows of Lougheed's

assault, was that many people who were tired of Social Credit anyway (or at least bored with it) began to seize on Lougheed's allegations as the "evidence" they needed to reinforce their beliefs and no amount of government explanation would sway them. After all, had not the Socreds been in power thirty-five years – and was that not *bound* to lead to complacency and stagnation? The Socreds' reputation for complacency and stagnation grew at the very time that the government was probably less complacent and stagnant than it had been for a generation. It was a powerful irony.

Harry Strom could perhaps have countered this trend by intervening boldly, personally, on the side of dramatic public change, but he did not. Harry was a consensus leader; he knew that Social Credit was internally divided already on the question of the direction and pace of change. He did not see that opinions – whether among the party rank and file or the voters – are fluid, that they can be bent by forceful manipulation of symbols and images. He was the prisoner of indecision. And so, day by day through the Strom administration, never by catching the government in a major scandal or failure but by an accumulation of small tactical victories, Lougheed chipped away at the government's credibility and stature.

For a brief golden moment early in the Strom administration there was a time when events, opinions, were ripe for change; with the election of a new leader the government was ripe for change, many of the people were expecting it. But the moment ebbed away, and there was no change – no shakeup in cabinet, no major policy initiatives, no dramatic change in the government's style. And so the magic moment passed. And with its passing, the initiative quietly slipped to Peter Lougheed.

CHAPTER THIRTEEN

Last Hurrah

It was to be the most sophisticated, the most cleverly planned, the most expensive election campaign that Social Credit had ever conducted. In previous years, Manning had made all the decisions of consequence, along with Orvis Kennedy; they had sat together, in the back of cars or, one year, in the barn at Manning's farm, and talked it out – what should be the issues, how they should advertise, who would make good candidates, how the cabinet should be composed. But this time it was to be different. The young men around Strom had a plan: the modernized, reshaped party would participate in planning a campaign that would draw upon the very best that theory had to offer. A whole new type of candidate would be sought out; these candidates would be given a thorough indoctrination in tactics and strategies which all were to follow. The advertising, for once, would be highly professional, and co-ordinated from the centre. And finally, a single campaign planning group would orchestrate all of these voices and instruments into a political symphony such as Alberta had never heard.

In the minds of Strom's planners, that was how it was to be. How it was to be in practice was another matter.

The first twenty-four months of the Strom administration were preoccupied with the tasks of government. As we have seen, reform of the Social Credit party and the Cabinet originally agreed to by Strom as a high priority, slipped into the background. These first twenty-four months were deeply introspective ones for Harry Strom, preoccupied as he was with maintaining "unity" in the cabinet and the caucus. But, by the autumn of 1970, Strom had to admit that the "political" questions were looming larger. The government's legal mandate – Manning's mandate – would expire in the summer of 1972. Tradition holds that governments should not try to remain in office their full legal term, but that an election should be called somewhat earlier, usually every four years. Those that try to go longer are accused of being afraid to face the people. Also, winter is not considered an acceptable time for elections. These two factors ruled out 1972 or the late fall of 1971. By a process of elimination, that left the spring, summer or early autumn of 1971, a decent one year earlier than the expiration of the mandate. Should it be the spring or fall? A debate on this point went on for many months, some Social Crediters maintaining stoutly that spring was better because that was when the farmers first planted their crops, and it was a time of cheerfulness and optimism; others said autumn was better because the harvest also brought the first cash payments to the farmers for their produce.

Of course there was another time when the election could have been held – right after the 1968 leadership convention (say, in the spring of 1969). Strom had considered going to the people then, for he was strongly conscious of the fact that the government had a Manning mandate, not a Strom mandate. He wavered, then decided to postpone the decision. He lacked confidence. It was too risky. It proved to be one of his most important decisions. Right after the leadership convention, he had momentum: to the public he was a new face.

By the spring of 1970 Strom agreed to begin sharpening the political consciousness of Alberta voters with some forays into partisanship. For many years, the tone of politics in the province – in comparison, say, with British Columbia or Saskatchewan – had been genteel; rarely did the opposition launch any really violent attacks on the government, or vice-versa. Manning had been untouchable; during his tenure, one could criticize the achievements of the government, but in the legislature it was considered bad form to attack "Mr. Manning" himself. As for Manning, he rarely attacked the opposition, preferring to act as if it did not exist. (Usually, it didn't.)

Strom's advisers felt that this must now end. Given Lougheed's appeal to many kinds of voters, especially to people who had traditionally voted Social Credit, it was imperative to begin chipping away at his image and polarizing his critics. Thus, in the spring of 1970, Strom began to attack Lougheed's "nice guy" image – the opposition's "crass" exploitation of current problems in the news, its stock reaction to the introduction of new government programs (which was that it had thought of it first and forced the government to take action), and Lougheed's "contradictory" promises of new programs and his criticism of Alberta's "big government" and high spending. The slogan of the 1970 Tory convention had been "The name of the game is winning"; Harry branded this a "cynical" slogan, saying, "nonsense, the name of the game is giving the people the kind of government they want and need."

But, while Strom became more receptive to rhetorical escalation, he remained unreceptive to suggestions that the government should begin getting itself in fighting trim organizationally. He would not reorganize cabinet and bring in new faces. He would not agree to do something dramatic to highlight the government's concern over the cost-price squeeze for farmers or the welfare of the cities.

And behind this surface activity was a cancer of doubt: how much of Social Credit's popular vote in previous years had been a Manning vote, and how much had been a Social Credit vote? With the exception of Alf Hooke and a few others, none of the major Social Credit decision-makers, Harry included, had ever been elected to the legislature save on a Manning coattail. Stripped of Manning, how would they fare, facing the people?

It was clear that the biggest issue in the election would have to be Harry himself. The "in" phenomenon of the day was charisma. Trudeau had it; W.A.C. Bennett certainly had it; in the heat of his election campaign, at least, Ed Schreyer seemed to have it. Unquestionably Lougheed had it, a kind of unshakeable cheerful confidence in himself, a sense of authority, of destiny. And Harry, for all of his fine qualities as a person, just didn't have this basic star quality. He mumbled through his speeches, often muffing the best lines; he let pass many priceless opportunities for defining, in a word or a phrase, the basic differences between himself and Lougheed. A social democrat to his fingertips, Strom lived in an ordinary house, sent his kids to an ordinary public school, shopped in Woodwards on Saturday like all the other middle-class fathers, took a holiday trailer on vacations. But these qualities did not add up to charisma; the voters, it seemed, wanted a feeling that the levers of government were in the hands of their betters, not their equals. It was not, for them, enough that Harry Strom be a humane and decent man.

Very well then, thought Strom's advisers, if Harry lacks charisma we must try and make him some. In 1969 they commissioned the Goodis, Goldberg, Soren advertising agency in Calgary to produce a half-hour film on Strom the Man, but this low-budget quickie was a disaster. Mostly shot in Harry's living room, it reinforced the very things the planners wanted to undermine. Through it, Strom scowled like everyone's crabby old grandfather, told the voters why they couldn't have what they wanted (there was no money) and mouthed banalities ("My philosophy of government? To do the very best I can."). His advisers cringed. The film was shown once on television, then locked away for good.

On the heels of this, the party received a proposal for another film. Edmonton television personality and music entrepreneur Tommy Banks came to Owen Anderson and told him that he had a film company which could produce a proper film on Harry Strom, a film that would at last bring out his real qualities of warmth, informality and humanity. The theme of the Banks film was to be change – how Alberta had changed, how Social Credit and Harry Strom had responded to change. The Banks film had its problems but the end result was more successful, portraying Harry on horseback, in an aircraft flying over the Alberta Resources Railway, walking through the old one-room rural school of his childhood. The film opened with Harry riding a horse (one place where he looked more at home than Lougheed) and meditating: "It's astonishing the number of changes that occur during one man's life. The country and the people have changed so much since I was a boy . . . and a person has to keep up with new ideas, new ways of thinking, new problems and new challenges . . . but you know, it often helps to overcome these new problems if a man can remember his roots every once in a while. Making adjustments isn't something new [for me]. We've all had to do it. . . . "

The film was begun in December 1970, and by April was in the can, ready for the election campaign. It was to be a key weapon in the Social Credit arsenal.

In the fall of 1970 Strom agreed to have the party begin a planning study for the election. The study was commissioned to Corporate Communications Ltd., a consulting company put together by Erick Schmidt and Don Hamilton. For a fee of $15,000 CORPCOM was told to prepare campaign manuals, a critical path for election planning, a suggested general strategy, a proposed election budget and a recommended organization plan. Schmidt, Hamilton, Owen Anderson and Preston Manning worked on the project.

In February 1971, they delivered their report, entitled *Project 71,* to Strom and the party executive.

The report recommended the creation of a centralized super-agency which could bypass both cabinet and the party executive to establish firm control over planning, programming and budgeting. A two-volume campaign manual was presented for use by candidates and their managers and staffs. A critical path was proposed, breaking the campaign into seven levels of activity: government activities; political planning; premier/candidate schedule; platform; information/analysis; province-wide media; constituency schedules. A campaign budget of $580,000 was proposed (a substantial increase over what Social Credit had ever spent before, partly to increase advertising and partly to pick up a larger share of local constituency costs).

This strong centralized super-agency would take charge of all advertising design, choose colours and ensure continuity of visual design. Advertising would begin before the election was actually called, but would tie in neatly with campaign advertising themes. A slogan was suggested: "Together we Build". "Many find in it a sense of personal involvement . . . and the concept of 'togetherness' relates well to the team style of Premier Strom" said *Project 71*.

The strong central super-agency would be called The Project 71 Task Force and would include representatives from all the various groups that had a legitimate role in campaign planning. It would report directly to the premier, by-passing cabinet and the party's provincial executive, "and should have the power to make final decisions regarding [all] campaign matters, subject only to the veto of the Premier . . . no individual group, including the Cabinet, should undertake unilateral decisions [during the campaign] without consultation with this Task Force."

Membership of the task force was to be:

Ray Speaker, Chairman (representing the premier and cabinet)
Bill Johnson (president of the party)
Mike Senych (representing rural backbench M.L.A.'s)
Don Hamilton (representing Edmonton and new candidates)
Jack Lowery (former Alberta Liberal leader, representing the rapidly-growing Calgary wing of the Socreds)
Orvis Kennedy (executive director of the party)
Owen Anderson (to conduct public opinion surveys)
Erick Schmidt (to monitor and direct advertising)
Preston Manning (to monitor the critical path), and
"A full-time executive" who was to be Robert Thompkins to maintain the information services and serve as task force secretary.

One of the central recommendations of the *Project 71* report was a $580,000 budget for the campaign. CORPCOM suggested that eight-six per cent of the budget be for advertising and fourteen per cent for headquarters, organization, surveys and planning. Of the $307,000 to be spent on advertising province wide, $72,000 would be for television, $28,000 for radio, $95,000 for daily newspapers, $36,000 for weeklies and $60,000 for a province wide direct mailer. Of the remainder, $150,000 was for printing and sign-painting (most to be supplied to local constituencies). No rationale was advanced for this particular split among the various advertising media. This recommendation had two fateful consequences: by downplaying TV, it abdicated control of this vital medium to Lougheed; and by advocating that the task force take control of all advertising concept design and execution, it opened the door for a struggle over control, and for a dangerous amateurism in execution. We will return later to the effects that these recommendations had in practice.

On the heels of the film production, Strom's advisers began to work with him on the improvement of his television performance. Owen Anderson visited campaign consultants to Ronald Reagan and Nelson Rockefeller and studied how they had "sold" their candidate. He wrote a report:

> . . . television is hurting Mr. Strom now because the viewer does not see him as he really is . . . television will not hurt the real Strom. It will only hurt the image that is received because he is received as something which he is not – cold, frowning, looking at the floor, unsure. The key, then, is for him to be natural, himself, just plain confident, smiling, pragmatic Harry Strom . . . above all, Mr. Strom has to look like a winner. A winner is self-assured . . . confident of his facts and his ability. Mr. Strom is all of these OFF screen. He must be all of these ON screen . . . when he loses his self-consciousness and has his mind firmly fixed on the subject and not his manner of expression then he comes over as the man in control with the short, snappy answers we saw in the last sequence of the [Banks] film . . . the experimental film [which we did] revealed certain 'dos' and 'don'ts':
> 1. Do not lean back when making a statement – looks like he is reclining.
> 2. Waist-high shots do him most credit.
> 3. Left profile is best.
> 4. Looks better from cue-cards than reading a statement. Cue-cards to be 12 inches wide with relatively small print.
> 5. Low lighting to reduce glasses shadow.
> 6. Clasped hands OK – but keep below chin.
> 7. Keep the questions short and the answers even shorter.

This concern about effective use of television took on added urgency because of growing evidence that Lougheed was able to use the medium with great effectivenesss. Lougheed had worked long and hard with professional media announcers (one of whom was a key member of his Edmonton organization) and public relations advisers to master his use of the medium.

Lougheed learned television the way he had learned sports and law and business and politics. He learned not to stare into the camera, not to follow the floor directors' movements with his head, he learned how to time himself so that an apparently spontaneous statement would meet the second hand at the top of the clock, learned how to polish and repolish his on-camera technique (for his last, five-minute election message to the people in August, Lougheed ran through five tapes to get one with right ring of spontaneous sincerity. TV was Lougheed's medium and long before the 1971 election he had taken the key decision to devote 85% of the party's advertising kitty to the tube. . . . *

Compared with Lougheed, Harry laboured under several burdens as a television personality. Lougheed was better educated, he had a lot of experience in executive boardrooms, he had travelled the whole law school/fraternity/debating society circuit. Harry was a farmer and a rural school trustee; he had been a cabinet minister, but only much later in his life. He could never hope to command Lougheed's polish and mastery of the language. The only course left open to Strom's advisers, then, was to focus on Harry's strengths – his easy warmth, his decency and sincerity, his charm with people – and to use a professional narrator to do the "voice over" whenever it became appropriate to speak of the accomplishments of the government.

Strom was made uneasy by all this talk of images and perceived impressions. It seemed to him phony and insincere. And his advisers had to tread carefully in spelling out his faults: he was a vulnerable man, and they didn't want to hurt his feelings.

As Strom's "television lessons" went on through the winter of 1971, a struggle for control of the campaign began to mount, both within the Project 71 task force, and down in the constituencies.

At long last, the drive to reform the party began to manifest itself at the grass-roots level as new men came forward to contest nominations. In north-east Edmonton the wife of a wealthy Polish building contractor, Irene Domecki, beat the hand-picked nominee of old Socred original Bill Tomyn, who had held the seat since 1935 and retired. On Edmonton's south side, young Edmonton alderman Cec Purves engaged feisty old Doctor J. Donovan Ross for the nomina-

* Walter Stewart, "The Upwardly Mobile Mr. Lougheed", *Maclean's,* January 1972.

tion – and then, to the surprise of almost everyone, lost. (Ross's supporters came to the nominating meeting; Purves's supporters, confident that he would win in a walk, didn't.) In Edmonton Parkallen the Socred banner was picked up by Gordon Rasmussen, an accountant and man of deep integrity and human concern who had first worked as a fund-raiser for the Strom leadership campaign in 1968. In other Edmonton ridings, as well, Socred candidates were young, educated and vigorous (like Don Hamilton, Strom's executive assistant, who ran in the south-west constituency of Whitemud, against Lougheed lieutenant Don Getty, and Werner Schmidt, a former Alberta School Trustees executive director, who ran in the north-east), or older, well-respected newcomers to politics, like land developer Lou Letourneau, who contested Lou Hyndman's seat in Edmonton's wealthy West End, and Alex Romaniuk, a hard-working school principal and hugely successful amateur sports promoter who ran in the suburban constituency of Meadowlark.

In Calgary, the renewal of the party began earlier, and hence was even more dramatic. New Socred candidates included George Ho Lem, a Chinese-Canadian alderman, Jay Salmon, the city solicitor, Don Luzzi, famous Calgary Stampeder lineman, Father Pat O'-Byrne, an activist Roman Catholic priest (whose campaign manager was Rabbi Lewis Ginsburg), and Roy Wilson, an energetic housing developer.

When the election came, 37 of the 75 Social Credit candidates were new faces, and many of them were impressive new faces – men and women of diverse backgrounds far more representative of the human complexity of Alberta than any previous Social Credit slate since 1935. Renewal was happening. For the first time, people could see it. The question was, would it happen in time for the average voter to comprehend and appreciate it?

As the campaign for renewal at the constituency level took place, there developed a behind-closed-doors contest for the control of the Project 71 task force. The task force had been conceived by CORP-COM as a way of ensuring that certain key Strom aides and advisers – Erick Schmidt, Don Hamilton, Owen Anderson and Preston Manning – would have a direct pipeline to the premier and control over not only campaign planning but also the day-to-day direction of the campaign. What CORPCOM wanted to avoid at all costs was interference in the planning or running of the campaign by either cabinet or the provincial executive of the party. Both groups would have nominal representation on the task force; but the composition of the task force was carefully engineered to assure that decisive control was in the hands of the reformers.

As the winter of 1971 wore on there was a struggle for the internal control of the task force itself, a struggle brought on, ironically, by the very man CORPCOM brought in to run the task force's administrative affairs, Robert G. Tompkins.

Tompkins was an incongruous choice for several reasons. He was a newcomer to Social Credit whose previous exposure to the party had been limited to acting as organizer of the Premier's Spring Conference in 1970. Erick Schmidt had recruited him then; at the time, Tompkins had been administrative assistant in the University of Alberta's Sociology Department. Tompkins was an effective academic mover and shaker, there was no doubt about that; in the badly divided Sociology Department, torn by a tenure controversy, he had parlayed his modest position into the job of some considerable influence. Schmidt persuaded Ray Speaker to let Tompkins organize the premier's Spring Conference, which he did efficiently. When the task force was formed, Schmidt and Hamilton then nominated Tompkins for the position of "full time executive" (his actual title became "Campaign Consultant"), and this was accepted. Offices were secured for the task force in a penthouse apartment overlooking the Saskatchewan River valley at 116th Street and Tompkins began assembling a staff.

At first Tompkins was a friend to all factions. His only previous political experience was as a worker for the Liberals in the Northwest Territories; he realized that the older people in Social Credit were suspicious of him, and he sought to obtain their confidence.

The task force was ripe for a takeover. Harry Strom would not find the time to participate in its meetings. Ray Speaker thus became the link with cabinet, but Speaker was indecisive and worried about the opinions of his older cabinet colleagues (he once turned on Erick Schmidt and cried, "why is it that everything you get me to do gets me into trouble, Erick?"). The cabinet had no intention of surrendering all of its prerogatives to the task force; it refused to allow the task force to draft the final platform, co-ordinate the travels of ministers, or integrate announcements from the party and announcements from the government. As the man in the middle, Speaker bore the brunt of the task force's criticism of cabinet, and the cabinet's criticism of the task force.

The other man who, in other years, might have been a force to reckon with on the task force was Orvis Kennedy, the party's executive director, Manning's old virtuoso, the political organizer *par excellence*. At 64 years of age, Orvis lacked the energy he once had, but he was still enthusiastic and a deep wellspring of experience in constituency-level organizing. But, in the winter of 1971, Orvis's wife Gladys fell ill with terminal cancer, and he was not able to play the kind of role he was capable of. This had far-reaching consequences: not only was Orvis Kennedy a valuable source of experience, he was also very open to change and reform. Both qualities were needed on the task force.

As the election campaign drew nearer men like Speaker, Hamilton and Senych – M.L.A.s or hopefuls – were able to spend less and less time on task force matters as they concentrated on their own re-election. People came and went; Bev Brooker was added to the task force to represent the party in Edmonton, Ray Nelson to represent it in rural areas; the one constant factor, always there, was Tompkins with his hand-picked staff.

A decision was made not to keep minutes of meetings. Today no record survives to describe the decisions which the task force made, or to enumerate who supported what (or whom).

Then the crucial moment came. Erick Schmidt had proposed, in *Project 71,* that the task force do its own creative and concept work on all advertising and employ an advertising agency to simply buy media time and do the legwork of placement. He then entered into negotiations with the James Lovick advertising agency, which had traditionally handled the Socred account, to reach an arrangement whereby, in return for not having to do the creative and concept work in advertising, Lovick's would rebate a part of their normal fifteen per cent commission to the task force, which in turn would use the funds to pay for the costs of doing their own creative and concept work internally.

Tompkins somehow obtained the correspondence between Schmidt and Lovick's and brought it to a meeting of the task force. He threw it on the table dramatically, asking whether this involved Schmidt in a conflict of interest. Schmidt tried to explain the background behind the correspondence, but Tompkins had made his point. Schmidt's group came under a cloud. The Schmidt plan for advertising was scrapped.

Tompkins brought in two small advertising agencies, Jim Ford in Edmonton and Gordon Reid in Calgary, to do the advertising in the conventional way. The task force would only act as advisers to these ad-men; Tompkins would exercise final control over advertising.

The consequence for the party's campaign advertising was disastrous.* The consequence for the management of the task force was

* Not only was much of the print advertising amateurish and badly executed, but the budget consequences were serious; because neither Ford nor Reid was accredited with the major media, neither could place advertising on credit. This meant the party had to pay for all advertising in cash. This almost exhausted the party's cash reserves and left it, after the election, virtually broke.

decisive: Tompkins was in effective control. At first, the task force was supposed to meet every Friday afternoon for the whole afternoon; eventually it met once a week for lunch over cold corned beef sandwiches in Ray Speaker's office. A basic shift of power had taken place. Schmidt was shunted to one side. Hamilton spent more and more time on his own campaign. Preston Manning drifted away in disgust. Owen Anderson spent more time with the premier, especially after the campaign got underway. Many of the day-to-day decisions were made by Bob Tompkins.

While Tompkins must bear some of the responsibility for the inept advertising of the Socred campaigning, it must not be thought that better advertising could have turned the tide; advertising cannot counter an idea whose time has come.

The pressure began to build on Harry Strom to name a date for the election. June was getting closer, and June had always been a favourite time for Alberta elections. But talk of June dissolved when Owen Anderson brought in the results of his province-wide public opinion survey, which had been carried out in mid-April. This bombshell left Strom and the cabinet in a state of shock: it showed that if the election were to be held immediately, Lougheed held a slight edge over the Socreds, with about thirty-one per cent of the popular vote to Strom's twenty-eight per cent, and a huge number of voters (twenty-five) per cent ominously "undecided". Voters characterized Harry as "honest" but "boring", "a poor speaker" and "uninteresting"; Lougheed was characterized as "man of ideas", "wants the best for the people" and "sincere."

To make matters even worse, someone leaked the main findings of the survey to the *Lethbridge Herald.* The premier's office, and the party, issued fierce denials; incredibly, other papers in the province didn't pick the story up. The self-doubt induced by the findings of Anderson's survey were reinforced in June when Ross Thatcher's incumbent Liberal government went down to defeat in Saskatchewan. All across the country, incumbent governments were toppling like dominoes. Jean-Jacques Bertrand had fallen in Quebec, Ike Smith in Nova Scotia, Louis Robichaud in New Brunswick, Walter Weir in Manitoba. And now Thatcher, a tough, imaginative politician, was also gone. The gloom grew perceptible. Among the Elders one heard mutterings: why was this happening to us? We never had these problems in the old days!

Sensing a June election, Lougheed stepped up his rhetoric. At the Conservative convention at the Palliser Hotel in Calgary on January 23 he had sounded his battle cry for an election. It was a vintage Lougheed speech full of bristling confidence ("this is a slate of candidates without parallel in the history of Alberta politics – there are

234

at least three capable of filling each cabinet position") and admonishments of challenge ("we enter the election campaign knowing the odds are against us – that the so-called experts have already written us off – but we start the campaign with certain positive factors in our favor – a clear two party battle; a far stronger slate of candidates than Social Credit, constituency by constituency; a platform that reflects the hours of participation by all of you . . . a peoples' party dominated by no group . . . facing a public who have not yet made up their minds but are at least open to our challenge.").

In earlier months Lougheed had built his position around the slogan "people first". That night he added to it a new Tory campaign slogan – "NOW!"

> These times of turmoil – of protest – of change – of confrontation – require a government party NOW where its members place people before party . . . we also look to the future – convinced this province could be doing very much better – that time has run its course – that NOW Alberta needs a new responsible government in touch with the issues and aspirations of the people – a party of the future, not of the past . . . the present [Social Credit] group struggling to preserve office and themselves simply cannot do so – cannot adjust – why? . . . they are locked in their perspective of their record – they are caught – they have become so smug about Alberta that they have convinced themselves that Alberta's development has been due to their efforts – not due to the fortunate presence of natural resources in the province – they are not prepared to accept the fact that the revenues from such natural resources in the past 20 years have been of such a magnitude to have permitted any government of any stripe to appear effective. . . .

It was pure John Kennedy ("let's get this country moving again") and John Lindsay ("he is fresh and they are tired"), an appeal for an election in which the issue would be style and form. It was an admission that there were no substantive issues on which an election could be fought – only the intangible but growing feeling on the part of many people that Social Credit had been in office long enough.

How could Social Credit cope with such a feeling? Not with statements about the good job the government had done – most people agreed that it had done a good job. Not with an attack on Lougheed as a dangerous man who would somehow ruin the province's prosperity – he was obviously a responsible leader. But how to combat an attack based on personality and style, and coming from the Right?

In one sense, Lougheed laboured under a disadvantage – no substantive traditional issues (eg., scandal, depression or inflation). In another sense, he had a major advantage – a growing popular readiness for change in government. This readiness for change was to become the only real issue in the election. Naturally there was talk of other issues, by all parties. But even this was for the purpose of influencing the basic mass psychology of undecided voters. A survey carried out for the Socreds in 1969 showed that 36.4 percent of the voters intended to vote Social Credit in the next provincial election versus 24.1 per cent for the Conservatives and twenty-four per cent who didn't know. The Anderson survey in April had shown that Lougheed's popular support had risen to thirty-one per cent, Social Credit's had dropped to twenty-eight per cent and the undecided had risen slightly. For this many voters to still be undecided twenty-eight months after Strom had taken office was not a good sign for Social Credit.

It was decided to inaugurate the "pre-campaign campaign". As a pilot project a series of sixty-second "Reports from your Premier" were taped for radio broadcast. Built around the standard closing "We've done a lot – together, we'll do more" (which in turn would build public receptivity for the campaign slogan, "Let's build Alberta together"), the commercials were aimed at injecting more dynamism and energy into Strom's image. But they failed to do this. The super-dramatic theme music and announcer's introduction contrasted too strongly with Strom's wooden delivery. Many of the spots reinforced the very impressions of Harry they were intended to erase. The survey evidence was that people generally didn't feel any strong animosity to the government, they were simply bored with it. The radio spots didn't change this.

The Banks organization was commissioned to do three basic sixty-second television commercials, and a number of radio commercials, for the campaign. To get around Strom's speaking style, the basic commercials were a montage of film of Strom going places and doing things, with a professional announcer doing the voice over.*

Part of the manoeuvring that took place in the spring was aimed at an unofficial alliance between the Socreds and the Liberals. No alliance was formed; there was, instead, an arrangement. Not long after Calgarian Jack Lowery had resigned as provincial Liberal leader in February 1970, he asked Strom to come to a secret meeting in the Chateau Lacombe and there proposed an actual merger be-

* For reasons never explained, only one of the three commercials was used during the campaign, over-exposing it and wasting the others. Just as incredible, once these excellent commercials were in its hands, the Task Force made no attempt to increase its $90,000 TV budget even after it became obvious Lougheed would concentrate on television.

tween the two parties. (Strom never was told if the offer had the authorization of the federal party, or indeed even the provincial Liberal executive.) Strom rejected the offer but welcomed all interested Liberals into the Social Credit party if they were willing to apply for membership. Not long after, Lowery joined the task force and played a large role in helping to reorganize the party and find new candidates in Calgary. Some of these candidates – e.g., "Chick" Thorssen, former head of the Alberta Universities Commission – had been Liberals. At the local level, a number of Liberals came to work on individual Social Credit campaigns. Edmonton Liberal Joe Shoctor brought his tremendous shoe-biz flair to the organization of the party's big rally at the Jubilee Auditorium August 25th. Liberal advertising man Gordon Reid took one-half of the advertising account. Beyond this, however, it is doubtful whether the Liberal "arrangement" helped the Socreds much. The provincial Liberals had long been the sick man of Alberta politics, could deliver very few votes (their own popular vote had dropped from 19.7 per cent in the 1963 election to 10.8 per cent in 1967 and was to drop to one per cent in 1971), and there was no great traditional friendship between Liberals and Socreds – many Socreds were inclined to view the Liberals as slick city sharpies, while many upper-middle class professional Liberals, for their part, were inclined to view the "Social Credit style" (particularly its religiosity) with disdain or amusement. As Edmund Burke said, "bodics tied together by so unnatural a bond of union as mutual hatred [of someone else] are only connected to their ruin."

By late June the Social Credit organization was in place and ready to begin the election campaign. All it awaited was a campaign platform and a decision from Harry Strom on a date.

The platform was late coming. The task force had been developing platform planks for several months, but cabinet had insisted that platform-building was their responsibility and Strom had concurred. The task force continued to submit ideas, but cabinet reviewed each one, priced it out, and frequently rejected it on the grounds of cost. Many of the proposals were viewed from the perspective of administrative convenience, rather than political appeal. Even on the eve of an election campaign, many cabinet members couldn't stop thinking like department administrators instead of politicians.

In previous elections Manning had always unveiled at least one major new policy at a critical time. In 1955 it was the payment of a cash "oil dividend" to every adult resident of the province. In 1959 it was his "five year plan" to build the famed Senior Citizens Lodges. In 1963, one day before the election, it was the announcement of an agreement between the province and the doctors to operate a voluntary medicare plan. (This was the year after the Saskatchewan medicare battle and Manning's handling of the issue stood in sharp contrast to the tactics of the C.C.F.) In 1967 it was the Alberta Resources Railway. Yet when the 1971 election was called the Social Credit platform had not yet been finalized.

Cabinet had final say on the platform. It insisted that each plank be economical and "workable" (i.e., acceptable to the civil service). Hence, Lougheed had promised $50,000,000 in loans for new industrial development; cabinet responded with a promise of $10,000,000. Lougheed promised free medicare for the aged; cabinet responded with medicare for a dollar a month for those receiving the old age pension and Guaranteed Income Supplement. Lougheed promised universal kindergartens offered through the public schools; Social Credit offered PROJECT ACCESS, a program to provide kindergarten for the mentally and physically handicapped, and a pre-school educational television series, produced in Alberta and aimed at meeting the unique cultural needs of Canadian children (Son of Sesame Street).

Each proposed plank that came to cabinet from the task force was dissected at length and pondered for its cost implications. There was a real fear of seeming to offer too much.

The only two "glamour" planks consented to by cabinet dealt with housing and recreation. The housing plank was borrowed from W.A.C. Bennett and aimed at young married couples: a promise of a $1,000 "one time only" cash grant to assist in the purchase of a first house. And, partly in response to Edmonton's long clamour for a multi-purpose sports "Omniplex", the platform promised per-capita cash grants to all the cities to permit them to build such facilities.

Strangely, the Social Credit platform was weakest of all in the area where one might have expected its greatest strength – agriculture. A reduction in crop insurance premiums and increased loans for farm purchase were the only two farm planks in the platform. For Social Credit to claim, as it did, that these two proposals would make a meaningful contribution to the "preservation of the family farm" was a sad commentary on the kind of political leadership the Agriculture Department had been given.

The reception of the Social Credit platform and the Lougheed platform by the commentators of the province was deeply ironic. The Social Credit platform, inhibited at every turn by an over-concern for economy, was roundly criticized for its "massive give-aways". The

Calgary Herald attacked the housing plank as "bad public policy" and *The Edmonton Journal* rapped Strom saying, "12 months ago Mr. Strom said we couldn't afford all this and now the money is suddenly available. This has stretched the government's credibility."

The Tories received little criticism from the commentators for their many proposals. In a sense, though, this reaction had been anticipated privately by Strom's advisers when they told him, in 1969, that actions speak louder than words. In several areas, the Social Credit promises came on the heels of several years of inaction or apparent inaction, and thus seemed a deathbed conversion.

Strom was determined to arrive at his own date for an election. Where he did, he made the decision in style. On July 22 he rode a brown-and-white horse down Edmonton's Jasper Avenue as a part of the Klondike Days Parade, and received sincere, spontaneous applause as he went. When the parade was over, he caught the media (and Lougheed, who was vacationing in Banff) off guard with an announcement that the election would be held August 30th.

The week before the announcement was a harried one for those who took part in the creation of the campaign advertising. Said a voice in one planning meeting: "We'll either win fifty seats or it'll be a disaster, like the U.F.A. in 1935." Said Bob Clark: "I agree." But this feeling of urgency did not seem to be shared by Ford and Reid, the two advertising men. Ford admitted he was entirely new to political advertising. Reid, who had more experience, felt that advertising was the most important thing in the election: "You get a funny feeling that somewhere else, in some other hotel room, they've got a group like ours and the masses out there aren't getting much involved one way or another. It's really just a question of who's better at advertising – our guys, or theirs."

The advertising group was forced to operate in an atmosphere where no one was sure of their authority. They requested a copy of the original Owen Anderson public opinion survey of April because it contained vital information for planning; but it was not provided. Robert Tompkins wanted to get all of the advertising designed, approved, and finalized immediately and was very stubborn when it was pointed out to him that this would destroy any possibility of re-writing ads to respond to new issues as the campaign went on. On July 19 Tompkins was asked whether it was wise to concentrate so heavily on print and radio advertising and virtually to vacate television to Lougheed. He said, "nobody watches television in the summer anyway."

Cabinet found it hard to shake its old habits and begin getting in fighting trim for the campaign. Two days before the campaign was called by Strom, cabinet spent an entire day wrangling over who would be appointed the next president of the Northern Alberta Institute of Technology.

Harry Strom's call for an election, right on the heels of the Klondike Days parade, generated a good press response. (The *Edmonton Journal* headline: "Sly Harry fools 'em".) On another note, someone went around and plastered "Support pollution, vote Social Credit" stickers on all the parked cars at the Klondike Days exhibition grounds.

Election Diary

It became apparent in the first week of the campaign that the media was going to be hostile to Social Credit, almost uniformly. An open-line radio personality talked about the departure of one of the Socred executive assistants (he had left to take another job outside the government) and said this was proof the Strom advisers were jumping ship just before it sank. A writer in *The Lethbridge Herald* wrote, "prominent Social Crediters are coming to me and saying they're going to vote Tory this time", and the *Red Deer Advocate* wrote, "the Socreds are trying to persuade Alf Hooke to come in at the last minute [in Rocky Mountain House] and save the Party." Stories like these almost seemed intended to create a defeatist psychology among the Social Crediters, and certainly succeeded in getting on the nerves of some of the party's candidates and workers.

The big move in the first week of the campaign (Alberta campaigns are thirty-nine days long) was Lougheed's success in making his platform public first on July 25. It contained a few surprises but did stipulate free medicare for those over sixty-five and massive aid for recreation complexes – two planks the Social Crediters were still fighting over in their own draft platform. On July 28 Strom apparently still hadn't read the final draft of the Socred platform because he visited three candidates' offices in Calgary and was quoted by *The Albertan* as being against both recreational centres and free medicare for people over sixty-five. "Where would we find the money?", he asked. The cabinet wrangled for days over the final composition of the platform and the strategy for its release. The medicare plank was watered down badly – from free medicare for those over sixty-five to medicare for a dollar a month for those receiving both the Old Age Pension and the Guaranteed Income Supplement. Although not significantly different in their effect on provincial spending, the two proposals were a world apart in political effect. Cabinet decided not to release the platform all in one piece but to deal it out in sections.

Strom would announce the agriculture part in Willingdon-Two Hills, a farm riding, within the next week. The rest would be announced later, at other meetings.

The first materials arrived at candidates' offices from campaign headquarters – posters, lawn signs, brochures. Some candidates liked them. Some didn't; Doctor J. Donovan Ross refused to use any of them, referring to them as "crap".

An eyeball survey of southern Alberta in the first week came away with the conclusion that the government was still secure in most of the ridings south of Calgary. Election interest was low, but most of what there was seemed pro-Socred. Few Tory bumper stickers were in evidence. This is dryland farming and cattle country, Baptist and Mormon country, a land of sun and wind and big properties. Here there were no signs of any weakening of government support. But north of Calgary, the party was like an old bear, snappy and still dangerous but not as fast or smart as he used to be, hoping to get through just one more winter on his meagre supply of fat.

August 6 was the one-third mark of the campaign and the assessment of the media (and many Social Credit insiders) was that both sides were having difficulty "getting untracked" (as they say in sports). The campaign was still low key. Strom's public appearances were mainly confined to visits to constituency headquarters, where the candidates were supposed to bring out the voters to meet the premier. Sometimes this worked; mostly it only resulted in Strom meeting a group of already-dedicated Social Crediters. The Social Credit newspaper advertisements had begun but so far there was little or no Conservative print advertising, leading Socred planners to wonder: were the Tories saving their print advertising for late in the campaign? Or were they going to simply ignore print?

It had been a clean campaign although the "sign war" was puzzling. The Socreds couldn't keep their signs up more than one night in Edmonton, except for the big display signs (painted on a four-foot by eight-foot plywood sheet and nailed to four-inch-square posts). *The Journal* said the Tories were complaining about the same thing. Either someone was lying or Edmonton had a lot of nonpartisan vandals going the rounds. *Journal* reports said all parties were getting a noncommital voter response in street canvassing so far; this was congruent with the Social Credit experience thus far. One Social Credit candidate who had already knocked once on every door in the riding (about 7,000 doors) said the voters were friendly, not hostile, but still uncommittal.

It was increasingly obvious that this was Social Credit's first non-Manning election. A debate raged in the task force over whether to use Manning in the campaign. Bob Clark, who was opposed, felt Manning should be saved for the big rallies planned for the end of the campaign, that to use him immediately would diminish Harry's stature. This question aside, it was obvious that there was a sense of drift within the party. The Socreds had some of the same troubles as the few Liberals who were now beginning to turn up at Socred constituency offices to offer their help: they lacked a sense of mission or purpose and often seemed to drift from day to day hoping something would turn up. Said one Social Credit campaign manager: "My first priority is to win this election. My second is to find us a new leader afterwards."

Two kinds of rumours swept through the Social Credit ranks in the second and third weeks of August. The first rumours were wildly optimistic: Lougheed was in trouble, Lougheed was spending more time in southern Alberta because he was afraid of losing his own seat, a Charley Gray (Lougheed's Social Credit rival) blitz through Lougheed's own constituency, Calgary West, showed Lougheed was in trouble, Lougheed was being hurt by his promise to sell forty-nine per cent of Alberta Government Telephones, former Lougheed supporters were saying they would support the government this time.

The other rumours, spoken in more guarded tones, were black: remember Alberta history, when the vote starts the swing it doesn't happen small it happens big, if it starts to swing this time, it's all over for Social Credit; the campaigns being conducted by some Socred candidates are pathetic – one is parking his van on various streets and waiting for people to come and talk to *him;* many young people, if we can believe what they say spontaneously, openly prefer Lougheed; the Tory rank and file seem frighteningly self-confident of victory. A man who took a group of boys on a canoe pageant through Saskatchewan just prior to Ross Thatcher's downfall, told Socreds the election there showed little popular interest or commitment during the first two-thirds of the campaign, and then a tide swept to the C.C.F. and there was nothing Thatcher could do to stop it. There isn't any obvious swing to the Tories yet, but otherwise the first half of the description sounded familiar.

One Social Credit worker remarked: "Positive thinking is the most dangerous thing in a campaign. Sure, you need a certain amount of it to keep your people working. But beyond that amount, it warps your judgement and you start believing your own propaganda. How do we walk that thin line and not step over?" The rumours continued. One cabinet minister said he had it from a reliable source that a Tory strategy meeting in Calgary had recommended a major change of strategy to downplay Lougheed and start swinging harder.

An unpublished *Edmonton Journal* telephone survey was reported to the Social Crediters. Taken around August 10 it was said to have shown the vote going twenty-five per cent Socred, twenty-one per cent Tory and forty-three per cent undecided. Complaints mounted in party ranks about *The Journal's* strong Tory biases in handling campaign news. One *Journal* reporter travelling with the two campaigns through the countryside, wrote of the Lougheed campaign only in the most glowing of terms. At the same time, it was obvious that Lougheed's campaign, in the small towns and rural areas especially, was far better organized – advance teams got out the citizenry, there were marching bands, all the meals, hotel reservations and cable facilities for accompanying media were taken care of, and so on. The Strom cavalcade wasn't nearly as well organized, and the party must take the rap for this, not Strom; several times the tour reached its destination to find no one waiting.

With the media right there to record the event, this was profoundly embarrassing.

Lougheed was not only drawing good crowds in the countryside, he was impressing people with his style. Said one reporter covering the Lougheed tour, Lougheed bounds off his bus "like a boxer answering the bell. He walks so fast that this reporter has lost five pounds trying to keep up to him as he visits every store on main street, shakes hands with everyone walking around and then runs-walks back to the bus. Once he even raced a group of kids down the street." Some of the Socred meetings were drawing disappointing crowds. A big meeting August 21 in Grande Prairie was planned for 700 people, but less than 400 showed up. The same day, Lougheed got out 300 people in Daysland for a main street tour with bands (Daysland has a population of only 700).

At the same time it was not clear even to the Tories whether they were making sufficient headway. On August 18 *The Journal's* senior legislative reporter, Bob Bell, wrote, "Peter Lougheed may be seeing the momentum his Conservative Party built up over the past four years being absorbed in an election campaign that has yet to generate anywhere near the enthusiasm that some were willing to predict several months ago . . . instead it appears that neither Social Credit nor the Conservatives have been able to make notable impact on the swing voter who will decide which party forms the next government."

On August 19 Robert Tompkins informed the advertising planning group that he was cutting back advertising planned for the last week of the campaign "because we're winning".

Individual "voters forums" so far were inconclusive.

On August 21st *The Journal* conducted interviews with fifty people chosen at random on Jasper Avenue. The only issue that emerged was whether or not it was "time for a change"; thirty-two per cent said they would vote Tory, twenty-four per cent Socred, fourteen per cent N.D.P. and two per cent Liberal. Yet – strangely enough, given their support for the Conservatives – only three of the fifty people thought the Tories would win. What would happen, Socred planners worried, if everyone voted Tory on the assumption that it didn't matter because everyone else would be voting Socred?

As the campaign entered its final weak tempers grew shorter and rhetoric intensified. One Conservative candidate said, "in 1935 Aberhart said vote for me and I will give you $35. In 1971 Harry Strom said vote for me and I will give you $1,000. Obviously the price of votes has gone up." On August 23d Lougheed blitzed the City Market and the Northgate Shopping Centre in Edmonton. Spotting two kids wearing "Apathy Club" tee-shirts, he went over and said, "I've been looking to find a Socred all day."

In the last week an extraordinary rumour swept through the upper echelons of the Social Credit organization: the JAPEX project was about to be announced! The candidates and workers were desperate for an ace in the hole and this seemed to be it. All through the 1960s JAPEX, a subsidiary of the Japan Petroleum Development Corporation, had been in the news off and on with talk of a huge development project in the Athabasca tar sands. Such a project would cost hundreds of millions of dollars, create thousands of new jobs and investment opportunities. Each previous time, the stories had petered out, only to start afresh a few years later. But now a "reliable source" close to the party said that the premier and Russ Patrick had been negotiating with the JAPEX group and that the deal was complete and ready to be announced. It would include a provision for all Albertans to buy stock at a very low price and would "turn the election upside down". And so the faithful waited, day after day for the announcement which never came. The deal, it turned out, wasn't quite a deal yet after all.

On August 25 came the big test of the Edmonton Social Credit campaign, a large public rally to be held at the Jubilee Auditorium. For its organizers, this was to be a traumatic day: the Socreds had had difficulty getting out the crowds almost everywhere in the province and the night of the rally was also the night of a football game between the Edmonton Eskimos and the Winnipeg Blue Bombers. The first officials to arrive after 7:00 p.m. felt their hearts fall: the building was virtually deserted, the parking lot likewise. The rally was due to start at 8:00 p.m. One of the Edmonton candidates, John

B. Ludwig and his workers, were passing out balloons and bravely trying to work up some enthusiasm.

And then, incredibly, the people started to come. By a few minutes after 8:00 p.m. the auditorium was miraculously full to its full 2,700 capacity, the biggest Social Credit crowd anyone had seen in years. Most of the candidates had brought up to 200 supporters (a good sign in itself); Don Hamilton, the "man from Whitemud" was there in a white suit, and the auditorium was ringing to war-whoops, cheers and campaign songs. The crowd's enthusiam seemd to feed on itself. The entertainment, arranged by Edmonton Liberal Joe Shoctor, was superb: the Strutters Drum Corps electrified the place with a close-order marching drill.

Harry Strom's speech was a recapitulation of campaign themes and promises. Then the master of ceremonies, Cec Purves, called on the keynote speaker, Ernest Manning. Manning gave the crowd what they had been craving all through the campaign: a give-'em-hell partisan attack on the opposition and its tactics. He called Lougheed "a Madison Avenue glamour boy" with an "ultra-brite toothpaste smile" and the "charm of an Avon Lady". Said Manning: "This is not the time to sacrifice our unique position of strength to experiment with a new man no matter how nice he may look on television . . . people have the right to keep a government as long as they desire . . . if it doesn't perform, four years is too long. If it continues to serve the interests of the people, there is no logical argument why it should not continue indefintely."* The party's supporters went home elated and confident.

But the next night, in the same auditorium, Lougheed drew up to 4,000 to a Conservative rally, and they were equally enthusiastic and noisy. Alf Hooke came to the meeting and told a reporter, "it looks ominous for the Stromites." And the next day *The Edmonton Journal,* as Strom predicted, came out editorially for Lougheed calling him "alert, thoughtful and experienced" and arguing that the Socreds "cannot dispel the feeling that today [they] are uncertain, uninspired and increasingly smug."

The following night, in Calgary, the Social Crediters held their second rally. On the evidence of the Social Credit campaign in Calgary, which had been conducted with more flair (and which had attracted more bodies) than its counterpart in Edmonton, feeling in party ranks was that a massive turnout could be expected. But the Jubilee Auditorium in Calgary was only half-full, and spirits fell.

* Public feedback over the next week ran counter to the audience reaction. Many noncommitted voters felt that bringing in Manning to attack Lougheed was somehow not fair.

As the campaign moved into its last days, neither side was absolutely confident of victory. Alluding to the large preponderance of Social Credit seats, Lougheed told one reporter, "I'm happy about everything but the arithmetic" and even *The Edmonton Journal* wrote that "few predict that the Goliath of Alberta political power will be defeated – but there is a growing consensus that there will be seats taken away (from Social Credit).*

August 30 dawned hot and clear everywhere in the province, a day made to order for a record voter turnout.

On the day of the election Peter Lougheed telephoned the sitting Tory M.L.A.s and found them subdued, "even Horner". He sat around his home in Calgary drinking coffee and reminiscing about the campaign. At 10:00 a.m. one of his aides drove him to Earl Gray School to vote; he then returned home to talk to party organizers over the telephone and get progress reports. The laughter was nervous and distracted as the tension grew. Lougheed changed the family barometer from "very dry" to "change" and hoped it would be a good omen. After lunch he visited the Tory campaign headquarters in Calgary and met and thanked volunteer workers. Then he went home at 3:00 p.m. to sit it out privately with his family. "It's just like the Grey Cup kick-off," he told one reporter. To another he said, "well, I don't think we made it."

Strom spent election day touring various polls and party offices and telephoning Orvis Kennedy to get reports on the situation in various constituencies. In late afternoon, with a deep sense of apprehension, he went home to the suburbs to have dinner with his family.

At about 7:30, thirty minutes before the close of the polls, party workers began to drift into the constituency offices to eat cold ham and potato salad, perhaps have a glass of beer, and watch the election returns. The tension was palpable: the long trial was finally over, the jury was about to come in.

At 8:00 o'clock the television networks came on the air with their election night coverage and there was a brief spell of fifteen minutes of commentator small talk while everyone waited for the returns from the first polls.

For the anxious Socreds, the first polls in Edmonton were not reassuring: they showed small Tory leads in many constituencies. Husbands reassured their wives, campaign managers reassured their candidates: it's too early to say that this means anything. But a clear

* In 1967 the Socreds took fifty-five seats with forty-five per cent of the vote and Lougheed took six seats with twenty-six per cent of the vote. Between 1967 and 1971 Lougheed added four more seats: two in by-elections and two when two already-elected opposition MLA's joined the Tories.

trend began to develop. The polls were coming in in larger numbers now, from every part of every constituency; the results could not be written off as unrepresentative. In Whitemud, Don Getty had a good lead on Don Hamilton and the lead was widening. In seats where the Socreds felt secure – like Parkallen and Norwood – the Conservative candidates had opened up sizeable leads. Socred party workers desperately telephoned the returning officers – perhaps there were errors in the figures being received by the television stations. No, the figures were correct.

At 8:25 CFRN anchorman Bruce Hogel said, "well, ladies and gentlemen, we may be viewing a major upset tonight." Ten minutes earlier his statement would have been greeted, in a dozen Socred committee rooms, with derisory hoots and anger. Now it was greeted with silence and grim concentration.

A pattern was beginning to emerge. The early Socred popular vote was still high, within several points of the forty-five per cent it gained in 1967. But the N.D.P. was down from fifteen per cent to ten per cent, the Liberals had completely collapsed from eleven per cent to one per cent, and the Tory vote was running at about forty-six per cent. The solid south was still solid, although one or two ridings were close. In Calgary the Tories were ahead in about ten ridings, the Socreds in about five. In the central rural area, it was a mixed bag, with substantial Tory inroads even where the Socreds were running attractive new faces. The far north, never a Socred stronghold, was showing pockets of N.D.P. strength – N.D.P. leader Grant Notley was ahead in Spirit River, although not by much. Edmonton was a disaster area, with only a handful of Socreds even in the running.

Thirty minutes later the scene at the Jubilee Auditorium, where the Socreds had set up their Edmonton headquarters, was one of stunned desperation. White-faced men bravely tried to look optimistic and women sat crying as they surveyed the wreckage on a large chalkboard on stage at the front. Orvis Kennedy wrote down the unbelievable numbers: the Tories ahead, or declared victors, in every single Edmonton seat, and with a commanding lead in Calgary and the countryside. A television team stood with Dr. J. Donovan Ross as he conceded his seat to the Conservatives and then left. Time seemed to be speeding up. The evening, the decade were slipping past. Someone handed Ruth Strom a bunch of roses and suddenly Harry Strom stepped forward before the audience, thanked everyone for their support and help, and began to concede the election. He spoke calmly, clearly and well. It was winding up.

The numbers spoke for themselves: the Tories ahead or elected in forty-nine seats, Social Credit ahead or leading in twenty-five, and one doubtful.* Strom and his wife left for the airport to fly to his home near Medicine Hat. Outside in the corridor, someone had set up a television monitor, which was showing scenes of unrestrained jubilation at Conservative headquarters in Calgary.

By 11:00 p.m. it was over. In Edmonton's west end, a get-together that was to have been a victory party was quickly unravelling. Most of the invited guests hadn't shown up, and the host went quickly around putting away the bottles and turning off the lights. Outside, on the front sidewalk, a small knot of Strom advisors stood discussing the night's events. It had been hot that day, and clear, but now the sky was scudding with clouds and a cold wind was blowing out of the north. It was only August, but it was almost winter.
[August, 1935 – August, 1971.]

---

* The final results: Tories forty-nine seats, 46.4 per cent of popular vote; Social Credit twenty-five seats, 41.9 per cent of popular vote; N.D.P. one seat, 11.4 per cent of popular vote; Liberals no seats, one per cent of popular vote.

Index

A

Aalborg, Anders, 170, 171, 172-4, 180, 181, 193, 195, 197, 220
Aberhart, William 16, 25, 27, 30, 35, 49, 107, 121, 122, 124, 127, 150n, 157-58
  and Agriculture Committee, 61-2
  background and character of, 37-39
  death of, 118-119, 120
  and Depression, 48, 50
  and Douglasites, 55-65
  and early Social Credit movement, 49, 50, 51-53, 65-68
  as educator, 38, 69, 117-118
  and financial policy of, 1935-39, 94-99
  and first days as Premier, 83-89
  and first legislative session, 90-93
  and first Socred convention, 72-74
  and friendship with Manning, 47-48
  and Interim Program, 114
  and insurgency, 100-106
  and political organization, 67-68, 72
  and press, 67-68, 75, 87-88, 95-96, 108-109, 112-13, 117
  and Prophetic Bible Institute, 44-46, 48
  and radio broadcasts, 40, 43, 48, 50, 51, 52, 69, 71, 108, 152
  and relations with Douglas, 53-55, 61-63, 76, 86, 87, 91, 93-94
  and religion, 38-40, 69
  resignation and reinstatement of, 61-64
  and theory of Social Credit, 56-61
  and tours with Manning, 51-52, 68, 71
  and U.F.A. convention, 70-71
  and 1935 election, 69-71, 74-80
  and 1938 session, 112

  and 1940 election, 115-117
Accurate News and Information Act, 109
Advisory Committee, 74, 75, 80, 170
agrarian democracy, 31
agrarian radicals, 16, 17, 121, 159
agrarian socialism, 32, 66
Agriculture Committee, 61-63, 64-65, 94n, 107
Alberta Bankers' Association, 92
Alberta Bill of Rights Act, 126-128
Alberta Credit House Act, 97, 99
Alberta Gas Trunk Line Ltd., 142
Alberta Government Telephones, 181, 195, 197, 242
Alberta Investment Fund, 142-43
Alberta Liquor Control Board, 134n, 136, 137
Alberta Service Corps, 144, 170
Alberta Social Credit Act, 103
Alberta Social Credit Chronicle, 68
Alberta Social Credit League, 50, 54, 55, 87, 109, 124, 126, 129, 153, 157-601, 203n, 204
  reform of, 210-14
Alberta Supreme Court, 34, 101, 126, 135
Alberta Teachers' Association, 21-22
Alberta Wheat Board, 14
Albertan, The, 55, 240
Americans
  influence of, 14
  and oil, 139-40
Anderson, Fred, 74, 80
Anderson, Owen, 143, 170, 173, 180, 190-92, 198, 203, 210, 227, 228, 229, 231, 234, 236, 239
Andison, Robert, 90, 104
Ansley, Earl, 124, 130
Atkinson, Roy, 200

B

Baich, B.V., 145, 146

Baker, Floyd, 105, 160-61
Bank Act, 65, 113
Bank of Canada, 16, 99-100
Bank Employees' Civil Rights Act, 107
Bank Taxation Act, 109
"Bankers' Toadies," 109-110, 111
Barnes, S.A.G., 95
Barons, the, 195-99
Batten Commission, 221
Bennett, R.B., 31, 66, 76, 84, 85
Bennett, W.A.C., 153, 158, 226, 238
Berry, Adrian, 155
Bertrand, Jean-Jacques, 234
Blair Report, 221, 222
Blue, A.L., 102
Blue Book, the, 56, 57, 60, 67, 70
Board of Credit Commissioners, 126
Bourcier, A.V., 102, 103, 128
Boyd, Herbert, 53, 93, 94n
British North America Act, 54, 60, 65, 76, 83, 98, 126
British Social Credit Movement, 100-101
Brown, Don, 112-113
Brown, Dr. Harry, 103, 104, 106
Brownlee, John Edward, 18, 30-31, 149n
  scandal, 32-36, 75
  and U.F.A., 31, 35-36
Buck, Walter, 176, 177, 183, 184, 199
Butnap, J.A., 111
Byrne, L. Denis, 105, 107, 128, 129-30

C

Calgary Herald, 55, 76, 75, 99, 108, 239
Campbell, Peter, 111
Caouette, Real, 112, 205-206
Canadian Bankers' Association, 193
Canadian Bar Association, 134-35
Canadian Federation of Agriculture, 22n
Canadian Farm Loans Board, 16
Canadian Red Cross, 20
C.C.F., 32, 73, 77, 121-22, 123, 124, 133, 139, 156, 159, 215
Central Council, 55, 63, 64
Chant, William N., 84, 101, 105

Clark Robert, 144, 173, 181, 195-96, 220, 239, 242
Clark, Ron, 159
Clement Committee, 135
Cockcroft, Charles, 84, 85, 93, 101
Colborne, Fred, 144, 162, 220
Colbourne, Maurice, 49
Collins, Larkham, 53, 54, 93, 94n
Commission on Agricultural Credit, 16
Communist Party of Canada, 23, 110
communists, 18, 23, 57, 67, 97, 123, 127
Community Development Program, 145, 146
Conservatives
  federal, 205, 207, 209
  opposition with Lougheed, 167, 209, 216-19, 221-23
  provincial, 15, 53, 65, 75, 76, 80, 100, 109, 111, 116, 121, 122, 159, 163-64, 184, 209, 210, 215
  and 1967 election, 217-20
  and 1971 election, 234-36, 238-48
Consort Enterprise, 68-69
Courtiers, the, 190-92
Credit of Alberta Regulation Act, 107
Credit House. See State Credit House
Credit and Loan Agreements Act, 138
Cross, W.W., 84, 105, 121

D

Davis, Arthur J., 159
Davis, Mr. Justice, 35
Davison, Andy, 115, 117
Debt Adjustment Act, 97, 99, 121, 138
Debt Adjustment Board, 97
Debtors' Assistance Board, 138
Depression, the, 14, 16, 17, 18, 19, 27, 77, 112, 117, 118, 132, 138, 149, 151, 182, 188
  and Aberhart, 48, 50
  effects of in Alberta, 20-23, 65
  and U.F.A., 32, 63, 66
Devenish, O.G., 80
Diefenbaker, John G., 200, 205, 207,

Dominion-Provincial Loan Council,
91, 94, 101
Douglas, Clifford Hughes, 25, 32,
65, 75, 80, 107
  and capitalism, 25-28
  economic theory of, 26-28, 57-59,
    62, 98
  and insurgents, 104-105, 109, 110,
    120
  political philosophy of, 29-30
  and relations with Aberhart, 53-
    55, 61-63, 76, 86, 87, 91, 93-94
  as reconstruction advisor, 76, 86,
    107
  and Say's Law, 25-26
  and visit to Alberta, 61-63
  and world conspiracy, 127-29
Douglas Credit League of Canada,
54
Douglas Social Credit Advocate, 95
Douglas Social Credit Council, 130
Douglasites, 27, 30, 53-54, 55, 59,
  60, 61-62, 64, 65, 68, 73, 86, 104-
  105, 109, 110, 120, 126-30, 178
Downey, Lorne, 195
Downton, Bill, 179, 212
Duggan, D.M., 109
Dunn, Kant B., 70

E

Economic Safety League, 79-80
Edmonton Bulletin, 22, 33, 35n, 122
Edmonton Journal, 85, 90, 112-13,
  123, 153n, 197, 213, 239, 240,
  241, 243, 244, 245, 246
Elders, the, 188-90, 191, 198, 211,
  212, 234
Elections
  1935, 69-71, 74-80
  1940, 115-117, 122
  1944, 121-124
  1967, 163-64, 217-19
  1971, 194n, 196, 224-48
Ergil, Jim, 143

F

Fallow, W.A., 84, 96, 105
federal government, 15, 16, 21, 24,
  60, 62, 76, 98, 107, 113, 127, 138,
144, 217, 219
  and loans to Alberta, 85, 89-90,
    94
"Fifty Big Shots," 56, 57
Financial Post, 97

G

Gerhart, Edgar, 176, 177, 182, 183,
  195, 196
Getty, Don, 219, 231, 247
Gibeau, Philip, 138
Giles, Mabel, 45
Gilles, John Patrick, 129
Gladstone, William Ewart, 168-69
Globe and Mail, 185
Gostick, Edith, 80, 90, 117
Gray, E.L., 111
Great Canadian Oil Sands, 142-43
Greenfield, Herbert, 31
Greenshirts, 80, 100

H

Hamilton, Don, 144, 170, 171, 173,
  190-92, 198, 227, 231, 232, 233,
  234, 245, 247
Hansell, E.G., 40
Hargreaves, John, 80, 100-101
Harradance, Milton, 155, 216
Harvey, Chief Justice, 34
Haslam, H.O., 105
Henderson, James, 195, 220
Hinman, E.W., 163, 197
Hollingworth, Frank, 68
Holowach, Ambrose, 194, 220
Ho Lem, George, 231
Hooke, Alf, 102, 118, 124, 129-30,
  163, 178, 182, 189-90, 193, 199,
  225, 240, 245
Horner, Dr. Hugh, 219
House of Commons, 15, 98, 205, 206
House of Commons Banking
  Committee, 27, 32
Huckvale, Keith, 193-94
Hugill, John, 80, 83, 84, 101, 105,
  108
Human Resource Development
  Program, 146-48, 169, 171, 178,
  189, 194, 195
Hunter, David, 155
Hutchinson, Cyril, 47-48

Hyndman, Louis, 219, 231

I

Independents, 115, 116, 122, 123, 215
Interim Program, 114, 124
Irvine, Andrew, 23
Irvine, William, 32, 67
Ives, Mr. Justice, 23, 34, 101

J

Jenson, Paul, 182, 189-90
Johnson, Bill, 190, 209, 212, 228
Johnson, Hewlett, 80, 87
Judicature Act Amendment Act, 107
Judicial Committee of Privy Council, 121
Just Price, 28, 57, 79, 89, 95, 127

K

Kelln, Martin, 206
Kelso, Louis, 202
Kennedy, Ed, 153
Kennedy, Orvis, 124, 153, 157-58, 159, 161, 182, 183-83, 206-207, 212, 224, 228, 232-33, 246, 247
Kerslake, C.V., 54, 68
Keynes, J.M., 25, 27
Keys, A.F., 74
King, W.D., 92
King, W.L. Mackenzie, 77, 113, 114
Kirby, Cam, 155
Knott, Dan, 19

L

Landeryou, Jack, 163
Landeryou, Ruth, 159
Lawson, Ross, 159
Leduc, 120, 130-31, 139, 168, 185
Lee, Roy, 163
Lethbridge Herald, 234, 240
Letourneau, Louis, 231
Liberals
 federal, 15, 76, 77, 205-206
 provincial, 14, 15, 35-36, 53, 64, 75, 76-78, 80, 111, 115, 116, 121-124, 149, 155, 156, 159, 167, 215, 220, 232, 234, 236-37, 241, 244, 247, 248n

Little, Walter, 80
Logan, A.J., 53, 64
Lougheed, Sir James, 31
Lougheed, Peter, 164, 167, 180n, 200, 209, 210,
 in opposition, 220-23
 and rise of Conservatives, 215-19
 and 1967 election, 217-20
 and 1971 election, 225, 229, 230, 234-36, 238-248
Low, Solon, 101, 103, 117, 119, 124, 129
Lowery, Jack, 228, 236, 237
Ludwig, John B., 245
Luzzi, Don, 231

M

Maccagno, Mike, 155, 215
MacDonald, Bill, 194n
MacEachen, Allen, 135
MacLachlan, G.L., 102, 104, 105
Maclean's, 88
MacMillan, A.C., 33-36
MacMillan, Vivian, 33-36
Magor, Robert J., 86
Mandarins, the, 192-95
Manderville, Fred, 161
Manning, Elizabeth Mara, 41-42
Manning, Ernest Charles, 40, 187, 188, 189, 190, 192, 194, 197, 203-206, 215, 218, 220, 221, 224, 225, 232, 242, 245
 achievements of, 168-69
 as acting Premier, 83-84, 85-86
 background and character of, 41-43, 151-52, 154-55
 and capitalism, 59
 and early Socred movement, 51-53, 64
 and financial policy, 124-26
 and first Socred convention, 72-74
 and free enterprise, 135-38, 143, 147
 and friendship with Aberhart, 43-44, 47-48
 and foreign capital and oil development, 132, 139-43, 185
 and government organization, 133-35, 157
 and human resources, 143-48
 and insurgency, 100, 106, 126-130

as Minister of Trade, 88-89, 91-93,
   96, 99, 121
and one-party government, 149-51,
   156-57, 163-64
political beliefs of, 133
and political realignment, 170,
   205-210
and Prophetic Bible Institute, 43-
   47
and religion, 152-53
and succession, 167, 169-72, 174,
   181, 183
and Social Credit League, 157-61
and tours with Aberhart, 69-71,
   74-75, 80
and 1937 session, 112
and 1940 election, 117
and 1944 election, 121-24
and 1944 session, 119-21
Manning, George Henry, 41
Manning, Keith, 154
Manning, Murial, 44, 154-55
Manning, Preston, 143, 146, 161,
   170, 171, 172, 173, 180, 190, 208,
   209, 227, 228, 231, 234
Manning, Roy, 41-42
Manning, William, 42
Manning Era, 120, 123, 130, 142,
   147, 157, 158, 161, 186
Manufacturers' Association, 91
Marketing Board, 124-25
McClellan, George, 135
McFarland, John, 111
McGeer, Gerry, 78
McGrath Report, 221, 222
McGregor, Gilbert, 55, 63, 64
McKinnon, Randy, 170, 219
monetary reform, 32, 51, 66, 67,
   178, 182, 201
Montreal Gazette, 113-14

N

National Credit Authority, 28
National Dividends, 28, 57, 58, 79,
   89, 95, 99-100, 114, 126, 127
National Farmers' Union, 200, 201
N.D.P., 133, 134, 137, 159, 167,
   181, 189, 204, 209, 247, 248n
New Age Club, 53-54, 55
Notley, Grant, 184, 247

O

O'Byrne, Father Pat, 231
oil
   development of, 139-43
   discovery of, 120, 130-32, 149, 185
   revenue from, 134, 141-42
Oil and Gas Conservation Board,
   140
Olson, Bud, 161, 206
Olson, Perry, 161
Orderly Payments of Debts Act, 138
Ottawa Citizen, 62

P

Page, J. Percy, 117, 155
Palmer, Charles G., 53, 54, 55, 64
Patrick, Russ, 170, 171, 244
Pearson, Lester B., 153
People's League, 100, 110, 111
Perceval, J.F., 101
populism, 14, 159, 201-202
Porter, Francis, 159, 189
Potter, Don, 191n
Powell, George Frederic, 105, 106,
   109, 110
Press Gag Bill, 112
Priestly, Norman, 32, 74, 77
Progressive Conservatives, 205, 208
Progressive Party, 27
Project 71, 227-28, 233
Prophetic Bible Institute, 38, 43-45,
   47, 48n, 50, 51-52, 55, 70, 72, 80,
   107
   curriculum of, 45-46
Prowse, J. Harper, 123, 155, 167,
   215
Pugh, Ken, 193
Purves, C., 199, 230-31, 245

R

Rasmussen, Gordon, 231
Rebel, The, 108
Recall Act, 91, 111
Red Deer Advocate, 240
Reduction and Settlement of Lands
   Debt Act, 97, 101
Regina Conference, 32
Regina Manifesto, 32
Reid, Eva, 68
Reid, R.G., 35, 69, 75, 76, 77, 78,

80

Reierson, Roy, 171, 172, 195, 197, 220,
   and leadership campaign, 172-75, 177, 180, 181, 183
Robarts, John, 153, 216
Robichaud, Louis, 234
Robinson, J.L., 112-13
Roblin, Duff, 153, 216
Rogers, Edith, 117
Romaniuk, Alex, 231
Roper, Elmer, 123, 124
Ross, Alex, 85
Ross, C.C., 84, 101, 220
Ross, J. Donovan, 199, 230-31, 241, 247
Rowe, P.J., 101
Ruste, Henry, 146, 181, 191n, 220
Royal Commission on Transportation, 22n

S

Salmon, Jay, 231
Sanders, Douglas, 212
Saskatchewan, 15, 16, 19, 22, 139, 234
Say, Jean-Baptise, 25
Scarborough, Charles M., 49
Schmidt, Erick, 143, 144, 146, 161, 170, 171, 173, 178, 190, 194, 209, 227, 228, 231, 232, 233, 234
Schmidt, Werner, 231
Schreyer, Ed, 225
Seduction Act, 35
Senych, Mike, 228, 233
Smallwood, Joey, 153
Smith, Earl, 159
Smith, Ian, 159
Smith, Ike, 234
Smith, Norman, 32, 67
Somerville, Hubert, 193
Speaker, Roy, 144, 195-96, 211-12, 228, 232, 233, 234
Social conservatism, 205, 208, 209
Social Conservative Society, 209
Social Credit, 14, 31, 33, 35-37, 50n, 64-67, 72, 73, 88
   and Aberhart's introduction to, 50-52
   and Aberhart's theory of, 56-61
   achievements of, 185-86

   and change of image, 185-87, 199-202
   and debt and loan legislation, 96-98
   and Douglas's theory of, 26-28, 49, 53, 57-59, 62
   and Douglasites, 53-55, 59-64, 100-106, 126-130
   as federal party, 88, 205-209, 210
   first convention of, 72-74
   first session of, 90-93
   and human resources, 143-48
   as government 1935-39, 83-85
   and leadership convention, 180-84,
   and opposition to Aberhart, 102-106, 111, 112
   organization of, 67-68
   and reform campaign, 203-204, 210-214
   rise of, 13, 14, 25, 50-53
   and rise of Conservatives, 215-18
   and second income plan, 202
   and social change, 150-51
   stagnation of, 162-63, 169, 215-16
   and U.F.A., 64-71
   and 1935 election, 69-71, 74-80
   and 1937 session, 108-11
   and 1938 session, 113
   and 1940 election, 115-17, 122
   and 1943 session, 121
   and 1944 election, 122
   and 1971 election, 224-48
Social Credit Board, 103, 104, 106, 107, 109, 114, 127-29
Social Credit League. *See* Alberta Social Credit League
Social Credit Measures Act, 91
Social Credit Secretariat, 53, 54, 55
social democracy, 14
socialists, 29, 99, 121, 127, 204
Spenser, 93
Stanfield, Robert, 209, 216
State Credit House, 57, 58, 96, 99n, 101, 103
Sterling, George, 159
Stewart, Charles, 23
Strom, Harry Edwin, 120n, 170, 171
   background and character of, 171-72, 188
   and the Barons, 195-99
   and cabinet unity, 198-99

and the Courtiers, 190-92
and the Elders, 189-90, 211
first days in office of, 185-87
and leadership campaign, 170-84
with Lougheed in opposition, 220-23
and public change, 185-87, 199-201
and 1971 election, 224-48
Sunday Express, 80
Supreme Court of Canada, 35, 109, 111, 112, 219

T

Tanner, E. Nathan, 90, 101, 130
Taylor, Gordon, 171, 172, 195, 220
    and leadership campaign, 172-74, 176-78, 180, 181, 182, 183, 184
Thatcher Ross, 153, 234, 242
Thompkins, Robert, 228, 232-34, 239, 243
Thompson, Robert, 206-207
Tomyn, Bill, 230
Tories. *See* Conservatives
Toronto Star, 207
Trade and Industry Act, 92
Treasury Branches, 93, 114, 115, 124-25, 185, 202
Trudeau Pierre Elliott, 169, 200, 225
Turcott, Garth, 163

U

Underwood, Charles, 68
unemployment relief, 18, 19, 20, 21, 24, 85, 94
Unemployment Relief, Commission, 21
U.F.A., 14, 24, 30, 31, 32, 33, 35, 50, 53, 61, 66, 67, 70-71, 88, 90, 107, 136, 149, 200, 215
    and Social Credit, 64, 65-71
    and 1935 election, 68, 69, 70, 74, 75, 76-78, 80
United Grain Growers, 14, 31
Unwin, Joe, 110
Usher, C.L., 144

V

Vancouver Sun, 54

W

Walker, James, 115
Walsh, William L., 84, 90
Watkins, Ernest, 155-56, 216
Webster, Herbert A., 88
Weir, Walter, 234
Whitford, Jim, 144-45, 146
Wilmott, Charles, 69
Wilson, Roy, 231
Wood, Henry Wise, 31, 149n
Workman's Compensation Act, 112

Y

Young, Henry, 32
Young Socreds, 170, 182, 212
Yurko, Bill, 209

Z

Zubick, J.J., 108